The Software Developer's Guide to Linux

A practical, no-nonsense guide to using the Linux command line and utilities as a software developer

David Cohen

Christian Sturm

BIRMINGHAM—MUMBAI

The Software Developer's Guide to Linux

Senior Publishing Product Manager: Aaron Tanna

Acquisition Editor – Peer Reviews: Gaurav Gavas

Project Editor: Parvathy Nair

Content Development Editor: Matthew Davies

Copy Editor: Safis Editing

Technical Editor: Karan Sonawane

Proofreader: Safis Editing

Indexer: Tejal Soni

Presentation Designer: Ganesh Bhadwalkar

Developer Relations Marketing Executive: Meghal Patel

First published: January 2024

Production reference: 1230124

Published by Packt Publishing Ltd.

Grosvenor House

11 St Paul's Square

Birmingham

B3 1RB, UK.

ISBN 978-1-80461-692-5

www.packt.com

Contributors

About the authors

David Cohen has, for the past 15 years, worked as a Linux system administrator, software engineer, infrastructure engineer, platform engineer, site reliability engineer, security engineer, web developer, and a few other things besides. In his free time, he runs the *tutorialinux* YouTube channel where he's taught hundreds of thousands of people the basics of Linux, programming, and DevOps. David has been at Hashicorp since 2019—first as an SRE, then as a reference architect, and now as a software engineer.

Thank you, Aleyna, for your unwavering support over the past few years as I've been developing and writing this book. Without you, this would just be another of my promising-but-unfinished projects languishing in some forgotten "Archive" directory. Thanks to Christian, who has stuck with me for over a decade as a friend and a partner on practically every wild tech project idea I've come up with since we met. Finally, a big "thank you" is also due to my friends and colleagues at Hashicorp and everywhere else I've been over the past 15 years, who have made me a better engineer and encouraged projects like this.

Christian Sturm is a consultant on software and systems architecture, having worked in various technical positions for well over a decade. He has worked as an application developer for the frontend and backend at companies large and small, such as zoomsquare and Plutonium Labs. On top of that, he is also an active contributor to various open source projects and has a deep understanding of fields including operating systems, networking protocols, security, and database management systems.

About the reviewers

Mario Splivalo works as a consultant dealing with databases extended into modern cloud-based architectures. He also helps companies design their infrastructure using IaaC tools such as *Terraform* and *AWS Cloudformation*. For five years, Mario worked with *Canonical* as an OpenStack engineer.

Mario's fascination with computers started back when Commodore 64 dominated the user space. He took his first steps using BASIC on his dad's C64, quickly shifting to Assembler. He gradually moved to PCs, finding a great love for programming, systems design, and database administration. He switched to Linux (Knoppix, then Ubuntu, and never looked back) in the early 2000s, continuing as a database administrator, programmer, and system administrator.

Nathan Chancellor is an independent contractor working on the Linux kernel, based in Arizona, US. As a developer, his focus is on improving the compatibility between the Linux kernel and the LLVM toolchain. He has used Linux since 2016 and it has been his primary development operating system since 2018. His distributions of choice are Arch Linux and Fedora.

Learn more on Discord

To join the Discord community for this book – where you can share feedback, ask questions to the author, and learn about new releases – follow the QR code below:

https://packt.link/SecNet

Table of Contents

Chapter 12: Automating Tasks with Shell Scripts 151

Preface

Many software engineers are new to Unix-like systems, even though these systems are everywhere in the software engineering world. Whether developers know it or not, they're expected to work with Unix-like systems running in their work environment (macOS), their software development process (Docker containers), their build and automation tooling (CI and GitHub), their production environments (Linux servers and containers), and more.

Being skilled with the Linux command line can help software developers go beyond what's expected of them, allowing them to:

- Save time by knowing when to use built-in Unix tools, instead of writing thousand-line scripts or helper programs
- Help debug complex production outages, often involving Linux servers and their interface to the application
- Mentor junior engineers
- Have a more complete understanding of how the software they write fits into the larger ecosystem and tech stack

We hope that the theory, examples, and projects included in this book can take your Linux development skills to the next level.

Who this book is for

This book is for software developers who are new to Linux and the command line, or who are out of practice and want to quickly dust off their skills. If you still feel a bit insecure about your abilities when you're staring at a Linux command-line prompt on a production server at 2:00 in the morning, this book is for you. If you want to quickly fill a Linux skills gap to advance your career, this book is for you. If you're just curious, and you want to see what kind of efficiency gains you can make in your day-to-day development setup and routines by adding some command-line magic, this book will serve you as well.

What this book is not

One of the ways we have tried to fulfill our vision for this kind of uniquely useful book is by being extremely careful about what's included. We've tried to cut out everything that isn't essential to your life as a developer, or to a basic understanding of Linux and its core abstractions. In other words, the reason this book is useful is because of *all the things we left out*.

This book is not a full Linux course. It's not for people working as Linux system engineers or kernel developers. Because of this, it's not 750+ pages long, and you should be able to work through it in a few days, perhaps during a quiet sprint at work.

What this book covers

Chapter 1, How the Command Line Works, explains how a command-line interface works, what a shell is, and then immediately gives you some basic Linux skills. You'll get a bit of theory and then begin moving around on the command line, finding and working with files and learning where to look for help when you get stuck. This chapter caters to new developers by teaching the most important command-line skills. If you read nothing else, you'll still be better off than when you started.

Chapter 2, Working with Processes, will take you on a guided tour of Linux processes. You'll then dive into useful, practical command-line skills for working with processes. We'll add detail to a few aspects that are a common source of process-related problems that you'll encounter as a software developer, like permissions, and give you some heuristics for troubleshooting them. You'll also get a quick tour of some advanced topics that will come up again later in the book.

Chapter 3, Service Management with systemd, builds on the knowledge about processes learned in the previous chapter by introducing an additional layer of abstraction, the systemd service. You'll learn about what an init system does for an operating system, and why you should care. Then, we cover all the practical commands you'll need for working with services on a Linux system.

Chapter 4, Using Shell History, is a short chapter covering some tricks that you can learn to improve your speed and efficiency on the command line. These tricks revolve around using shortcuts and leveraging shell history to avoid repeated keystrokes.

Chapter 5, Introducing Files, introduces files as the essential abstraction through which to understand Linux. You'll be introduced to the **Filesystem Hierarchy Standard** (**FHS**), which is like a map that you can use to orient yourself on any Unix system. Then it's time for practical commands for working with files and directories in Linux, including some special filetypes you probably haven't heard of. You'll also get a taste of searching for files and file content, which is one of the most powerful bits of knowledge to have at your fingertips as a developer.

Chapter 6, Editing Files on the Command Line, introduces two text editors – nano and vim. You will learn the basics of using these text editors for command-line editing while also becoming aware of common editing mistakes and how to avoid them.

Chapter 7, Users and Groups, will introduce you to how the concepts of users and groups form the basis for the Unix security model, controlling access for resources like files and processes. We'll then teach you the practical commands you'll need to create and modify users and groups.

Chapter 8, Ownership and Permissions, builds on the previous chapter's explanation of users and groups to show you how access control works for resources in Linux. This chapter teaches you about ownership and permissions by walking you through file information from a long listing. From there, we'll look at the common file and directory permissions that you'll encounter on production Linux systems, before engaging with the Linux commands for modifying file ownership and permissions.

Chapter 9, Managing Installed Software, shows you how to install software on various Linux distributions (and even macOS). First, we introduce package managers, which are the preferred way of getting software onto a machine: you'll learn the important theory and practical commands for the package management operations you'll need as a software developer. Then we'll introduce a few other methods, like downloading install scripts and the time-honored, artisanal Unix tradition of compiling your own software locally, from source (it's not as scary as it sounds!).

Chapter 10, Configuring Software, piggybacks off the previous chapter's focus on installing software by helping you with configuring software on a Linux system. You will learn about the places that most software will look for configuration ("the configuration hierarchy"). Not only will this knowledge come in handy during late-night troubleshooting sessions, but it can actually help you to write better software. We'll cover command-line arguments, environment variables, configuration files, and how all of this works on non-standard Linux environments like Docker containers. There's even a little bonus project: you'll see how to take a custom program and turn it into its own `systemd` service.

Chapter 11, Pipes and Redirection, will give you an introduction to what is possibly the "killer feature" of Unix: the ability to connect existing programs into a custom solution using pipes. We'll move through the prerequisite theory and practical skills you need to understand: file descriptors and input/output redirection. Then you'll jump into creating complex commands using pipes. You'll be introduced to some essential CLI tools and practical pipe patterns, which you'll still find yourself using long after you finish this book.

Chapter 12, Automating Tasks with Shell Scripts, serves as a Bash scripting crash course, teaching you how to go from typing individual commands in an interactive shell to writing scripts. We assume you're already a software developer, so this will be a quick introduction that shows you the core language features and doesn't spend a lot of time re-explaining the basics of programming. You'll learn about Bash syntax, best practices for script writing, and some important pitfalls to avoid.

Chapter 13, Secure Remote Access with SSH, explores the Secure Shell Protocol and the related command-line tools available to you. You'll learn the basics of **public-key cryptography (PKI)**, which is always useful for a developer to know, before diving into creating SSH keys and securely logging into remote systems over the network. You'll build on this knowledge and get some experience copying files over the network, using SSH to create ad-hoc proxies or VPNs, and see examples of various other tasks that involve moving data over an encrypted SSH tunnel.

Chapter 14, Version Control with Git, shows you how to use a tool you probably already know well – git – from the command line, instead of through your IDE or a graphical client. We quickly go through the basic theory behind git and then jump into the commands you'll need to use in a command-line environment. We'll cover two powerful features that it pays to understand – bisecting and rebasing – and then give you our take on best practices and useful shell aliases. Finally, the *Poor man's GitHub* section presents a small but legitimately useful project that you can do to practice and integrate the Linux skills you've learned up to this point.

Chapter 15, Containerizing Applications with Docker, gives you the basic theory and practical skills that will make it easy to work with Docker as a developer. We'll explore the problems that Docker solves, explain the most important Docker concepts, and take you through the core workflow and commands you'll use. You'll also see how to build your own images by containerizing a real application. And because we're approaching this from a software development and Linux perspective, you'll also develop a good intuition for how containerization works under the hood, and how it's different from virtual machines.

Chapter 16, Monitoring Application Logs, gives an overview of logging on Unix and Linux. We'll show you how (and where) logs are collected on most modern Linux systems using systemd, and how more traditional approaches work (you'll come across both in the real world). You'll build practical command-line skills finding and viewing logs and learn a bit about how logging is being done in larger infrastructures.

Chapter 17, Load Balancing and HTTP, covers the basics of HTTP for developers, with a special focus on the complexities that you'll come across when working with HTTP services in larger infrastructures. We'll correct some common misunderstandings about HTTP statuses, HTTP headers, and HTTP versions and how applications should handle them. We'll also introduce how load balancers and proxies work in the real world, and how they make the experience of troubleshooting a live application quite different from troubleshooting a development version on your laptop. Many of the Linux skills that you will have learned up to this point will come in handy here, and we'll introduce a new tool – curl – to help you troubleshoot a wide variety of HTTP-related issues.

To get the most out of this book

If you can get yourself to a Linux shell prompt – by installing Ubuntu in a virtual machine or running it as a Docker container, for example – you can follow along with everything in this book.

You can get away with even less – on Windows, there's WSL, and macOS is a bona-fide Unix operating system, so almost all of the practical commands you learn in this book (except those called out as Linux-only) will work out of the box. That said, for the best experience, follow along on a Linux operating system.

The skills required to get the most out of this book are only the basic computer skills that you already have as a software developer – editing text, working with files and folders, having some notion of what "operating systems" are, installing software, and using a development environment. Everything beyond that, we'll teach you.

Download the color images

We also provide a PDF file that has color images of the screenshots/diagrams used in this book. You can download it here: https://packt.link/gbp/9781804616925.

Conventions used

There are a number of text conventions used throughout this book.

CodeInText: Indicates code words in text, database table names, folder names, filenames, file extensions, pathnames, dummy URLs, user input, and Twitter handles. For example: "The -f flag stands for 'follow,' and the -u flag stands for 'unit.'"

A block of command line is set as follows:

```
/home/steve/Desktop# ls
anotherfile  documents  somefile.txt  stuff
/home/steve/Desktop# cd documents/
/home/steve/Desktop/documents# ls
contract.txt
```

Bold: Indicates a new term, an important word, or words that you see on the screen For instance, words in menus or dialog boxes appear in the text like this. For example: "When a file is set to be executable, Unix will do its best to execute it, either succeeding in the case of **ELF** (**Executable and Linkable Format**, probably the most widely used executable format today) or failing."

 Warnings or important notes appear like this.

 Tips and tricks appear like this.

Get in touch

Feedback from our readers is always welcome.

General feedback: Email feedback@packtpub.com, and mention the book's title in the subject of your message. If you have questions about any aspect of this book, please email us at questions@packtpub.com.

Errata: Although we have taken every care to ensure the accuracy of our content, mistakes do happen. If you have found a mistake in this book we would be grateful if you would report this to us. Please visit, http://www.packtpub.com/submit-errata, selecting your book, clicking on the Errata Submission Form link, and entering the details.

Piracy: If you come across any illegal copies of our works in any form on the Internet, we would be grateful if you would provide us with the location address or website name. Please contact us at copyright@packtpub.com with a link to the material.

If you are interested in becoming an author: If there is a topic that you have expertise in and you are interested in either writing or contributing to a book, please visit `http://authors.packtpub.com`.

Share your thoughts

Once you've read *The Software Developer's Guide to Linux*, we'd love to hear your thoughts! Scan the QR code below to go straight to the Amazon review page for this book and share your feedback.

https://packt.link/r/1804616923

Your review is important to us and the tech community and will help us make sure we're delivering excellent quality content.

Download a free PDF copy of this book

Thanks for purchasing this book!

Do you like to read on the go but are unable to carry your print books everywhere?

Is your eBook purchase not compatible with the device of your choice?

Don't worry, now with every Packt book you get a DRM-free PDF version of that book at no cost.

Read anywhere, any place, on any device. Search, copy, and paste code from your favorite technical books directly into your application.

The perks don't stop there, you can get exclusive access to discounts, newsletters, and great free content in your inbox daily

Follow these simple steps to get the benefits:

1. Scan the QR code or visit the link below

https://packt.link/free-ebook/9781804616925

2. Submit your proof of purchase
3. That's it! We'll send your free PDF and other benefits to your email directly

1

How the Command Line Works

Before we dive into practical Linux commands, you need to have a basic understanding of how the command line works. This chapter will give you that understanding.

For new developers, we'll explore the initial skills that you need to get started on the Linux command line. For those with a little more experience, there are still some nuances to discover, such as the difference between "shell" and "command line." It pays to know the difference!

In this chapter, we will cover the following topics:

- The basic idea of a command-line interface, or CLI
- The form that commands take
- How command arguments work and how they look when you're typing commands and when you're looking up documentation
- An introduction to "the shell," and how it differs from the "command line"
- The core rules that the shell uses to look up commands

To begin with, we'll start off with the basic idea of a command-line interface. We will get ourselves up to speed with how a CLI works and run through a quick example.

In the beginning...was the REPL

What is a **command-line interface (CLI)**? It's a text-based environment for interacting with your computer that:

1. Reads some input from you,
2. Evaluates (or processes) that input,

3.　Prints some output to the screen in response, and then

4.　Loops back to the beginning to repeat that process.

Let's look at what happens at each step, on a practical level, with the ls (list) command, which you'll see in a few pages. For now, it's enough to know that the ls command lists the contents of a directory.

Step	What it means
1. Read input	You type the ls command and press *Enter*.
2. Evaluate command	The shell looks up the ls binary, finds it, and tells the machine to execute it.
3. Print output	The ls command emits some text – the names of all files and directories it found – and the shell prints that output to your terminal window.
4. Loop back to 1 (repeat the process)	Once the programs called by the command have exited, repeat the process by accepting more user input.

If you read steps 1-4 again, you'll notice that the first letter of each step spells "REPL", which is a common way of referring to this kind of Read-Eval-Print Loop in the languages that invented and refined this workflow, such as Lisp.

To put this into programming terms, you can translate the REPL instructions above into code:

```
while (true) { // the loop
  print(eval(read()))
}
```

Indeed, you can create a REPL capable of doing basic calculations with just a few lines of code in most programming languages. Here's a one-liner "shell" program written in Perl:

```
perl -e 'while (<>){print eval, "\n"}'
1+2
3
```

Here, we write the code as a parameter, printing the output of the evaluation as long as there is input to read from. At the end, we append a new line and exit.

This program is tiny, but it's enough to implement an interactive Read-Eval-Print Loop in a command-line environment – a **shell.** The shells you'll use in Linux and Unix are significantly more complex than this Perl mini-shell, but the principles are the same.

The point is simple: as a developer, you might already be using REPLs without realizing it, because almost all modern scripting languages come with one. In essence, the Linux (or macOS, or other Unix) command line functions like the "interactive shells" that interpreted languages give you. So even if you're not familiar with the Lisp REPL, the Perl snippet above should remind you of a very basic Ruby or Python shell.

Now that you understand the basic mechanics of the command-line interfaces you'll be using in Linux, you're ready to try out your first commands. To do that, you'll need to know the correct command-line syntax to use.

Command-line syntax (read)

All REPLs start by reading some input. On the Linux command line, commands that the shell reads in need to have the correct syntax. Commands take this basic form:

```
commandname options
```

In programming terms, you can think of the command name as a function name, and the options as any number of arguments that will be passed to that function. This is important, because there is no single fixed syntax for all the options – each command defines which parameters it will accept. Because of this, the shell can do very little to validate a command's correctness beyond checking that the command maps to an executable.

Note

The terms "program" and "command" are used interchangeably in this chapter. There's a very slight difference because some shell builtins are defined in the shell's code and are therefore not technically separate programs of their own, but you don't need to worry about it – leave that distinction to the Unix greybeards.

Let's dive into more complex variations on this "command [options]" syntax, which you'll see frequently:

```
command [-flags,] [--example=foobar] [even_more_options ...]
```

This is the conventional format you'll see used in help documentation such as the program manual pages (manpages) included in most Linux environments, and it's fairly simple:

- command is the program you're running

- Items in brackets are optional, and brackets with ellipses ([xyz ...]) tell you that you can pass zero or more arguments here
- -flags means any valid option ("flag," in Unix-speak) for that program, e.g. -debug or -foobar

Some programs will also accept short and long versions of a parameter, usually denoted by single- vs. double-hyphenation: so -l and --long might do the same thing. It's not consistent across commands, though; this kind of behavior requires that the command's creator implemented short and long arguments that set the same parameter.

Not all commands will implement all these ways of passing configuration when invoking them, but these represent the most common forms you'll see.

By default, a space denotes the end of an argument, so just like in most programming languages, an argument string that includes spaces must be single- or double-quoted. You'll read more about this in *Chapter 12, Automating Tasks with Shell Scripts.*

In just a moment, we'll follow the process of how the shell interprets a command that you issue using this syntax, but first we want to clearly define the difference between two sometimes-interchangeable terms we've been using in this chapter: "command line" and "shell."

Command line vs. shell

In this book, we refer to a "command-line environment." We define this as any text-based environment that acts as a kind of REPL, specifically for interacting with the operating system, programming language interpreter, database, etc. A "command-line" environment or interface describes the general idea of how you're interacting with a system.

But there's a more specific term which we'll use here: shell.

A shell is a specific program that implements this command-line environment and lets you give it text commands. Technically, there are lots of different shells which provide the same kind of REPL-based command-line environment, often for wildly different things:

- Bash is a common shell environment for interacting with Linux and Unix operating systems.
- Popular databases like Postgres, MySQL, and Redis all provide a shell for developers to interact with and run commands in.
- Most interpreted languages provide a shell environment to speed up development. In these, valid commands are simply programming language statements. See irb for Ruby, the interactive Python shell, etc.

- Zsh (the Z shell) is an alternative operating system shell (like Bash), which you might see on some developers' laptops if they've customized their environments.

When we talk about a *shell* in this book, we're referring to a Unix shell (generally Bash), which is a command-line interface specifically designed to let you interact with the underlying Linux or Unix operating system.

How does the shell know what to run? (evaluate)

After *reading* in a command, the shell needs to *evaluate* it, by executing a program, fetching some information, or doing something else that's actually useful to you.

Note

Such a detailed description of how shells work may seem tedious at first, but we promise that this knowledge will come in handy when you have to troubleshoot an issue with a missing or incorrectly permissioned program.

When you type a command like `foobar -option1 test.txt` in a shell like Bash and press *Enter*, a few things happen:

1. If the command has a path specified, it will be used. This can take various forms:

   - A full path, like `/usr/bin/foobar` in the command `/usr/bin/foobar -option1 test.txt`.

   - A relative path, like the current working directory in the command `./foobar-option1 test.txt` (the `.` denotes the current directory, which we'll cover in the *Absolute vs. Relative Filepaths* section below; this command essentially says "please execute the "foobar" file that's in my current directory").

   - The path may be based on variables and symbols either in:

     - The shell's environment (env vars) like `$HOME/foobar`, or

     - Provided by the shell, like `~/foobar` (the `~` character means "this user's home directory")

2. If not, the shell checks to see whether it knows what `foobar` means:

   - It could be a built-in shell command.

   - It could be an *alias*, which is a way to set up macros or shortcuts for commands.

3. If not, the shell generally looks at the $PATH environment variable, which contains a few different locations to check for commands: /bin, /usr/bin, /sbin, etc. Users can add locations to this $PATH list, and various software will modify your $PATH: version managers for scripting languages, Python's virtual environments, and many other programs make heavy use of this mechanism. The shell tries those places specified in your $PATH, in the order it finds them in the $PATH variable, to see if any of them contain an executable with the name foobar.

If the shell still hasn't found anything, it'll return an error like bash: foobar: command not found:.

On the other hand, if at any point the shell indeed finds an executable file named foobar, it executes that file and passes -option1 and test.txt (in that order) as arguments.

At this point, the shell knows what program to use to evaluate the command, and it does so. As the command is evaluated, any output is printed to the user, completing the third step of the REPL process. Now all that's left to do is to loop back to the beginning and start the process over again, accepting another command as input from the user.

The shell tries its best to guess which program the user wants to run, using the general process we outlined above to resolve ambiguity. However, ambiguity can be a bad thing and lead to misunderstandings or bugs. During troubleshooting, you'll often want to find out which command is really being run. To accomplish this, you can use the command which <command>, which will print the full path (or the alias or script being run) and will let you know whether that command is a shell builtin. Depending on the system, which might not be available. In these situations, you can use command -v instead. This is the POSIX equivalent, which we'll learn about next:

```
bash-3.2$ which ls
/bin/ls
bash-3.2$ command -v ls
/bin/ls
```

A quick definition of POSIX

Wikipedia tells us that "the **Portable Operating System Interface (POSIX)** is a family of standards specified by the IEEE Computer Society for maintaining compatibility between operating systems." Practically speaking, it's an attempt at defining some common standards between Unix systems, which can otherwise have wildly different sets of basic commands available.

POSIX basically says things like, "every POSIX-compatible OS should have a list command called ls"; in this case, "every POSIX-compatible OS should have a way to check to see if a matching executable exists for a given command name."

If your scripts need to be portable across Unix operating systems, restricting yourself to POSIX commands is a good thing to do. However, it's still not a guarantee – many extremely popular Linux distributions divert from POSIX in numerous ways, most of which you won't notice until they bite you.

Understanding POSIX is the last brick in the foundation you need before getting started with the practical job of working on the command line. We've covered a lot of ground so far:

- You learned about REPLs and saw how this basic process maps to how all modern shells work
- We explored the basic command syntax you'll be using while working with Linux

You saw how your shell decides how to take your command input and "evaluate" it correctly. You learned important terminology that you'll come across frequently: shell, command-line interface, POSIX, and a few more terms that will pay dividends if you learn them now. Armed with this knowledge, you're ready to move from theory to practice. In the next section, we'll talk about the Linux-specific context that you'll be in while running commands. You'll learn the absolute basics of the Linux filesystem and how different kinds of paths work. After that, the rest of the chapter is all about running Linux commands!

Basic command-line skills

To work effectively with Linux, you need to know the absolute basics: how the system is structured, how to look and move around on the system, and how to read and edit files. In this section, we'll cover all of that, and get you comfortable with the very basics of navigating a Linux system.

Throughout the rest of this book, we'll dive deeper into each of these topics and commands, but we want to make sure you have a minimal, functioning set of skills by the time you get to the end of this chapter.

Unix filesystem basics

In graphical user interfaces, **directories** (called *folders* in macOS) are represented by icons. Perhaps you're used to seeing neat little rows of these in your home directory - Desktop, Documents, Videos, and so on. Double-clicking on a directory icon opens a new window with a new view from inside that directory.

When we use the term "filesystem," we mean exactly this – a collection of directories and files that organizes all data on the system. The underlying concept is exactly the same in a command-line environment, it just looks a bit different.

Instead of seeing lots of windows and icons, everything is represented as text, and the contents of directories are only shown when you ask for them. However, files and directories still work exactly the way that you're used to.

Keeping the filesystem in your head as you navigate seems difficult at first, but once you get used to it, it's often a more efficient way of dealing with a computer. After a few days of working this way, most people have no problem holding a detailed view of the filesystem in their heads as they work on a system and verify this view only occasionally.

Absolute vs. relative file paths

When beginners work with Linux, they often get caught up on the difference between an **absolute path** and a **relative path**. This simple misunderstanding results in frustrating amounts of time wasted staring at errors like this one:

```
No such file or directory
```

Because you need to understand paths as a prerequisite for almost every Linux command you run, we'll cover them first.

An absolute path is the full path to any file on the filesystem, starting from the root directory. You can recognize this because it starts with a /, which references the root directory (the very top, or beginning, of the filesystem, which contains all other files and directories).

Here are some examples of absolute paths:

- `/home/dave/Desktop`
- `/var/lib/floobkit/`
- `/usr/bin/sudo`

These **absolute paths** are like a full set of driving directions, giving turn-by-turn instructions from a known starting point (your apartment, or in the case of a Unix system, the root directory).

You can immediately recognize an absolute path by the fact that it starts with a "/" character. No matter where you are on the filesystem, absolute paths will work, since they are full, unique addresses for file objects.

A **relative path** is a partial path, and it's assumed that it starts at *the current location* instead of at the root directory. You can recognize an absolute path by the fact that it *doesn't* start with a / character.

Relative paths are like driving directions that use your current location as the starting point. If you've pulled off the road because you're lost and you need new directions, you want directions that start from your *current location*, not your home address. Relative paths give you exactly this.

As a result, relative paths are often more convenient to type: if you're already sitting in your /home/Desktop directory, it's easier to reference a file as mydocument.txt than as /home/Desktop/mydocument.txt (even though both ways are valid, given your location on the filesystem). The real difference comes when you change directories. When you move up a directory from /home/Desktop to /home, the absolute path will still reference the same file, while the relative path reference won't (now, typing mydocument.txt would reference /home/mydocument.txt).

Imagine a partial directory structure like this – in our example, we'll say this is a directory tree listing of /home/dave/Desktop:

```
Desktop
├── anotherfile
├── documents
│   └── contract.txt
├── somefile.txt
└── stuff
    ├── nothing
    └── important
```

You're sitting in this desktop directory; in other words, your current directory (which you can see by running the pwd command) is /home/dave/Desktop.

Here are some example relative paths to files in this desktop directory:

- anotherfile
- documents/contract.txt
- stuff/important

Here are the absolute paths for those same files:

- /home/dave/Desktop/anotherfile
- /home/dave/Desktop/documents/contract.txt
- /home/dave/Desktop/stuff/important

You'll notice that a relative path is just an absolute path with the path to the current working directory chopped off from the beginning.

Absolute vs. relative pathname review

Recall our example:

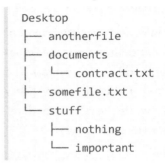

```
Desktop
├── anotherfile
├── documents
│   └── contract.txt
├── somefile.txt
└── stuff
    ├── nothing
    └── important
```

Now imagine that you're in a shell environment and your current working directory is this Desktop directory. You want to list the contract.txt file. How do you reference that file? You've got two options:

1. ls /home/dave/Desktop/documents/contract.txt: This is the absolute path, which works from everywhere.

2. ls documents/contract.txt: This is a relative path to that file, from your current directory.

Opening a terminal

On Ubuntu Linux and macOS, you can get to a command-line prompt by opening the "Terminal" application.

Looking around — command-line navigation

As a beginner, the first thing you'll want to do when you open a shell is to have a look around the system. In this section, we'll cover the most important commands for navigating around and looking at a Linux environment through a shell window.

That said, let's dive into some basic Linux commands!

pwd - print working directory

pwd stands for "print working directory," and when you type it into your terminal, your shell will print out the directory that you're currently sitting in. The Unix filesystem is often compared to a tree, but for now you can just think of it as a messy desktop with lots of directories inside. If each directory is like a room, pwd lets you see which room your command-line environment is currently visiting.

New shell sessions will usually start in your home directory. If you're following along on Linux, this will look something like:

```
→  ~  pwd
   /home/dave
```

If you're running another flavor of Unix, it may look slightly different. Here's what you'd see on macOS:

```
→  ~  pwd
   /Users/dave
```

Regardless of where you are on the filesystem, you can still reference files in all directories (see the *Absolute vs. relative file paths* section in this chapter), but sometimes moving around makes things easier. We'll get into the details of filesystem structure in a later chapter.

ls - list

ls lets you "list" the files in a directory. If you run this command without any arguments, it'll just list the files and directories in your current directory. If you pass it a path to a directory as an argument, it'll try to see what's in that directory and list it out for you:

```
ls /var/log
```

List will also take arguments ("flags"). There are many flags, but two commonly useful ones are -l ("long") and -h ("human-readable").

```
ls -l -h

# same thing; you can combine flags
ls -lh

# List a specific directory
ls -lh /usr/local/
```

A long listing will produce the following output format:

```
-rw-r--r--  1 dcohen  wheel  0 Jul  5 09:27 foobar.txt
```

Let's go through it, column by column:

- -rw-r--r--: The filetype (the first character) and permissions (three groups of three bits that represent permissions for the owning user, the owning group, and everyone else on the system, respectively).

- 1: The number of references (hardlinks) to this file.
- dcohen: The user who owns this file.
- wheel: The group that owns this file.
- 0: The amount of disk space used by the file (this one is empty). The -h flag changes this output from the default, number of bytes to something "human-readable," meaning it'll show megabytes or gigabytes when appropriate.
- Jul 5 09:27: File modification time.
- foobar.txt: The filename.

This shows you output that requires some knowledge that we haven't covered yet (users, groups, and permissions). That's okay – we'll get there in *Chapter 7, Users and Groups*.

Moving around

Now that you've learned the most basic Linux commands for getting your bearings, let's talk about navigating to where you want to go in a command line environment.

cd – change directory

cd lets you "change directory" to anywhere on the filesystem. Using the rooms metaphor from before, this is the equivalent of teleporting out of your current room and going into a different one.

After you successfully change directory, the pwd command will show your new (updated) location:

```
bash-3.2$ cd /etc/ssl

bash-3.2$ pwd
/etc/ssl

bash-3.2$ ls
README  cert.pem  certs  misc  openssl.cnf private

bash-3.2$ cd certs

bash-3.2$ pwd
/etc/ssl/certs
```

find — find files

find allows you to search for files. It is one of the few commands that does not follow the convention of long options (e.g., --name). Instead, its flags are specified with a single dash. Here is an example:

```
bash-3.2$ find / -type d -name home
/home
...
```

The above will search / (the whole system) for a directory (-type d) with the name home. Keep in mind that when you are not executing this as the all-powerful root (administrator) user, find will not have permissions to list the contents of many directories, so you will receive output like find: '/root': Permission denied in addition to what is being found.

Another common use case is to execute commands based on the output of find:

```
bash-3.2$ find . -exec echo {} \;
.
./foobar
```

This will run the echo command with any found files in place of {}. The resulting output will be much like an invocation of ls.

If, instead of running echo for each found file, we want to pass them as arguments to echo, we can replace + instead of \.

```
bash-3.2$ find . -exec echo {} +;
. ./foobar
```

find has many more flags. Which ones, exactly? That depends on the version of find your operating system ships with.

Here are some typical use cases:

- find -iname foobar: Searches for foobar, but be case-insensitive
- find -name "foobar*": Searches for files starting with foobar
- find -name "*foobar": Searches for files ending with foobar

Reading files

Now that you've learned how to find the files you're looking for, let's see how to actually read file content on the command line.

less — page through a file

less allows you to read a file, one "page" (based on the size of your terminal window) at a time.

```
less somefile.txt
```

Running less will open the file and allow you to scroll through it, one line (up/down arrow keys) or one page (spacebar) at a time.

To search inside the file, type /, followed by your search string, and hit *Enter*. Navigate matches with n (for next) and SHIFT-n (previous).

To quit, type q.

Making changes

Now that you can find and read files, let's look at how to change them or create new ones.

touch — create an empty file, or update modification time for an existing one

touch creates a file, and therefore requires a file path as your argument. If the path you give it doesn't exist yet (and presuming you have permissions to do so), an empty file is created at that path.

If a file already exists at the specified path, its access and modification timestamps are updated to the current time. If you only want to update access-time OR modification-time, you can use the -a or -m flags, respectively.

mkdir — create a directory

mkdir requires a file path argument and uses it to create ("make") a directory:

```
bash-3.2$ mkdir foobar
bash-3.2$ ls
foobar
```

Optionally, you can feed it additional arguments if you want to create multiple directories:

```
bash-3.2$ mkdir foo bar baz
bash-3.2$ ls
foo
bar
baz
```

If you want to create multiple directories nested inside of each other (or if you simply want to ensure that they all exist), you can use the -p flag:

```
bash-3.2$ mkdir -p /var/log/myapp/error
bash-3.2$ ls /var/log/myapp
error
```

Even if /var/log/myapp didn't exist before, running mkdir with the -p flag would have ensured that /var/log/myapp was created, before creating /var/log/myapp/error inside of that. On the other hand, if a directory in the path you're giving to mkdir -p *does* already exist, -p won't hurt it in any way, so it's safe to run multiple times in a row ("idempotent"). This makes the -p flag standard for scripting use.

rmdir — remove empty directories

rmdir removes empty directories. They have to be empty for this command to work, meaning it's a relatively safe command to run. Most Linux users end up just using rm instead, because it can do the same thing.

rm — remove files and directories

To delete a file, use the rm command:

```
rm filename
```

In practice, most people use rm to delete directories as well, because unlike rmdir, it works on directories that are *not* empty. You'll need the -r flag to apply the command *recursively* (to all directories contained by the one you're deleting), and the -f flag to "force" deletion without a confirmation for each file and directory:

```
rm -rf /path/to/directory
```

Note

Be extremely careful when using `rm -rf` because Linux will let you delete directories that are critical to the operation of your system. For example, `rm -rf /` is telling `rm` that you'd like to delete the root directory, which contains everything on the system.

Some Linux distributions and Unix operating systems get around this in creative ways (Ubuntu ships with a version of the `rm` command that has a `--no-preserve-root` option as a way of asking "are you *sure* you want to do this?" and Solaris intentionally used a loose interpretation of what `rm` should do to avoid deleting the root directory). In practice, these safeguards are easily circumvented. Be careful when using `rm`, and take care when pasting commands into your shell from the Internet!

mv — move or rename files and directories

`mv` is a clever one, because it can do two different things using the same syntax. Either it "moves" files from one directory to another, or – alternatively – it can rename a file, keeping it in the same directory.

First, we'll create a file using touch:

```
bash-3.2$ touch foobar.txt
bash-3.2$ ls
foobar.txt
```

Then, we'll rename the file in place:

```
bash-3.2$ mv foobar.txt foobarbaz.txt
bash-3.2$ ls
foobarbaz.txt
```

Note that the command above would overwrite any existing file named `foobarbaz.txt`, if one existed, so be careful when renaming things.

To move the file to a new directory, we'll create a new directory and then move the file there:

```
bash-3.2$ mkdir targetdir
bash-3.2$ mv foobarbaz.txt targetdir/
bash-3.2$ ls targetdir/
foobarbaz.txt
```

You can combine the operations, too. If you want to move a file to a different directory *and* rename it at the same time, you can:

```
bash-3.2$ mv foobarbaz.txt targetdir/renamed.txt
bash-3.2$ ls targetdir/
renamed.txt
```

Getting help

All but the most minimal environments tend to come with manual pages (manpages), which are documentation that you can use to learn (or remember) how to use the command-line programs you have available to you.

Use man $COMMANDNAME to get information on a command. For example, man ls will print something like this:

```
LS(1)                                           General Commands
Manual                                          LS(1)


NAME
     ls - list directory contents


SYNOPSIS
     ls [-@ABCFGHILOPRSTUWabcdefghiklmnopqrstuvwxy1%,] [--color=when] [-D
format] [file ...]


DESCRIPTION
     For each operand that names a file of a type other than directory, ls
displays its name as well as any requested, associated
     information.  For each operand that names a file of type directory,
ls displays the names of files contained within that directory,
     as well as any requested, associated information.


     If no operands are given, the contents of the current directory are
displayed.  If more than one operand is given, non-directory
     operands are displayed first; directory and non-directory operands
are sorted separately and in lexicographical order.


     The following options are available:
```

```
       -@        Display extended attribute keys and sizes in long (-l)
    output.

       -A        Include directory entries whose names begin with a dot ('.')
    except for . and ...  Automatically set for the super-user
                 unless -I is specified.
```

Since manual pages are automatically opened in a pager application, scrolling, searching, and quitting works using the same shortcuts that you're used to from the less command.

Keep in mind that man is an old utility which tries to resemble an actual book, with different sections (chapters) that cover different topics. In the example above, the (1) in ls(1) denotes which manual section we're being shown.

Sometimes a man page with the same name will exist in different sections. To specify a section, add a number before the command name. For example, to receive the same manual as above one might run man 1 ls.

The sections on most Unix-like operating systems are as follows:

1. General commands, so commands that you typically run on the command line

2. System calls

3. Library functions, covering the C standard library

4. Special files (usually devices, those found in /dev) and drivers

5. File formats and conventions. This includes configuration files

6. Games and screensavers

7. Miscellaneous

8. System administration commands and daemons

So, if you want to dig deeper into one of the topics we cover in this book, you'll likely start by looking in manpage sections 1, 5, and 8.

If you are unsure about what the name of the manual page you are looking for is, you can use apropos <keyword> or man -k <keyword> to find it. It will print a list of all manual pages containing the specified keyword.

Shell autocompletion

If you're in an interactive shell session (i.e., not executing from a script or creating a Dockerfile), you can use **shell autocompletion**, also known as **tab-completion**, to construct commands with fewer keystrokes and a lower chance of typos.

To make use of shell autocompletion, start typing a file or directory name and press *Tab*. The shell will progressively narrow your choices, displaying possible matches below the line you're typing on. When there's only one choice left based on what you've typed, the shell will autocomplete that command or argument and you can press *Enter*. Let's walk through an example.

If you're sitting in your home directory on a Linux desktop system, the view might look like this:

```
→  ~ pwd
/home/dave

→  ~ ls
Desktop
Documents
Downloads
Library
Movies
Music
Pictures
Public
code
go
```

If you want to move to the Documents directory, you'll use the cd (change directory) command to do that:

```
→  ~ cd Documents
```

First, type cd D and hit *Tab*:

```
→  ~ cd D
Desktop/    Documents/   Downloads/
```

You'll see that the shell has narrowed the ten possible choices down to three. Type another letter and press *Tab* again. You'll see that only two items match:

```
→  ~ cd Do
Documents/   Downloads/
```

Typing another letter, c, will narrow the choices to just one and another *Tab* will autocomplete the directory name for you:

```
→  ~ cd Documents/
```

As soon as you reach an autocompletion for a directory name, you can execute the command as usual with *Enter* or continue autocompleting inside of that directory. For example, pressing *Tab* again here will start the autocompletion process again inside of the Documents directory, leaving the Documents/ prefix and autocompleting valid items to the right of the slash. Your shell's current working directory won't change until you have a valid path and press *Enter*.

This small trick will save you a LOT of typing over the years. Start using it sooner rather than later!

Conclusion

In this chapter, you learned all the basic theory you need to know before working effectively on the command line. You saw practical examples of command-line syntax and learned the basics of how most commands accept arguments.

We also introduced the concept of shells and walked through how executables are looked up once you type a command and press the *Enter* key. Surprisingly, there are many advanced users who don't fully understand these two concepts, and it hinders their ability to quickly and efficiently use command-line environments.

Finally, you've learned the most important basic commands for getting around a system on the command line. You'll use these commands almost every single time you work on a Linux system – they represent the absolute basics anyone needs to master before going further. You even learned your first time-saving trick, shell autocompletion.

If you're following along and trying all of this on a real Linux system (and you *should* be!), make sure to practice what you've learned for a few minutes before moving on to the next chapter. We'll build on that knowledge throughout the rest of this book.

Learn more on Discord

To join the Discord community for this book – where you can share feedback, ask questions to the author, and learn about new releases – follow the QR code below:

https://packt.link/SecNet

2

Working with Processes

As a developer, you are already intuitively familiar with processes. They are the fruits of your labor: after writing and debugging code, your program finally executes, transforming into a beautiful operating system process!

A process on Linux can be a long-running application, a quick shell command like ls, or anything that the kernel spawns to do some work on the system. If something is getting done in Linux, a process is doing it. Your web browser, text editor, vulnerability scanner, and even things like reading files and the commands you've learned so far all spawn a process.

Linux's process model is important to understand because the abstraction it gives you – the Linux process – is what all the commands and tools you'll use to manage processes depend on. Gone are the details you're used to seeing from a developer's perspective: variables, functions, and threads have all been encapsulated as "a process." You're left with a different, external set of knobs to manipulate and gauges to check: process ID, status, resource usage, and all the other process attributes we'll be covering in this chapter.

First, we'll take a close look at the process abstraction itself, and then we'll dive into useful, practical things you can do with Linux processes. While we're covering the practical aspects, we'll pause to add detail to a few aspects that are a common source of problems, like permissions, and give you some heuristics for troubleshooting processes.

In this chapter, you'll learn about the following topics:

- What a Linux process is, and how to see the processes currently running on your system
- The attributes a process has, so you know what information you can gather while troubleshooting

- Common commands for viewing and finding processes
- More advanced topics that can come in handy for a developer actually writing programs that execute as Linux processes: Signals and inter-process communication, the /proc virtual filesystem, seeing open file handles with the lsof command, and how processes are created in Linux

You'll also get a practical review of everything you've learned in an example troubleshooting session that uses the theory and commands we cover in this chapter. Now, let's dive into what exactly a Linux process is.

Process basics

When we refer to a "process" in Linux, we're referring to the operating system's internal model of what exactly a running program *is*. Linux needs a general abstraction that works for *all* programs, which can encapsulate the things the operating system cares about. A process is that abstraction, and it enables the OS to track some of the important context around programs that are executing; namely:

- Memory usage
- Processor time used
- Other system resource usage (disk access, network usage)
- Communication between processes
- Related processes that a program starts, for example, firing off a shell command

You can get a listing of all system processes (at least the ones your user is allowed to see) by running the ps program with the aux flags:

```
root@localhost:~# ps aux
USER        PID %CPU %MEM    VSZ   RSS TTY      STAT START   TIME COMMAND
root          1  0.2  0.3 167308 12816 ?        Ss   18:55   0:01 /sbin/init
root          2  0.0  0.0      0     0 ?        S    18:55   0:00 [kthreadd]
root          3  0.0  0.0      0     0 ?        I<   18:55   0:00 [rcu_gp]
root          4  0.0  0.0      0     0 ?        I<   18:55   0:00 [rcu_par_gp]
root          5  0.0  0.0      0     0 ?        I<   18:55   0:00 [slub_flushwq]
root          6  0.0  0.0      0     0 ?        I<   18:55   0:00 [netns]
root          8  0.0  0.0      0     0 ?        I<   18:55   0:00 [kworker/0:0H-ever
root         10  0.0  0.0      0     0 ?        I<   18:55   0:00 [mm_percpu_wq]
root         11  0.0  0.0      0     0 ?        S    18:55   0:00 [rcu_tasks_rude_]
root         12  0.0  0.0      0     0 ?        S    18:55   0:00 [rcu_tasks_trace]
root         13  0.0  0.0      0     0 ?        S    18:55   0:00 [ksoftirqd/0]
root         14  0.0  0.0      0     0 ?        I    18:55   0:00 [rcu_sched]
root         15  0.0  0.0      0     0 ?        S    18:55   0:00 [migration/0]
root         16  0.0  0.0      0     0 ?        S    18:55   0:00 [idle_inject/0]
root         17  0.0  0.0      0     0 ?        I    18:55   0:00 [kworker/0:1-cgrou
root         18  0.0  0.0      0     0 ?        S    18:55   0:00 [cpuhp/0]
root         19  0.0  0.0      0     0 ?        S    18:55   0:00 [cpuhp/1]
root         20  0.0  0.0      0     0 ?        S    18:55   0:00 [idle_inject/1]
root         21  0.0  0.0      0     0 ?        S    18:55   0:00 [migration/1]
root         22  0.0  0.0      0     0 ?        S    18:55   0:00 [ksoftirqd/1]
root         23  0.0  0.0      0     0 ?        I    18:55   0:00 [kworker/1:0-event
```

Figure 2.1: List of system processes

We'll cover the attributes most relevant to your work as a developer in this chapter.

What is a Linux process made of?

From the perspective of the operating system, a "process" is simply a data structure that makes it easy to access information like:

- **Process ID** (**PID** in the ps output above). PID 1 is the init system – the original parent of all other processes, which bootstraps the system. The kernel starts this as one of the first things it does after starting to execute. When a process is created, it gets the next available process ID, in sequential order. Because it is so important to the normal functioning of the operating system, init cannot be killed, even by the root user. Different Unix operating systems use different init systems – for example, most Linux distributions use systemd, while macOS uses launchd, and many other Unixes use SysV. Regardless of the specific implementation, we'll refer to this process by the name of the role it fills: "init."

Note

In containers, processes are namespaced – in the "real" environment, all container processes might be PID 3210, while that single PID maps to lots of processes (1..n, where n is the number of running processes in the container). You can see this from outside but not inside the container.

- **Parent Process PID (PPID)**. Each process is spawned by a parent. If the parent process dies while the child is alive, the child becomes an "orphan." Orphaned processes are re-parented to init (PID 1).

- **Status (STAT** in the ps output above). man ps will show you an overview:

  - D – uninterruptible sleep (usually IO)
  - I – idle kernel thread
  - R – running or runnable (on run queue)
  - S – interruptible sleep (waiting for an event to complete)
  - T – stopped by job control signal
  - t – stopped by debugger during tracing
  - X – dead (should never be seen)
  - Z – defunct ("zombie") process, terminated but not reaped by its parent

- **Priority** status ("niceness" – does this process allow other processes to take priority over it?).

- A process **Owner** (USER in the ps output above); the effective user ID.

- Effective **Group ID** (EGID), which is used.

- An **address map** of the process's memory space.

- Resource usage – open files, network ports, and other resources the process is using (**VSZ** and **RSS** for memory usage in the ps output above).

(Citation: from the *Unix and Linux System Administration Handbook, 5th edition*, p.91.)

Let's take a closer look at a few of the process attributes that are most important for developers and occasional troubleshooters to understand.

Process ID (PID)

Each process is uniquely identifiable by its process ID, which is just a unique integer that is assigned to a process when it starts. Much like a relational database with IDs that uniquely identify each row of data, the Linux operating system keeps track of each process by its PID.

A PID is by far the most useful label for you to use when interacting with processes.

Effective User ID (EUID) and Effective Group ID (EGID)

These determine which system user and group your process is running as. Together, user and group permissions determine what a process is allowed to do on the system.

As you'll see in *Chapter 5, Introducing Files*, files have user and group ownership set on them, which determines who their permissions apply to. If a file's ownership and permissions are essentially a lock, then a process with the right user/group permissions is like a key that opens the lock and allows access to the file. We'll dive deeper into this later, when we talk about permissions.

Environment variables

You've probably used environment variables in your applications – they're a way for the operating system environment that launches your process to pass in data that the process needs. This commonly includes things like configuration directives (LOG_DEBUG=1) and secret keys (AWS_SECRET_KEY), and every programming language has some way to read them out from the context of the program.

For example, this Python script gets the user's home directory from the HOME environment variable, and then prints it:

```python
import os
home_dir = os.environ['HOME']
print("The home directory for this user is", home_dir)
```

In my case, running this program in the python3 REPL on a Linux machine results in the following output:

```
The home directory for this user is /home/dcohen
```

Working directory

A process has a "current working directory," just like your shell (which is just a process, anyway). Typing pwd in your shell prints its current working directory, and every process has a working directory. The working directory for a process can change, so don't rely on it too much.

This concludes our overview of the process attributes that you should know about. In the next section, we'll step away from theory and look at some commands you can use to start working with processes right away.

Practical commands for working with Linux processes

Here are some of the commands you'll use most often:

- ps – Shows processes on the system; you saw an example of this command earlier in the chapter. Flags modify which process attributes are displayed as columns. This command is usually used with filters to control how much output you get, for example, (ps aux | head -n 10) to cut your output down to just the top 10 lines. A few more useful tricks:

  - ps -eLf shows thread information for processes
  - ps -ejH is useful for seeing the relationships between parent and child processes visually (children are indented under their parents)

```
root@40086047ef36:/# ps -eLf
UID        PID  PPID   LWP  C NLWP STIME TTY          TIME CMD
root         1     0     1  0    1 22:30 pts/0     00:00:00 /bin/bash
root         9     1     9  0    1 22:31 pts/0     00:00:00 ps -eLf
root@40086047ef36:/# ps -ejH
   PID  PGID   SID TTY          TIME CMD
     1     1     1 pts/0     00:00:00 bash
    10    10     1 pts/0     00:00:00   ps
```

Figure 2.2: Examples of outputs of the ps command with flags

- pgrep – Find process IDs by name. Can use regular expressions.

```
root@localhost:~# pgrep nginx
1589
1592
1593
root@localhost:~# pgrep ^n
6
584
1589
1592
1593
root@localhost:~# █
```

Figure 2.3: Examples of outputs of the pgrep command with flags

- `top` – An interactive program that polls all processes (once a second, by default) and outputs a sorted list of resource usage (you can configure what it sorts by). Also displays total system resource usage. Press *Q* or use *Ctrl* + *C* to quit. You'll see an example of this command's output later in this chapter.

- `iotop` – Like top, but for disk IO. Extremely useful for finding IO-hungry processes. Not installed on all systems by default, but available via most package managers.

```
Total DISK READ:        0.00 B/s | Total DISK WRITE:        0.00 B/s
Current DISK READ:      0.00 B/s | Current DISK WRITE:      0.00 B/s
   TID  PRIO  USER     DISK READ  DISK WRITE  SWAPIN      IO>    COMMAND
     1 be/4 root        0.00 B/s    0.00 B/s  ?unavailable? init
     2 be/4 root        0.00 B/s    0.00 B/s  ?unavailable? [kthreadd]
     3 be/0 root        0.00 B/s    0.00 B/s  ?unavailable? [rcu_gp]
     4 be/0 root        0.00 B/s    0.00 B/s  ?unavailable? [rcu_par_gp]
     5 be/0 root        0.00 B/s    0.00 B/s  ?unavailable? [slub_flushwq]
     6 be/0 root        0.00 B/s    0.00 B/s  ?unavailable? [netns]
     8 be/0 root        0.00 B/s    0.00 B/s  ?unavailable? [kworker~_highpri]
    10 be/0 root        0.00 B/s    0.00 B/s  ?unavailable? [mm_percpu_wq]
    11 be/4 root        0.00 B/s    0.00 B/s  ?unavailable? [rcu_tasks_rude_]
    12 be/4 root        0.00 B/s    0.00 B/s  ?unavailable? [rcu_tasks_trace]
    13 be/4 root        0.00 B/s    0.00 B/s  ?unavailable? [ksoftirqd/0]
    14 be/4 root        0.00 B/s    0.00 B/s  ?unavailable? [rcu_sched]
    15 rt/4 root        0.00 B/s    0.00 B/s  ?unavailable? [migration/0]
    16 rt/4 root        0.00 B/s    0.00 B/s  ?unavailable? [idle_inject/0]
    18 be/4 root        0.00 B/s    0.00 B/s  ?unavailable? [cpuhp/0]
    19 be/4 root        0.00 B/s    0.00 B/s  ?unavailable? [cpuhp/1]
    20 rt/4 root        0.00 B/s    0.00 B/s  ?unavailable? [idle_inject/1]
    21 rt/4 root        0.00 B/s    0.00 B/s  ?unavailable? [migration/1]
    22 be/4 root        0.00 B/s    0.00 B/s  ?unavailable? [ksoftirqd/1]
    23 be/4 root        0.00 B/s    0.00 B/s  ?unavailable? [kworker~ercpu_wq]
keys:  any: refresh  q: quit  i: ionice  o: active  p: procs  a: accum
sort:  r: asc  left: SWAPIN  right: COMMAND  home: TID  end: COMMAND
CONFIG_TASK_DELAY_ACCT not enabled in kernel, cannot determine SWAPIN and IO %
```

Figure 2.4: Example of output of the iotop command

- nethogs – Like top, but for network IO. Groups network usage by process, which is incredibly convenient. Available via most package managers.

```
NetHogs version 0.8.6-3

   PID USER    PROGRAM                    DEV       SENT       RECEIVED
  2064 root    curl                       eth0      0.580       8.730 KB/sec
   719 root    sshd: root@pts/0           eth0     11.067       0.412 KB/sec
     ? root    45.33.83.163:445-201.91..            0.021       0.024 KB/sec
     ? root    45.33.83.163:6379-47.57..            0.011       0.014 KB/sec
     ? root    45.33.83.163:7777-139.1..            0.000       0.000 KB/sec
  2062 root    curl                       eth0      0.000       0.000 KB/sec
     ? root    45.33.83.163:9010-79.12..            0.000       0.000 KB/sec
  2060 root    curl                       eth0      0.000       0.000 KB/sec
     ? root    45.33.83.163:50153-66.7..            0.000       0.000 KB/sec
     ? root    45.33.83.163:36198-35.2..            0.000       0.000 KB/sec
     ? root    45.33.83.163:37464-35.2..            0.000       0.000 KB/sec
     ? root    45.33.83.163:2443-66.29..            0.000       0.000 KB/sec
     ? root    45.33.83.163:57240-23.2..            0.000       0.000 KB/sec
     ? root    unknown TCP                          0.000       0.000 KB/sec

 TOTAL                                              11.679      9.181  KB/sec
```

Figure 2.5: Example of output of the nethogs command

- kill – Allows users to send signals to processes, usually to stop them or make them
  re-read their configuration files. We'll explain signals and kill command usage later in
  this chapter.

Advanced process concepts and tools

This marks the beginning of the "advanced" section of this chapter. While you don't need to
master all the concepts in this section to work effectively with Linux processes, they can be extremely helpful. If you have a few extra minutes, we recommend at least familiarizing yourself
with each one.

Signals

How does systemctl tell your web server to re-read its configuration files? How can you politely
ask a process to shut down cleanly? And how can you kill a malfunctioning process immediately,
because it's bringing your production application to its knees?

In Unix and Linux, all of this is done with signals. Signals are numerical messages that can be
sent between programs. They're a way for processes to communicate with each other and with
the operating system, allowing processes to send and receive specific messages.

These messages can be used to communicate a variety of things to a process, for example, indicating that a particular event has happened or that a specific action or response is required.

Practical uses of signals

Let's look at a few examples of the practical value that the signal mechanism enables. Signals can be used to implement inter-process communication; for example, one process can send a signal to another process indicating that it's finished with a particular task and that the other process can now start working. This allows processes to coordinate their actions and work together in a smooth and efficient manner, much like execution threads in programming languages (but without the associated memory sharing).

Another common application of process signals is to handle program errors. For example, a process can be designed to catch the SIGSEGV signal, which indicates a segmentation fault. When a process receives this signal, it can trap that signal and then take action to log the error, dump core for debugging purposes, or clean up any resources that were being used before shutting down gracefully.

Process signals can also be used to implement graceful shutdowns. For example, when a system is shutting down, a signal can be sent to all processes to give them a chance to save their state and clean up any resources they were using, via "trapping" signals.

Trapping

Many of the signals can be "trapped" by the processes that receive them: this is essentially the same idea as catching and handling an error in a programming language.

If the receiving process has a handler function for the signal that's being sent, then that handler function is run. That's how programs re-read their configuration without restarting, and finish their database writes and close their file handles after receiving the shutdown signal.

The kill command

However, it's not just processes that communicate via signals: the frighteningly named (and, technically speaking, incorrectly named) kill is a program that allows users to send signals to processes, too.

One of the most common uses of user-sent processes via the kill command is to interrupt a process that is no longer responding. For example, if a process is stuck in an infinite loop, a "kill" signal can be sent to force it to stop.

The kill command allows you to send a signal to a process by specifying its PID. If the process you'd like to terminate has PID 2600, you'd run:

```
kill 2600
```

This command would send signal 15 (`SIGTERM`, or "terminate") to the process, which would then have a chance to trap the signal and shut down cleanly.

>
>
> **Note**
>
> As you can see from the included table of standard signal numbers, the default signal that `kill` sends is "terminate" (signal 15), not "kill" (`SIGKILL` is 9). The `kill` program is not just for killing processes but also for sending any kind of signal. It's really confusingly named and I'm sorry about that – it's just one of those idiosyncrasies of Unix and Linux that you'll get used to.

If you don't want to send the default signal 15, you can specify the signal you'd like to send with a dash; to send a `SIGHUP` to the same process, you'd run:

```
kill -1 2600
```

Running man `signal` will give you a list of signals that you can send:

```
     Name        Default Action      Description
 1   SIGHUP      terminate process   terminal line hangup
 2   SIGINT      terminate process   interrupt program
 3   SIGQUIT     create core image   quit program
 4   SIGILL      create core image   illegal instruction
 5   SIGTRAP     create core image   trace trap
 6   SIGABRT     create core image   abort program (formerly SIGIOT)
 7   SIGEMT      create core image   emulate instruction executed
 8   SIGFPE      create core image   floating-point exception
 9   SIGKILL     terminate process   kill program
10   SIGBUS      create core image   bus error
11   SIGSEGV     create core image   segmentation violation
12   SIGSYS      create core image   non-existent system call invoked
13   SIGPIPE     terminate process   write on a pipe with no reader
14   SIGALRM     terminate process   real-time timer expired
15   SIGTERM     terminate process   software termination signal
16   SIGURG      discard signal      urgent condition present on socket
17   SIGSTOP     stop process        stop (cannot be caught or ignored)
18   SIGTSTP     stop process        stop signal generated from keyboard
19   SIGCONT     discard signal      continue after stop
20   SIGCHLD     discard signal      child status has changed
21   SIGTTIN     stop process        background read attempted from control
                                     terminal
22   SIGTTOU     stop process        background write attempted to control
                                     terminal
23   SIGIO       discard signal      I/O is possible on a descriptor (see
                                     fcntl(2))
24   SIGXCPU     terminate process   cpu time limit exceeded (see setrlimit(2))
25   SIGXFSZ     terminate process   file size limit exceeded (see
                                     setrlimit(2))
26   SIGVTALRM   terminate process   virtual time alarm (see setitimer(2))
27   SIGPROF     terminate process   profiling timer alarm (see setitimer(2))
28   SIGWINCH    discard signal      Window size change
29   SIGINFO     discard signal      status request from keyboard
30   SIGUSR1     terminate process   User defined signal 1
31   SIGUSR2     terminate process   User defined signal 2
```

Figure 2.6: Example of output of the man signal command

It pays – sometimes quite literally, in engineering interviews – to be familiar with a few of these:

- SIGHUP (1) – "hangup": interpreted by many applications – for example, nginx – as "re-read your configuration because I've made changes to it."

- SIGINT (2) – "interrupt": often interpreted the same as SIGTERM - "please shut down cleanly."

- SIGTERM (15) – "terminate": nicely asks a process to shut down.

- SIGUSR1 (30) and SIGUSR2 (31) are sometimes used for application-defined messaging For example, SIGUSR1 asks nginx to re-open the log files it's writing to, which is useful if you've just rotated them.

- SIGKILL (9) – SIGKILL cannot be trapped and handled by processes. If this signal is sent to a program, the operating system will kill that program immediately. Any cleanup code, like flushing writes or safe shutdown, is not performed, so this is generally a last resort, since it could lead to data corruption.

If you want to explore Linux a bit deeper, feel free to poke around the /proc directory. That's definitely beyond the basics, but it's a directory that contains a filesystem subtree for every process, where live information about the processes is looked up as you read those files.

```
/proc
```

In practice, this knowledge can come in handy during troubleshooting when you've identified a misbehaving (or mysterious) process and want to know exactly what it's doing in real time.

You can learn a lot about a process by poking around in its /proc subdirectory and casually googling.

Many of the tools we show you in this chapter actually use /proc to gather process information, and only show you a subset of what's there. If you want to see *everything* and do the filtering yourself, /proc is the place to look.

lsof – show file handles that a process has open

The lsof command shows all files that a process has opened for reading and writing. This is useful because it only takes one small bug for a program to leak file handles (internal references to files that it has requested access to). This can lead to resource usage issues, file corruption, and a long list of strange behavior.

Thankfully, getting a list of files that a process has open is easy. Just run lsof and pass the –p flag with a PID (you'll usually have to run this as root). This will return the list of files that the process (in this case, with PID 1589) has open:

```
~ lsof -p 1589
```

```
root@localhost:~# lsof -p 1589
COMMAND  PID USER   FD    TYPE     DEVICE SIZE/OFF    NODE NAME
nginx   1589 root   cwd   DIR         8,0     4096       2 /
nginx   1589 root   rtd   DIR         8,0     4096       2 /
nginx   1589 root   txt   REG         8,0  1240136   78096 /usr/sbin/nginx
nginx   1589 root   mem   REG         8,0   184904  262503 /usr/lib/nginx/modules/ngx_stream_module.so
nginx   1589 root   mem   REG         8,0   112264  262494 /usr/lib/nginx/modules/ngx_mail_module.so
nginx   1589 root   mem   REG         8,0   149760     867 /usr/lib/x86_64-linux-gnu/libgpg-error.so.0.32.1
nginx   1589 root   mem   REG         8,0   125488    1035 /usr/lib/x86_64-linux-gnu/libgcc_s.so.1
nginx   1589 root   mem   REG         8,0  2252096     837 /usr/lib/x86_64-linux-gnu/libstdc++.so.6.0.30
nginx   1589 root   mem   REG         8,0 29476472    8427 /usr/lib/x86_64-linux-gnu/libicudata.so.70.1
nginx   1589 root   mem   REG         8,0  1296312     840 /usr/lib/x86_64-linux-gnu/libgcrypt.so.20.3.4
nginx   1589 root   mem   REG         8,0  2062664    8432 /usr/lib/x86_64-linux-gnu/libicuuc.so.70.1
nginx   1589 root   mem   REG         8,0    96416   17716 /usr/lib/x86_64-linux-gnu/libexslt.so.0.8.20
nginx   1589 root   mem   REG         8,0   264632   17717 /usr/lib/x86_64-linux-gnu/libxslt.so.1.1.34
nginx   1589 root   mem   REG         8,0  1967384    5818 /usr/lib/x86_64-linux-gnu/libxml2.so.2.9.13
nginx   1589 root   mem   REG         8,0    27672  262485 /usr/lib/nginx/modules/ngx_http_xslt_filter_module.so
```

Figure 2.7: Example of list of files opened by the 1589 process using the lsof -p 1589 command

The above is the output for an nginx web server process. The first line shows you the current working directory for the process: in this case, the root directory (/). You can also see that it has file handles open on its own binary (/usr/sbin/nginx) and various libraries in /usr/lib/.

Further down, you might notice a few more interesting filepaths:

```
nginx   1589 root   DEL   REG                  0,1              11 /dev/zero
nginx   1589 root    0u   CHR                  1,3       0t0      5 /dev/null
nginx   1589 root    1u   CHR                  1,3       0t0      5 /dev/null
nginx   1589 root    2w   REG                  8,0        76 262197 /var/log/nginx/error.log
nginx   1589 root    3u  unix 0xffff8da007507300       0t0   23207 type=STREAM
nginx   1589 root    4w   REG                  8,0      2910 262196 /var/log/nginx/access.log
nginx   1589 root    5w   REG                  8,0        76 262197 /var/log/nginx/error.log
nginx   1589 root    6u  IPv4                23965       0t0    TCP *:http (LISTEN)
nginx   1589 root    7u  IPv6                23966       0t0    TCP *:http (LISTEN)
nginx   1589 root    8u  unix 0xffff8da007505540       0t0   23208 type=STREAM
nginx   1589 root    9u  unix 0xffff8da007504000       0t0   29795 type=STREAM
nginx   1589 root   10u  unix 0xffff8da007505dc0       0t0   29796 type=STREAM
```

Figure 2.8: Further opened files of the 1589 process

This listing includes the log files nginx is writing to, and socket files (Unix, IPv4, and IPv6) that it's reading and writing to. In Unix and Linux, network sockets are just a special kind of file, which makes it easy to use the same core toolset across a wide variety of use cases – tools that work with files are extremely powerful in an environment where almost everything is represented as a file.

Inheritance

Except for the very first process, init (PID 1), all processes are created by a parent process, which essentially makes a copy of itself and then "forks" (splits) that copy off. When a process is forked, it typically inherits its parent's permissions, environment variables, and other attributes.

Although this default behavior can be prevented and changed, it's a bit of a security risk: software that you run manually receives the permissions of your current user (or even root privileges, if you use sudo). All child processes that might be created by that process – for example, during installation, compilation, and so on – inherit those permissions.

Imagine a web server process that was started with root privileges (so it could bind to a network port) and environment variables containing cloud authentication keys (so it could grab data from the cloud). When this main process forks off a child process that needs neither root privileges nor sensitive environment variables, it's an unnecessary security risk to pass those along to the child. As a result, dropping privileges and clearing environment variables is a common pattern in services spawning child processes.

From a security perspective, it is important to keep this in mind to prevent situations where information such as passwords or access to sensitive files could be leaked. While it is outside the scope of this book to go into details of how to avoid this, it's important to be aware of this if you're writing software that's going to run on Linux systems.

Review – example troubleshooting session

Let's look at an example troubleshooting session. All we know is that one specific Linux server is running extremely slowly.

To begin with, we want to see what's happening on the system. You just learned that you can see a live view of processes running on a system by running the interactive top command. Let's try that now.

```
top - 19:06:27 up 10 min,  2 users,  load average: 0.08, 0.03, 0.01
Tasks: 108 total,   3 running, 105 sleeping,   0 stopped,   0 zombie
%Cpu(s): 46.8 us,  2.0 sy,  0.0 ni, 48.8 id,  2.3 wa,  0.0 hi,  0.0 si,  0.0 st
MiB Mem :   3924.0 total,   3260.3 free,    145.5 used,    518.2 buff/cache
MiB Swap:    512.0 total,    512.0 free,      0.0 used.   3552.6 avail Mem
```

PID	USER	PR	NI	VIRT	RES	SHR	S	%CPU	%MEM	TIME+	COMMAND
1763	root	20	0	10168	7820	1436	R	94.7	0.2	0:03.14	bzip2
1761	root	20	0	7324	3100	2872	S	3.0	0.1	0:00.11	tar
1	root	20	0	167308	12816	8300	S	0.0	0.3	0:01.82	systemd
2	root	20	0	0	0	0	S	0.0	0.0	0:00.00	kthreadd
3	root	0	-20	0	0	0	I	0.0	0.0	0:00.00	rcu_gp
4	root	0	-20	0	0	0	I	0.0	0.0	0:00.00	rcu_par_gp
5	root	0	-20	0	0	0	I	0.0	0.0	0:00.00	slub_flushwq
6	root	0	-20	0	0	0	I	0.0	0.0	0:00.00	netns
8	root	0	-20	0	0	0	I	0.0	0.0	0:00.00	kworker/0:0H-events_highpri
10	root	0	-20	0	0	0	I	0.0	0.0	0:00.00	mm_percpu_wq
11	root	20	0	0	0	0	S	0.0	0.0	0:00.00	rcu_tasks_rude_
12	root	20	0	0	0	0	S	0.0	0.0	0:00.00	rcu_tasks_trace
13	root	20	0	0	0	0	S	0.0	0.0	0:00.02	ksoftirqd/0
14	root	20	0	0	0	0	R	0.0	0.0	0:00.03	rcu_sched
15	root	rt	0	0	0	0	S	0.0	0.0	0:00.00	migration/0
16	root	-51	0	0	0	0	S	0.0	0.0	0:00.00	idle_inject/0
17	root	20	0	0	0	0	I	0.0	0.0	0:00.33	kworker/0:1-mm_percpu_wq
18	root	20	0	0	0	0	S	0.0	0.0	0:00.00	cpuhp/0
19	root	20	0	0	0	0	S	0.0	0.0	0:00.00	cpuhp/1

Figure 2.9: Example of output of the top command

By default, the top command sorts processes by CPU usage, so we can simply look at the first listed process to find the offending one. Indeed, the top process is using 94% of one CPU's available processing time.

As a result of running top, we've gotten a few useful pieces of information:

- The problem is CPU usage, as opposed to some other kind of resource contention.

- The offending process is PID 1763, and the command being run (listed in the **COMMAND** column) is bzip2, which is a compression program.

We determine that this bzip2 process doesn't need to be running here, and we decide to stop it. Using the kill command, we ask the process to terminate:

```
kill 1763
```

After waiting a few seconds, we check to see if this (or any other) bzip2 process is running:

```
pgrep bzip2
```

Unfortunately, we see that the same PID is still running. It's time to get serious:

```
kill -9 1763
```

This orders the operating system to kill the process without allowing the process to trap (and potentially ignore) the signal. A SIGKILL (signal #9) simply kills the process where it stands.

Now that you've killed the offending process, the server is running smoothly again and you can start tracking down the developer who thought it was a good idea to compress large source directories on this machine.

In this example, we followed the most common systems troubleshooting pattern in existence:

1. We looked at resource usage (via top in this example). This can be any of the other tools we discussed, depending on which resource is the one being exhausted.

2. We found a PID to investigate.

3. We acted on that process. In this example, no further investigation was necessary and we sent a signal, asking it to shut down (15, SIGTERM).

Conclusion

In this chapter, we took a close look at the process abstraction that Linux wraps around executing programs. You've seen the common components that all processes have and learned the basic commands you need to find and inspect running processes. With these tools, you'll be able to identify when a process is misbehaving, and more importantly, *which* process is misbehaving.

Learn more on Discord

To join the Discord community for this book – where you can share feedback, ask questions to the author, and learn about new releases – follow the QR code below:

```
https://packt.link/SecNet
```

3

Service Management with systemd

In the previous chapter, you learned about how processes work in Linux. Now it's time to look at how these processes are wrapped in an additional layer of abstraction: the *systemd service*.

The commands you've seen so far – ls, mv, rm, ps, and others – run in the foreground, attached to your shell session. You run them, the programs do their job, and then they exit. However, not all programs run like this.

Services, also frequently called daemons, are long-running processes that run in the background. These can be things like databases and web servers, but also regular system services like your network manager, your desktop environment, and so on. These long-running background services are typically started and controlled via an **init** system such as **systemd**.

init here refers to the first process your operating system kernel starts, and it is the job of this process to take care of starting any other processes.

systemd services are controlled using a command line utility called systemctl. It will be used for starting and stopping services, for example, to restart a service that's misbehaving or to reload one whose configuration has changed.

If you're bouncing around the book and haven't read the previous chapter yet, you can still get value out of this one. For now, just think of a process as any running command, application, or service. When you're ready to learn about how processes work in more detail, you can read *Chapter 2, Working with Processes*.

In this chapter, you'll learn all about:

- The command you'll use to interact with systemd services: systemctl
- A slightly deeper dive into what an init system does, and how systemd specifically fills this role
- Managing services with systemctl
- A few tips for working in container environments (like Docker containers), which usually don't have the kind of robust service management layer we describe in this chapter

Note

This chapter applies to Linux only – macOS and Windows (and even other Unixes) manage processes using different tools. In fact, different Linux distributions use different tools, however, systemd is the most widely used one. While the concepts are similar, knowing how modern Linux environments manage services is most useful for developers.

The basics

Linux services are background processes that run on a Linux system to perform specific tasks. They are similar to Windows services or daemons on macOS.

Most non-containerized Linux environments use systemd to manage services. The two tools you'll use to interact with systemd are:

- systemctl: Controls services (called 'units' in systemd nomenclature)
- journalctl: Lets you work with system logs

We'll cover systemctl in this chapter, and journalctl in *Chapter 16, Monitoring Application Logs*, later in the book.

systemd is a system and service manager for Linux that provides a standard way to manage services. It is now widely used as the default init system for most Linux distributions. Many Linux distributions previously made use of the SysV init systems, which come from Unix and are still used by many modern Unix operating systems. Others, such as Alpine and Gentoo Linux, use OpenRC as their init systems. There are many more init systems out there, however, the overwhelming majority of Linux distributions now use systemd. With systemd, services can be started, stopped, restarted, enabled (set to start at boot), and disabled, and their status can be checked. Services are defined by a *unit file*, which specifies exactly how the service should be managed by systemd.

To manage services with `systemd`, you can use the following basic commands (we'll dive into each one later in this chapter):

- `systemctl start <service>`: starts a service.
- `systemctl stop <service>`: stops a service.
- `systemctl restart <service>`: restarts a service.
- `systemctl status <service>`: displays the current status of a service.

Remember that only users with root privileges (e.g., using `sudo`) can manage system services with `systemd`.

init

Let's take a quick detour to define a common term that you'll see used often. In Linux, `init` – short for 'initialization' – is the first process that is started when the system boots up. Unsurprisingly, you can find it at PID 1. init is responsible for managing the boot process and starting all other processes and services that have been configured to run on the system. It also re-parents orphaned processes (processes whose original parent process has died) and keeps them as its own children, to ensure they still behave normally.

Like almost everything in the Linux world, there are several different, mutually exclusive programs that can fill this role. They are all referred to as *init systems*, which is the general name for any software that can fill this important bootstrapping, initializing, and coordinating role. As mentioned previously, there are several init systems available for Linux, including **System V init** (**SysV**), OpenRC, and `systemd`. Most modern Linux systems have switched to systemd, which is why that's the one we're covering here.

Which init system you're using will determine how services are defined and managed, so keep in mind that everything you see here applies only to systemd.

Processes and services

Let's talk about the subtle difference between processes and services. You can think of a service as some packaging around a piece of software that makes it easier to manage as a running process.

A service adds convenient features to how a program (and the resulting process spawned by that program) is handled by the system. For example, it lets you define dependencies between different processes, control startup order, add environment variables for the process to start with, limit resource usage, control permissions, and many other useful things. To tie a bow around the whole package, a service provides a simple name to reference your program. We'll show you how to create your own service in the later *Chapter 10, Configuring Software*.

In the rest of this chapter, we'll stick to managing existing services.

systemctl commands

systemctl is the tool you'll use to manage the services that have been defined on your system. These examples will use the foobar service, which doesn't really exist, as a stand-in for whatever service you might be managing.

Checking the status of a service

systemctl status <service> checks the status of the service. You'll get an assortment of data that's useful for all kinds of troubleshooting tasks. This is what the output for the nginx web server's service looks like:

```
root@localhost:~# systemctl status nginx
● nginx.service - A high performance web server and a reverse proxy server
     Loaded: loaded (/lib/systemd/system/nginx.service; enabled; vendor preset: enabled)
     Active: active (running) since Mon 2023-02-06 21:47:43 UTC; 3min 54s ago
       Docs: man:nginx(8)
    Process: 1503 ExecStartPre=/usr/sbin/nginx -t -q -g daemon on; master_process on; (code=exited, status=0/SUCCESS)
    Process: 1504 ExecStart=/usr/sbin/nginx -g daemon on; master_process on; (code=exited, status=0/SUCCESS)
   Main PID: 1598 (nginx)
      Tasks: 3 (limit: 4575)
     Memory: 5.4M
        CPU: 20ms
     CGroup: /system.slice/nginx.service
             ├─1598 "nginx: master process /usr/sbin/nginx -g daemon on; master_process on;"
             ├─1601 "nginx: worker process" "" "" "" "" "" "" "" "" "" "" "" "" "" "" "" "" "" "" "" "" "" "" "" "" ""
             └─1602 "nginx: worker process" "" "" "" "" "" "" "" "" "" "" "" "" "" "" "" "" "" "" "" "" "" "" "" "" ""

Feb 06 21:47:43 localhost systemd[1]: Starting A high performance web server and a reverse proxy server...
Feb 06 21:47:43 localhost systemd[1]: Started A high performance web server and a reverse proxy server.
```

Figure 3.1: nginx web server service output

Let's dissect the information that's displayed in the dense output that this command produces, line by line:

- **Service name:** The name of the service as defined in its unit file.
- **Load state:** Whether the service unit file has been successfully loaded and is ready to be started.
- **Active state:** The current state of the service – whether it is running, inactive, or failed – and how long it's been that way.
- **Docs:** The main page where you can find relevant documentation if it's been installed.
- **Main PID and child processes:** The **process ID (PID)** of the main process associated with the service, with additional entries for any child processes that have been launched.
- **Resource usage:** RAM (memory) and CPU time.
- **CGroup:** Details about the control group to which this process belongs.

- **Log preview**: A few loglines from the service's output, to give you an idea of what's happening.

This information provides a detailed overview of the service and its status and can be useful for debugging issues or checking the health of the service.

If the service has failed, the output will usually provide details on why it failed, such as the exit code or a description of the error.

Starting a service

```
systemctl start foobar
```

This starts the service. If the service was already running, this command would have no effect.

Stopping a service

```
systemctl stop foobar
```

This stops the service. If the service wasn't running, then it should have no effect.

Restarting a service

```
systemctl restart foobar
```

This stops and then starts a service. It is equivalent to running:

```
systemctl stop foobar
systemctl start foobar
```

> **Note**
>
> Be careful with this command: if a service's configuration file has changed on disk since it was started, and that config file has a bug that prevents the program from successfully starting, then restart will happily stop your running service and then fail to start it again.
>
>
>
> This logical but potentially undesirable behavior has bitten many developers over the years, so take care to ensure that your service's configuration is still valid before restarting.
>
> Many popular programs have built-in configuration validation, e.g., for nginx, you can run:
>
> ```
> nginx -t
> ```
>
> to test the configuration on disk.

Reloading a service

```
systemctl reload foobar
```

Not all services support this subcommand – it's up to the person creating the service configuration to implement it. If a service does have a reload option, it is generally safer than restart.

Usually, a reload:

- re-checks the configuration on disk to ensure that it's valid
- re-reads the configuration into memory without interrupting the running process, if possible
- restarts the process only after validating the config and making sure the process will start successfully after being stopped

Like so many things in Linux, this is a convention rather than a strictly enforced requirement, so you may run into software that:

- doesn't implement a reload subcommand
- doesn't implement some of the safety features discussed above (config validation, etc.)
- does something else with a reload, because the developer or packager thought it was a good idea

In general, when updating the configuration file for an application, especially in production environments, you should prefer reload over restart.

Enable and disable

systemctl enable foobar – configures foobar to start automatically on boot. systemctl disable foobar – if foobar is configured to start automatically, gets rid of that configuration and turns foobar into a manually managed service.

The key difference here is that while start and stop have an immediate effect – they ensure that a service is running (or stopped) *right now*; enable and disable are about future system startups. However, they have no effect on that service's 'running' status at the time you run the command.

One common mistake that developers make is to assume that enable will start a service. It won't. If you want to start an nginx web server now and ensure that it automatically starts every time the VM is rebooted, you need to run two commands:

```
systemctl start nginx
systemctl enable nginx
```

Because of this, enable and disable come with an optional flag that also starts (or stops, in the case of disable) the service. This command is equivalent to the two commands above:

```
systemctl enable --now nginx
```

A note on Docker

While systemctl is a common tool for managing services on traditional Linux systems, it is generally not used in Docker containers due to containers' isolated and self-contained nature.

Docker containers ideally run a single process and therefore don't require a complex boot phase or process management. The container, in essence, *is* the process and doesn't have access to the host system's init system (including systemd).

Although it's possible to have access to these commands in a Docker container, it's usually undesirable to use any kind of service-management system inside of them.

Docker containers ideally contain a single application and launch a single process when they start. For this, no service management is needed – the running container is your service package, and your Docker container essentially *is* your process.

We don't recommend a Docker setup that includes multiple processes or significant internal service management, so we won't get into it here: much like families, all happy Docker images are alike in the same way, while each unhappy Docker configuration is unhappy in its own way.

Conclusion

In this chapter, you learned how services are managed in Linux, and we introduced the practical commands you'll use to control them. We gave you the theory you'll need to make sense of all the terminology you'll come across on a live system: what init is, what systemd does on Linux systems, and which commands you need to interact with it.

In the next chapter, we'll show you some useful tricks for interacting with your shell and your command history, so you can save time and look like a Unix wizard from your favorite movie (it will also make you faster and more efficient at your day job, but putting it that way just doesn't make it sound as fun).

Learn more on Discord

To join the Discord community for this book – where you can share feedback, ask questions to the author, and learn about new releases – follow the QR code below:

`https://packt.link/SecNet`

4

Using Shell History

To become skilled at the command line, you have to use it regularly. There are no shortcuts to becoming comfortable, but there are a few high-value tricks that you can learn early on, which will save you time and frustration. The earlier you build them into your muscle memory, the better.

In this chapter, you'll learn how to leverage your shell history to avoid the tedious re-typing of commands you've already run. You'll also see how to customize your shell's behavior or appearance via the shell configuration file. Finally, we'll show you the most useful shortcuts to edit and modify commands at the command prompt. All in all, this chapter will make you blazing fast on the command line.

We will go about this by covering the following topics:

- Shell history
- Executing previous commands with !
- Jumping to the beginning or end of a line

Let's begin by understanding shell history.

Shell history

Most shells keep a history of the commands you've run. This means that you can see every successful command that you've run just by pressing the arrow keys: the *Up-Arrow* key to go back one command and *Down-Arrow* to go forward one. Scrolling through your shell history like this can be very useful, especially if you find that you're re-running similar commands frequently.

Note that you can also edit commands that you find like this: use *Left-Arrow* and *Right-Arrow* to navigate to the line of text that is a command, and just type to edit the command.

An edited command is added to the end of your shell history (it doesn't actually modify the saved line in the history).

Together, these tricks allow you to easily go back and re-execute or modify previous commands.

Shell configuration files

Some of the tricks we'll talk about require changes to your shell's configuration file. The workflow is usually the following:

1. Change the option you want to change in your shell's config file.
2. Save the file.
3. Open a new shell session to see the changes.
4. For existing shell sessions, re-read your shell config file by running a command to `source` (execute) it: `source ~/path/to/config/file`.

Here are locations for the most common shells:

Common shells	Locations
Bash	`~/.bashrc` for interactive sessions, such as the one you get from opening a new terminal window in your graphical environment. You almost always want this one if you're changing the configuration on your work machine. "Interactive" here refers to situations where you as a user make use of the shell in a terminal, not to a script running (for example, a script automatically invoked by a cron job). You're in an "interactive shell" when you are in some form of terminal, manually being prompted for input and writing commands. `~/.bash_profile` for login shells – this might be a local login, but also what you get if you log in over SSH. Again this is in comparison to shell instances when running a script.
Zsh (the Z shell)	`~/.zshrc`

History files

Different shells keep history files in different places, and most can be configured to change the location. By default, you'll almost always be using Bash, which, by default, keeps its history file at `~/.bash_history`.

If you're ever unsure about where to find the shell history file, many shells have a shell configuration option named `HISTFILE` that contains the history file's location.

Here, I'm checking to see where my history file is, while running the zsh OS:

```
% echo $HISTFILE
/home/dcohen/.zsh_history
```

Bash has two configuration options that prevent your history file from growing indefinitely, to keep its size manageable and your history searches fast:

- HISTSIZE controls the maximum history kept in memory
- HISTFILESIZE controls the maximum size of the history file that's saved between shell sessions

If you want to increase the amount of history that Bash keeps, increase both of the preceding in your shell's configuration file.

To do so open the shell's configuration file (e.g., ~/.bashrc) and set these variables by appending the following lines to the end of the file:

```
export HISTSIZE=1000
export HISTFILESIZE=5000
```

Searching through shell history

You will often find yourself looking for a command you ran a week (or a month) ago. That command will likely be further back in your history, and it would be a waste of time to hit *Up-Arrow* hundreds of times to get there. If you have at least *some* idea of what you're looking for, an interactive shell history search is the trick that you're looking for. Here's how to search your shell history:

1. Press *CTRL + R* to invoke reverse-i-search.
2. Type a part of the command you are looking for.
3. Your shell will try to match the characters you type against your command history and come up with the closest, most recent match.
4. Repeatedly press *CTRL + R* to step through the history. Press *ENTER* to select a command or *Esc* to exit this mode.
5. If you accidentally skip backward past the command you wanted, *CTRL + SHIFT + R* will search forward to the next-most-recent match.

Exceptions

There are some exceptions to this feature depending on the shell and the configuration you are using.

Some shells forget about commands that failed with an error (exited with a non-zero exit code). Many shells also forget commands starting with a space character – those won't be added to the shell's history. However, in both scenarios you are typically still able to reach the history entry if you go back (*Up-Arrow*) right away, without executing any other commands.

Executing previous commands with !

Executing previous commands is done with exclamation marks. There are various ways to use this trick, which we'll look at now.

Re-running a command with the same arguments

The ! command will execute the last command with the previous arguments. For example, !ssh will go back and find the last ssh command you ran and execute it with the same arguments. You can use this to re-run commands that you frequently use with the same arguments, such as to quickly re-connect to the SSH server you connect to every day.

Prepending a command to something in your history

The !! command will execute the last command you ran, but with some other command in front of it. This may sound strange, but it's *very* useful for situations where you accidentally ran a command that requires root privileges without sudo at the beginning.

```
apt-get install nginx # fails with a permission error
sudo !!
# this is the command that runs:
sudo apt-get install nginx
```

After that previous command fails due to a lack of permissions, simply running sudo !! will re-run it with sudo prepended to the beginning.

Note

For security, don't make this an automatic habit: always make sure you know why a command needs more permissions and ask yourself whether you trust it enough to want to give it permission to do literally anything on your system. Careless misuse of sudo can make it easy to break things or allow an attacker to gain a foothold on your system.

Jumping to the beginning or end of the current line

It's not uncommon to need to jump to the beginning of a line when editing, perhaps to correct the spelling of a command or add a required argument. To do this, press *CTRL + A*.

Likewise, to jump back to the end of a line, use *CTRL + E*.

These two will come in handy quite often.

Conclusion

Working in a Linux shell environment entails a lot of typing. Making even the smallest improvements to your speed and accuracy as you construct and edit your commands can make the difference between feeling like basic tasks are taking forever and feeling like you're speeding along like a seasoned Unix wizard.

The tricks we've shared in this chapter are a few of the most common and most powerful shortcuts we use in our day-to-day work. Combining your new command-history-searching skills with the editing and command-modification shortcuts you just learned will have a massive impact on your comfort, efficiency, and speed on the command line.

Learn more on Discord

To join the Discord community for this book – where you can share feedback, ask questions to the author, and learn about new releases – follow the QR code below:

```
https://packt.link/SecNet
```

5

Introducing Files

In Linux, everything is – or can be represented as – a file. Files are organized into a filesystem, which is just a hierarchy of files and directories (directories are just a special kind of file). As a developer, just about everything you do on a Linux system will require knowledge about files: writing and copying source code, building Docker images, application logging, configuring dependencies, and more.

In this chapter, we'll cover the details of files in Linux. You'll learn about the difference between plaintext files and binary files, which are the two most common types of file content you'll be working with. We'll show you how those are laid out and organized into a filesystem "tree" in Linux, before diving into the practical commands you'll need to create, modify, move, and edit files. Then we'll complete our tour of the basics with a practical introduction to file editing, using the most commonly available command-line text editors.

However, in this chapter, we don't stop at the basics. Linux files are one topic where it pays (sometimes quite literally) to dive a bit deeper into some advanced knowledge. After all, "working with files" is one of the primary things you'll be doing on Linux as a developer: writing and reading source code and configuration files, searching for specific file content, copying and moving log files around, and more. The more efficient you are at these basics, the more competent you'll be as a well-rounded developer who doesn't have to google basic Linux commands over and over, or get embarrassingly stuck in a command-line text editor during a troubleshooting Zoom call with your peers.

First, we'll talk about searching for files in the filesystem tree and finding specific content or patterns inside individual files. Then, we'll talk about special files and alternate filesystems that you're likely to come across, and what you need to know to work with them effectively.

By the end, you'll know about:

- The many file types you might encounter, and what they're used for
- The most important kinds of file data you'll need to work with
- The Linux filesystem and the commands you'll use to work with it
- File editing basics
- Some common problems and how to avoid them

There's a lot of content in this chapter, and it's one of the most important foundations for the rest of your Linux skills. Make sure you understand each part before moving on – you don't have to memorize everything on your first readthrough, but try to get as much practical experience as you can in your own Linux environment while working through this chapter. There's a tangible payoff to knowing this stuff when you're troubleshooting real-world problems or interviewing for a job.

Files on Linux: the absolute basics

In order to break up the larger topic of files on Linux, let's cover some of the absolute basics that you probably already have some intuition of: plaintext files and binary files. We'll also cover a practical error that you might see if you move Windows files to a Unix system, or vice versa.

Plaintext files

One of the simplest forms of text files you'll encounter is the mighty plaintext file. While historically they were ASCII files, they are now typically UTF-8 encoded. You might come across other file encodings, but this is rare as they are generally considered obsolete.

What is a binary file?

Unix doesn't differentiate between binary and text files, the way many other operating systems do. All files can be streamed through pipes, edited, and appended to. A file is just a file. When a file is set to be executable, Unix will do its best to execute it, either succeeding in the case of **ELF** (**Executable and Linkable Format**, probably the most widely used executable format today) or failing – for example, when trying to execute an image or audio file.

This simple mechanism opens up some amazing possibilities. For example, executables can be piped through a compression utility, then a network tunnel (such as SSH), before being decompressed and written back into a file – all in one command, without any temporary files.

It also means, however, that you should be careful to avoid creating a situation where random files, for example, ones uploaded or modified by users of a website (including log files!), have any possibility of being executed. This can lead to serious security issues.

Line endings

While Unix files, especially text files, function similarly to files on other operating systems, it is worth mentioning that Windows (and DOS), among others, uses a different line-ending character, which can produce errors in many programs that use those text files. Although this is only the case for files that were created on one kind of system and then copied to another (for example, moving a file from Linux to DOS), it's worth knowing about.

The reasons for the different line endings are historical, and many tools (for example, Git and various text editors) will automatically handle that difference for you. However, in rare circumstances, you might have to convert files manually. There are famous commands like dos2unix to do so, but these have to be manually installed on most Unix-like operating systems.

There are, however, some methods to convert them using more traditional utilities.

- Using sed: `sed 's/^M$//' original_dos_file > unix_file`
- Using tr: `tr -d '\r' < original_dos_file > unix_file`
- In place, using perl: `perl -pi -e 's/\r\n/\n/g' original_file`

Now that we've talked about the crucial basic concepts you need to know to understand files on Unix-like systems, let's talk about the context that all of these files actually exist in: the Linux filesystem.

The filesystem tree

The **Filesystem Hierarchy Standard (FHS)** describes the conventional directory layout of Unix-like systems. Linux conforms to this standard, essentially making it "the official folder structure of Linux." The FHS is a standardized tree structure where every file and directory stems from the root (a directory simply named "/"). This hierarchy is crucial: although there's a place for end-users to go wild with their own directory structure, every single subdirectory inside of / (the root directory) has a specific purpose.

The basic layout of this filesystem hierarchy doesn't take long to learn, and by investing a few minutes now, you'll develop an intuition for where things go – whether they're application binaries, logs, data files, or external devices that your code needs access to. In other words, it eases both development and troubleshooting: when you know where things *should* be, you spend less time confused and unsure of where to look during an incident. Additionally, this knowledge is required when it comes to writing your own scripts and doing the light system administration tasks expected of a senior developer.

Here are some of the important places in the filesystem that you'll often see referenced, or have to use yourself:

- /etc: System and software configuration files go here, organized into many subdirectories.
- /bin and /sbin: System binaries go here. Don't mess with these.
- /usr/bin and /usr/local/bin: Your installed software and your own binaries go here, so that anyone on the system can see and execute them.
- /var/log and /var/lib: /var contains variable data, things that are prone to change while the system is running, such as application logs (/var/log) and dynamic libraries (/var/lib), files, and other state for running applications.
- /var/lib/systemd: One of several places on the filesystem that contain systemd configuration.
- /etc/systemd/system: A good place for custom system unit files, if you're creating services.
- /dev: A special filesystem used to represent hardware devices.
- /proc: A special filesystem used to query or change system state.

Basic filesystem operations

It's time to dive into the foundational Unix commands you'll use every single day as a developer. This set of commands will allow you to accomplish a range of basic command-line tasks you need to do on any system you interact with. Once you have learned and practiced the commands in this chapter, you'll be able to do things like:

- Follow your application logs in real time.
- Fix a broken configuration file to get your application working.
- Move from one directory to another in a Git repository on your local macOS development machine.

Let's get started with listing a directory. Make sure you're logged in to a Linux or Unix system (Ubuntu or macOS is fine), and have the Terminal application open, ready to follow along.

ls

List a file or directory. This command is similar to "opening a folder" in a graphical user interface. It lists the contents of the directory it's given. By default, it uses your current directory:

```
/home/steve# ls
my_document.txt
```

In this example, my shell's current location is the /home/steve directory, which contains a single file (my_document.txt).

You can ask ls to list any directory path on the system, though, by passing the directory as an argument:

```
/home/steve# ls /var/log/
alternatives.log  apt  bootstrap.log  btmp  dpkg.log  faillog  lastlog
wtmp
```

For a more orderly output, you may want to add the "-l" option. This will give you a "long listing," which means a single file or directory per line, along with extra information.

```
# ls -l /var/log/
total 296
-rw-r--r-- 1 root root   4686 Jun 24 02:31 alternatives.log
drwxr-xr-x 2 root root   4096 Jun 24 02:31 apt
-rw-r--r-- 1 root root  64547 Jun 24 02:06 bootstrap.log
-rw-rw---- 1 root utmp      0 Jun 24 02:06 btmp
-rw-r--r-- 1 root root 177139 Jun 24 02:31 dpkg.log
-rw-r--r-- 1 root root  32032 Oct 28 14:26 faillog
-rw-rw-r-- 1 root utmp 296296 Oct 28 14:26 lastlog
-rw-rw-r-- 1 root utmp      0 Jun 24 02:06 wtmp
```

In short, the ls command is how you "look around" on a Unix filesystem.

pwd

Short for "print working directory." This shows "where you are" on the filesystem, in the context of your current shell session. If I'm logged in to a Linux system as the steve user, and I'm in my home directory, I can expect to see pwd print something like this:

```
pwd
/home/steve
```

cd

Change the current working directory in your shell. The commands you run after using this command will run from the perspective of your new, changed location on the filesystem.

Here's an example directory:

```
Desktop
├── anotherfile
├── documents
│       └── contract.txt
├── somefile.txt
└── stuff
        ├── nothing
        └── important
```

If you're sitting in the Desktop directory, but then change to the documents directory with cd documents, you'll get a different listing from that new perspective when using the ls command. Let's see this in action:

```
/home/steve/Desktop# ls
anotherfile   documents   somefile.txt   stuff
/home/steve/Desktop# cd documents/
/home/steve/Desktop/documents# ls
contract.txt
```

Now that we can see our surroundings (ls), move around on the filesystem (cd), and find out where we are (pwd), let's get into actually affecting the filesystem by creating and modifying files.

touch

This operation is written as touch filepath.

Depending on whether the filepath you give it already exists or not, this touch command will do one of two things:

1. If a file does not already exist at that path, touch will create it:

   ```
   →   /tmp touch filepath
   →   /tmp ls -l filepath
   -rw-r--r--  1 dcohen  wheel  0 Aug  7 16:02 filepath
   ```

2. If a file *does* exist at that path, touch will update the access and modification times for that file:

   ```
   →   /tmp touch filepath
   →   /tmp ls -l filepath
   -rw-r--r--  1 dcohen  wheel  0 Aug  7 16:03 filepath
   ```

Notice that the only thing that's changed is the modification time shown in the long listing.

less

less is what's known as a "pager" – a program that allows you to view file content, one screen (page) at a time:

```
less /etc/hosts
```

It's interactive – once you're using it to view a file, you can:

- Scroll up or down, line by line, using your mouse wheel or arrow keys.
- Scroll down a whole page with **SPACE**.
- Search with / (enter your search pattern) *RETURN*.
- Go to the next match: **n**.
- Use **q** to quit the program.

Practice using it for a minute or two, and you'll be fine.

tail

tail is used to view the last few lines of a file.

```
tail /some/file
```

The -f (follow) option for tail is very useful for live-streaming logs to your terminal:

```
tail -f /var/log/some.log
```

Use **q** to quit out of tail.

mv

mv (move) is used to move and rename files.

Moving

Imagine you have a file named somefile.txt:

```
→   Desktop ls -alh somefile.txt
-rw-r--r--  1 dcohen  wheel    0B Aug  7 11:02 somefile.txt
```

Provided you're sitting in the same directory as the file, here's how you'd move it to the /var/log directory, without renaming it:

```
mv somefile.txt /var/log/
```

Renaming

Now you want to rename that file to `foobar`:

```
mv /var/log/somefile /var/log/foobar
```

That's it!

cp

To copy files and directories, use the `cp` command:

`cp file destination` copies a file named `file` to a destination filepath, `destination`. The most commonly used option is `-r`, or `-recursive`; if you're copying a directory, this will copy everything inside as well.

```
cp -r /home/dave /storage/userbackups/
```

mkdir

Create a new, empty directory named `directoryname` with:

```
mkdir directoryname
```

A useful option is `-p`, which allows you to create nested directories in a single command. For example, if you want to create a `Documents` directory that contains a directory named `school`, which in turn contains a directory named `reports`, you could run the following command:

```
mkdir -p Documents/school/reports
```

rm

`rm` removes (deletes) files and directories:

- `rm filename` deletes a file named `filename`.
- `rm -r directoryname` will delete a directory named `directoryname`, and every file and directory inside of it, recursively.

There's a separate command for deleting empty directories named `rmdir`, but it's usually only used in scripts where developers are being careful to limit the blast radius of an unintentional deletion.

Editing files

Whether it's updating configuration files, creating new Linux services, or taking notes during a troubleshooting session, your work on Linux is occasionally going to require you to edit files on the command line. We're going to cover command-line file editing in detail in *Chapter 6*, *Editing Files on the Command Line*, but we'll give you a very brief overview here.

If you're limited to a command-line-only environment, there are a few CLI text editors you might use:

- **nano**: Almost always installed or available; easy to use
- **vi**: Installed almost everywhere; takes a bit of getting used to
- **vim**: Easy to install everywhere; more full-featured than vi

If any of these are not installed, you can install them via your package manager. For example, if you're using Ubuntu Linux, that'll be a command like sudo apt-get install nano (or substitute nano for vim). We'll dive deeper into package management commands in *Chapter 9*, *Managing Installed Software*. Regardless of which editor you choose, you'll edit a file by simply typing [$EDITOR filename] on the command line; for example:

```
vi filename
vim /some/file
nano /another/file
```

- If the file exists, you'll be able to edit it in your editor.
- If it doesn't, but the directory exists, you'll create a new file at that path the first time you save it in the editor.
- If the directory doesn't exist, you might be able to edit the file, but the editor won't be able to write it to the filesystem without a few extra steps.

In the next chapter, *Chapter 6*, *Editing Files on the Command Line*, we're going to dive much more deeply into the practical skills involved in file editing on the Linux command line. If you absolutely need to edit a file before you finish this chapter, just type nano /path/to/the/file and follow the on-screen cheatsheet to save and quit. In the meantime, let's learn about the many kinds of files you'll run into as a developer on Linux.

File types

We've already covered "regular" files, such as plaintext files or the binary data in your image files and executable programs. But there are several other file types that you'll need to know how to recognize and work with in Linux. Whether you're looking for the USB stick or keyboard you just plugged into your machine, creating a link that points to a file, or inspecting the network sockets that a web process has opened, you'll want to know a bit about *all* of these.

Here are all of the Linux file types and what they're used for:

- **Regular file**: This is the most common file type, containing text or binary data. As a software engineer, you'll encounter regular files in nearly every programming task, whether you're writing code, editing configuration files, or executing programs. A typical example that you might see in a long listing could be a source code file like:

```
-rw-r--r-- 1 dave dave 210 Jan 04 09:30 main.c
```

- **Directory**: Directories are special files that are used to organize other files and directories. You're already familiar with directories if you've ever used Windows or macOS (where they're called "folders"); they contain other files and directories. In a long listing, a directory like /etc will appear as:

```
drwxr-xr-x 5 root root 4096 Jan 04 09:21 /etc
```

- **Block special**: This special file type provides buffered access to hardware devices, which makes them particularly useful for devices like hard disks where data is accessed in large, fixed-size blocks. You'll rarely work with these directly, except when mounting filesystems. An example could be a hard disk partition, shown as:

```
brw-rw---- 1 root disk 8, 2 Jan 19 11:00 sda2
```

This represents a block device with read and write permissions for the owner and group.

- **Character special**: Similar to block files, character files provide unbuffered, raw access to hardware devices, but they are designed for devices where data is not block-oriented, like keyboards or mice. You'll never need to worry about these, although you may occasionally use them in the course of your work (for example, /dev/urandom, /dev/null, or /dev/zero). A character device like a terminal might appear in a long listing as:

```
crw-rw-rw- 1 root tty 5, 1 Jan 19 22:00 /dev/tty1
```

- **FIFO special ("named pipes")**: Named pipes, not to be confused with the anonymous pipes frequently used in shells, are used for interprocess communication. You'll almost never have to deal with these, although you'll be using their anonymous cousins to become a Unix wizard in *Chapter 11, Pipes and Redirection*. You won't often come across these, but one example is a named pipe file, which might look like this:

```
prw-r--r-- 1 user user 0 Jan 21 10:00 mynamedpipe
```

- **Links**: Links are a kind of shortcut to another file. There are two types of links – hard and symbolic (soft). You'll almost never need to deal with hard links, but you might use symbolic links to create convenient paths to frequently accessed files or to ensure multiple paths lead to the same file. We'll cover these more below. A symbolic link may appear as:

```
lrwxrwxrwx 1 user user 7 Jan 21 10:30 versions/latest -> bin/app-3.1
```

This example indicates a link named latest that points to a file named app-3.1.

- **Sockets**: Unix sockets are used for IPC, similar to pipe files. You might encounter socket files when troubleshooting services that need to talk to each other ("Why is nginx not able to reach my application server?"). A socket file – in this case a socket used by nginx and php-fpm to communicate so that a WordPress application can run – might look like this:

```
srwxrwx--- 1 root socket 0 Jan 23 11:31 /run/wordpress.sock
```

This list has covered the additional, special file types you might encounter, and given you some intuition about how (and why) you might encounter them in the wild. To help you build useful practical skills, there are a few types in particular that we should explore in more detail. Let's start by getting some real-world experience with the most common of these special file types: links.

Symbolic links

Symbolic links, often referred to as symlinks or soft links, are a type of file that serves as a reference to another file or directory. Unlike a hard link, a symbolic link can point to a file or directory across different filesystems, and it maintains a separate inode from the file or directory it references.

You can create a symbolic link using this basic syntax:

```
ln -s document.txt /path/to/create/link
```

ln (lowercase L) is the "link" command.

For example, if you have a file named `file1.txt` in your current directory and you want to create a symlink to it named `link1`, you would use the command:

```
ln -s file1.txt link1
```

Now, if you do a long listing of your directory with `ls -l`, you will see `link1` listed as a link to `file1.txt`:

```
ls -l
total 0
-rw-r--r-- 1 root root 0 Oct 28 16:08 file1.txt
lrwxrwxrwx 1 root root 9 Oct 29 17:20 link1 -> file1.txt
```

When you access `link1`, for example, by printing out the file's contents using `cat link1`, the system will automatically dereference the link and give you the contents of `file1.txt`. If `file1.txt` is moved, deleted, or renamed, the symbolic link will not update automatically and will be left pointing to a non-existing file (a broken link).

Symbolic links are particularly useful for creating shortcuts, organizing files and directories, and maintaining flexible and logical filesystem structures.

Hard links

A hard link is an additional name for an existing file on the same filesystem, effectively acting as an alias. Both the original file and the hard link share the same inode, meaning changes to one are reflected in the other. Unlike symbolic links, hard links can't cross filesystem boundaries or link to directories. If the original file is removed, the hard link will still maintain the data. To create a hard link named `link1` to a file named `file1.txt`, you would use the command:

```
ln file1.txt link1.
```

The file command

The `file` command is a utility that can let you inspect the type of a file. The basic usage of the `file` command is simple: type `file` followed by the filename. For example:

```
file mysecret.txt
```

might output `mysecret.txt: ASCII text`, indicating that `mysecret.txt` is a plaintext file.

If you have a binary file, like a compiled program named `mybinary`, running `file mybinary` might output something like `mybinary: ELF 64-bit LSB executable`, indicating that `program` is a binary executable file.

For a directory, such as /home/user, running `file /home/user` will likely return /home/user: directory, signifying that /home/user is a directory.

The `file` command is a powerful tool for quickly understanding the types of files you're working with, especially when dealing with unknown or unfamiliar files.

If you feel like exploring, use the `file` command to inspect the following files:

- `file /bin/sh`
- `file /dev/zero`
- `file /dev/urandom`
- `file /dev/sda1`
- `file ~/.bashrc`
- `file /bin/ls`
- `file /home`
- `file /proc/1/cwd`

Advanced file operations

When you're working with files in Unix-like operating systems, you'll often want to perform actions on them, with them, or with their content, but without directly modifying them in an editor. For example, you may want to:

- Search a file to see if it contains some content you're looking for.
- Identify a batch of files that was modified at a specific time.
- Securely move a file to another system, instead of just copying it around with mv on the local machine.

You may even want to combine all three into a single action! This type of knowledge can really come in handy during troubleshooting (searching for a specific request ID or error code in a log), during development (finding recently modified source code files), or when you want to do some testing (copying updated application source code to a test system).

Here's a quick look at these kinds of file operations, to give you an idea of the tools and commands you'll use to accomplish them.

Searching file content with grep

Text matching is traditionally done with grep. On your personal or work laptop, you may want to install ag or rg, which are more programmer-friendly and faster versions of this idea (for example, `sudo apt-get install silversearcher-ag`), but on production systems, you'll always have grep.

Search for the pattern `search_pattern` in the file `path/to/file`:

```
grep "search_pattern" path/to/file
```

You can, of course, search for string literals like this, but grep is so powerful because it allows you to use regular expressions (regexes) to search for patterns. The following command will return lines that start with `startswith`:

```
grep ^startswith /some/file
```

And this command will return lines that end with `endswith`:

```
grep endswith$ /some/file
```

Regular expressions are tremendously useful, and every developer and Linux user should be familiar with the basics.

You can also use grep to search recursively through a directory – that is, search through all files in all directories it contains:

```
root@c7f1417df8d2:/tmp# grep -r -i "hello world" /tmp
/tmp/secret/dontlook.key:hello world
/tmp/hi.txt:hello world
/tmp/hi.txt:HeLlO WoRlD! You found me!
```

But what if you don't want to find strings *inside* of a file – what if you want to find specific files themselves?

Finding files with find

find can help you find files and directories by name, modification time, or other attributes. It's essentially a breadth-first search of the filesystem tree, which is quite useful for things like:

- Finding all application log files that were created or modified in the last day.
- Identifying all source code test files with names that end in `_test.go`.
- Locating all of the `php.ini` files left behind by an intern programmer so you can delete them.

In the following examples, `/search/path` is the part of the filesystem you want to search. If you want to search your current directory and all of its subdirectories, you can use the period character (.), for example, `find . -name 'file.txt'`:

- Find files by extension:

```
find /search/path -name '*.ext'
```

- Find files matching multiple path/name patterns:

```
find /search/path -path '**/path/**/*.ext' -or -name '*pattern*'
```

- Find directories matching a given name, in case-insensitive mode:

```
find /search/path -type d -iname '*lib*'
```

- Find files matching a given pattern, excluding specific paths:

```
find /search/path -name '*.py' -not -path '*/site-packages/*'
```

- Find files matching a given size range:

```
find /search/path -size +500k -size -10M
```

Copying files between local and remote hosts with rsync

rsync is an extremely useful tool that copies files and directories between and across hosts. It works just like cp, except it works when one or both hosts are remote.

rsync is essentially a combination of cp (for copying data) and ssh (for secure, encrypted transport). If you're unfamiliar with ssh, you'll need to learn how it works (and set up your own SSH keys and access) before trying rsync commands.

Here are a few sample invocations, thanks to the tldr project:

- Transfer a file from a local to a remote host:

```
rsync path/to/local_file remote_host:path/to/remote_directory
```

- Transfer a file from a remote host to the local host:

```
rsync remote_host:path/to/remote_file path/to/local_directory
```

- Transfer file in [a]rchive mode (to preserve attributes) and compressed ([z]ipped) mode with [v]erbose and [h]uman-readable [P]rogress:

```
rsync -azvhP path/to/local_directory remote_host:path/to/remote_
directory
```

That last example is one I've used a hundred times to make quick, automated backups.

Combining find, grep, and rsync

We'll take a detailed look at combining commands with the | character in *Chapter 11, Pipes and Redirection*, but here's a quick preview.

If, for example, you want to combine the examples you just saw, for example, to make a backup of all files in the /tmp directory that were modified in the last week, that's just one clever command away:

```
find /tmp -type f -mtime -7 -exec grep -l "hello world" {} \; | xargs -I _
backupscript.sh _ backup@backupserver.local:/backups_
```

First, we run find, looking for files that have a modification time of less than 7 days ago. We use find's -exec flag to execute a grep command with the -l flag, which simply returns the filename of the matching file. Then, we pipe those filenames into the xargs command, which applies an action to every line of input that it receives from the previous command. In this case, the action is to run a made-up backup script on each matching file, along with a made-up destination path that someone might want to back this file up to.

If we have the same files as in the grep section above, this wild-looking command will run two commands for you:

```
backupscript.sh /tmp/secret/dontlook.key backup@backupserver.local:/
backups/tmp/secret/dontlook.key

backupscript.sh /tmp/hi.txt backup@backupserver.local:/backups/tmp/hi.txt
```

It's doing exactly what we wanted: running the backup script on ONLY the two files that contain the "hello world" content we care about *and* that were modified in the last 7 days.

While a command like this can certainly take a few minutes (and some googling) to put together, it may save you hours in the long run. That's the power of the command-line environment, combined with small, focused Unix tools that you can arrange together however you need.

You'll learn more about Unix pipes and xargs in *Chapter 11, Pipes and Redirection*, but we've given you this example because it's important for you to get a taste of how you're going to combine all these simple commands together as you learn them.

Advanced filesystem knowledge for the real world

You've gotten an introduction to the various Linux filetypes now, and have some experience working with the most common ones. Now let's take a look at some less-common filesystem knowledge that will come in handy during your time working on Linux systems.

You'll meet these when you're:

- Troubleshooting your first Docker application that has mounted storage volumes.
- Working on an application that talks to industrial controllers, cameras, or other external hardware.
- Writing application code that needs access to randomness for securely generating passwords or API tokens. One of the special file types you'll see are **block devices**, which are devices resembling some form of disk, where data is fetched and read in blocks.

Classical disk devices are block devices, and you'll usually find them attached to your filesystem at these locations:

- `/dev/hdX`
- `/dev/sdX`
- `/dev/nvmeN`

Where `X` and `N` are alphabetical or numerical indices of the respective disks, such as `/dev/sda` or `/dev/nvme0`. **Partitions** look just like disks, but with an additional digit or character appended, such as `/dev/sda0`, for the first partition on the first drive.

Note that even once the operating system detects a new hard drive and attaches it (and any detected partitions) in one of these locations, you'll still have to intentionally "mount" the filesystem that's on the drive, using the `mount` command. This isn't a particularly common thing for developers to do, so we'll leave it at that.

There are also special "**software devices**." These range from `/dev/null`, which you might have seen output to be piped to in the form of `somecommand > /dev/null`, to `/dev/random` and `/dev/urandom`, which provide you with random bytes. This is where the programming language of your choice will most likely retrieve its cryptographically secure random numbers from.

Another directory is /proc, which is a filesystem popularized by the Plan 9 operating system, but envisioned in the early days of Unix. As the name suggests, it was created to represent processes as files. /proc contains directories named after process IDs, which contain files that can be used to read those processes' state. Particularly on Linux, it has been extended with various other interfaces, including ways to configure kernel drivers, read hardware information and sensor outputs, and even interact with BIOS and UEFI.

FUSE: Even more fun with Unix filesystems

As you've just seen, many things can be interpreted as files in Unix. The philosophy is that it's common to edit files, so commands and programming languages able to interact with files provide a well-understood interface. **FUSE**, short for **Filesystem in Userspace**, is an API that allows anyone to implement new Unix filesystems without having to become a kernel programmer. In other words, because lots of things can talk to files, it's useful to be able to "fake" the Unix file API for things that aren't the kind of normal, locally stored data that you'd expect a file to be. If this sounds a bit wild, check out some of the things people have written with FUSE. FUSE has been used to implement many classical filesystem drivers, for example, NTFS, so you can read your old Windows filesystems on a Linux machine. However, because of FUSE's flexibility and accessibility, there are also some pretty wild filesystems that have been implemented this way:

- sshfs, for example, allows you to locally mount a directory on another machine accessible via SSH.
- Other FUSE filesystems allow you to mount remote cloud storage (like Amazon's S3) as a local directory.
- Some even more obscure ones allow you to mount Wikipedia as a directory of files, or to represent protocols such as IRC and services like weather APIs as filesystems.

FUSE is so useful that it has found its way into many Unix-like operating systems besides Linux, and is now even available on Windows. It's worth knowing about, not just because it's a novel use of the file abstraction in Unix but because it can be extremely useful when you are dealing with information that's stored somewhere without a classical API that your application can use at the application layer. Any programming language you're likely to use has a standard library that lets you talk to files on a Unix filesystem, and FUSE is a way of creating that interface for just about any kind of information.

Conclusion

This chapter was an intense journey through the basics – and some of the more advanced bits – of files and the filesystem on Linux. You saw the difference between plaintext files and binary files, explored how the Linux filesystem tree is laid out, and learned all the basic commands you need to work with files. If you did it right, you also spent some time in your own Linux environment, practicing the important command-line file editing skills we showed you here.

After covering the basics, we jumped into the most critical intermediate and advanced topics that you'll need. You saw how to find files and search them for content, and we also gave you a taste of special files and filesystems.

All of this together arms you with the most important skills and knowledge you need in order to use Linux to solve real-world problems. We hope you had fun on this whirlwind tour!

Learn more on Discord

To join the Discord community for this book – where you can share feedback, ask questions to the author, and learn about new releases – follow the QR code below:

```
https://packt.link/SecNet
```

6

Editing Files on the Command Line

Editing text on the command line is often a hard requirement due to the constraints of production systems, which tend to lack a graphical user interface. However, becoming fluent at editing text on the command line has many benefits even outside of those systems – indeed, even when you have graphical text editors or **integrated development environments (IDEs)** available.

For example, many full-featured text editors and IDEs support the patterns you'll learn about in this chapter, which means the speed and efficiency you gain is transferrable to other tools. In fact, you can use the shortcuts you'll learn in this chapter for all kinds of things, from quickly finding and replacing text to correcting a misspelled word in the middle of a long shell command.

You might even find similar shortcuts built into your favorite tools (sometimes via plugins); for example, you're only a few Google searches away from discovering email clients, browser plugins, and web applications that support the vim keyboard shortcuts that you'll learn later in this chapter.

Learning how to think in the efficient patterns that these minimal, text-only interfaces require can help you find more efficient ways of doing things you'll have to do every day, preventing you from wasting time tediously clicking through graphical menus or wizards when you can accomplish the same task with just a few keystrokes.

Note

Many extremely minimal (or highly secure) environments also tend to strip text editors out of production images, although that doesn't improve security (cat, echo, mv, and input/output redirection are more than enough to improvise a workable text editor in a pinch). You — like hackers everywhere — will likely end up installing nano or vim in quite a few Docker containers over the course of your life.

In this chapter, you'll learn the basics of two text editors: one that we think is the easiest to get started with (nano) and another that we think is the best long-term learning investment for your career (vim). You'll get the basic context for how command-line text editing is done on Linux, dive into nano and vim, and finally, learn how to avoid the most common editing mistakes. We'll also show you how to tweak your shell to automatically use your preferred editor when possible.

Nano

Nano is a small and easy-to-use CLI text editor. One of the features of nano — you might even call it the main feature — is that it prominently has a keyboard-shortcut cheat sheet bolted to the bottom of your screen while you happily edit text in your terminal. This is particularly useful if you're under stress and not used to editing text on the command line.

Nano is good in a pinch, but you won't find it installed in more minimal environments (such as Docker containers or production VMs). Be aware that nano also tends to automatically make backup files (~yourfile.txt), thereby potentially polluting the filesystem.

Installing nano

On all the popular Linux distributions you're likely to use, the package name for nano is nano – use your preferred OS's package manager to install it (in this case, we're installing it on Ubuntu):

```
apt-get install nano
```

Nano cheat sheet

You can find an official, up-to-date nano cheat sheet here: https://www.nano-editor.org/dist/latest/cheatsheet.html

Some of the most useful commands are called out in the following sections.

File handling

- *Ctrl+S*: Save current file
- *Ctrl+O*: Offer to write file ("Save as")
- *Ctrl+R*: Insert a file into the current one
- *Ctrl+X*: Close buffer, exit from nano

Editing

- *Ctrl+K*: Cut the current line into a cutbuffer
- *Ctrl+U*: Paste contents of the cutbuffer
- *Alt+3*: Comment/uncomment a line/region
- *Alt+U*: Undo last action
- *Alt+E*: Redo last undone action

Search and replace

- *Ctrl+Q*: Start backward search
- *Ctrl+W*: Start forward search
- *Alt+Q*: Find next occurrence backward
- *Alt+W*: Find next occurrence forward
- *Alt+R*: Start a replacing session

Vi(m)

Vi (often referred to as ex-vi or nvi) is a command-line text editor. Vim (vi iMproved) is an extended version, that many people use as an entire IDE. vi and vim share the same basic commands and keyboard bindings, so if you just learn the basics, you'll be fine no matter what kind of ancient or modern system you log in to.

Fair warning: vim is complicated and has a relatively steep learning curve. It'll probably take a few weeks of spare time studying and experimenting to get comfortable with it – comparable to setting up your first Linux web server or writing your first 500-line program.

The wonderful thing about learning vim is that you can use it locally on your laptop or remotely on a server that has no GUI, and the editing experience is the same – beautifully efficient – in both places. To use it effectively, both a shift in mindset and an understanding of its vocabulary (the *commands* and *modes* we'll get into) are important.

As with learning any other skill, some dedicated practice followed by consistent use of the editor is essential to really build up an understanding and feel comfortable. Some initial struggle and confusion will likely be part of that. Please don't let this deter you!

Vim is a modal editor, meaning that the same keys do different things depending on which "mode" you're in. For example, when you're in insert mode, your keypresses will simply be written into the file (or buffer) you're editing – much like your IDE or Microsoft Word. However, in normal mode, pressing those same letter keys will execute whatever keybinding they are tied to. Once you've adjusted to that idea – **modal editing** – the rest of vi/vim is just practice.

For example, if you start vim and type a lowercase *i* twice, the first *i* will enter insert mode, while the second will actually write an *i* character in the editing window (buffer) that you're editing a file with. If this sounds confusing right now, it's okay. Even if you never choose to use vim as your regular IDE, you'll feel a lot more comfortable with its basics by the end of this chapter.

> **Note**
>
> It is also worth mentioning that another vim-like editor, nvim (neovim), has started gaining traction at the time of writing this book. Most of what applies to vim also applies to nvim, so there is no need to worry about which one to get started with. The major differences are around plugin development, so you won't lose anything if you decide to switch from vim to neovim down the road, as we have.

Vi/vim commands

Here are some basic vi(m) commands – hit *Escape* before using any of these, to make sure you're in Normal mode.

Modes

- *v* – enter visual mode. This feature only exists in vim (not vi) and can easily be overused in the beginning because it's familiar to people coming from other editors.
- *ESC* — exit whichever mode you're in and go to Normal mode, where you can give commands.

Command mode

Command mode can be reached from normal mode (hit *Escape*) by typing a colon (:). We've included the colon in the commands below for clarity.

Helpers

- `:set number` – show line numbers.
- `:set paste` – this is helpful if you want to paste things into vim and don't want it to interact with indentation. You can disable it again with `:set nopaste`.

Exiting

- `:q` – quit
- `:q!` – quit without saving (force quit)
- `:w` – write ("save") the file
- `:wq` – write and quit
- `:wqa` – only vim; helps when multiple panes are open, such as a plugin opening a file browser on the side

Normal mode

Normal mode is the mode you're in when you start vim, before typing anything. You can always get back to normal mode by hitting the *Escape* key.

Navigation

- *k* – move up
- *j* – move down
- *l* – move right
- *h* – move left

Alternatively, it is possible to use the arrow keys, but it can be helpful to think in terms of vi shortcuts, instead of trying to drive vi(m) like an ordinary editor. We've found that it helps to stick to vi's movement keys when you're practicing with it.

- *w* – next word
- *b* – beginning of the current word or previous word
- *^* or *0* – go to the beginning of the line
- *$* – go to the end of the line
- *gg* – go to the beginning of the file
- *G* – go to the end of the file

Editing

- *i* – enter insert mode (write actual text). *I* inserts at the beginning of the line.

- *a* – insert text, appending after the cursor. *A* appends on the end of the current line.

- *o* – open a new line (*O* opens a new line before the current one).

- */* – search for pattern (regexes work here; use *ENTER* to search and *n* and *SHIFT+n* to cycle forward or backward through search results).

- *dd* – delete (and cut) the current line.

- *y* – yank (copy) selected text.

- *yy* – yank (copy) the current line.

- *p* – put/paste text after the cursor.

- *u* – undo the last change.

- *CTRL+R* – redo.

- *nX* – where *n* is a number and *X* is a command, will execute *X n* times. For example, *3dd* will delete three lines.

Tips for learning vi(m)

Over a few weeks of normal editing tasks, you can become quite comfortable with vim. That said, it's not always easy to get started. Here are our tips for making the journey smoother.

Use vimtutor

Vim comes with a built-in tutorial. If you want to get started with vim, this is probably the very first thing you want to do. Just run `vimtutor` on your command line to open vim and the tutorial.

Think in terms of mnemonics

When using vi(m) to edit files, it's common to "build sentences" using the commands you saw above. For example, d2w means "delete two words." While we tried to mention fitting words in the command list above, different people prefer different mental concepts, so don't feel scared to build up your own vocabulary.

Avoid using arrow keys

Avoid using arrow keys and consider disabling this feature. It prevents you from thinking of vim as another editor and reduces the time it takes until you're comfortable with its standard keybindings. Don't worry; although this may feel strange at the beginning, you will get used to the basic vim keybindings after a few sessions.

Avoid using the mouse

While vim can be used with a mouse for visual selection, it makes sense to resist this temptation and keep training your working memory of the keyboard shortcuts. Otherwise, you'll switch back and forth and not be comfortable when it counts, like when you're troubleshooting on a remote server that has no mouse input at three in the morning.

Don't use gvim

While gvim (graphical/GUI vim) can be useful, it is not a good idea to use its graphical shortcuts when no proper terminal is available. The benefit of vi(m) is that it allows for effective text manipulation via the keyboard when you don't have a graphical environment available – like the many Linux servers you'll be troubleshooting after reading this book!

Avoid starting with extensive configuration or plugins

A typical beginner's mistake is starting with someone else's vim configuration. Although they seem useful at first, heavily customized vim setups can hinder you when you're just trying to learn the basic concepts. Extensive configurations will not magically make you more productive, especially not in the beginning. Once you become more confident, you will find yourself writing your own configuration.

Another thing to avoid is excessive plugin usage, especially early on. Occasionally, plugins break things, which can become a burden and lead to more issues. Vim plugin troubleshooting is not something you want to deal with when you are just getting started. Third-party configuration files and plugins can be amazingly useful, but they can also become a crutch: when you are suddenly thrown into an environment outside of your development machine, you won't be able to rely on all of that fancy stuff. If you've come to depend heavily on a custom workflow, even basic edits can become difficult and frustrating, especially under stress.

A more sensible approach is to start out with a minimal configuration and only add bits that you fully understand (and that you're sure you will need). Your time is much better spent actually using the editor on real projects, because it trains you to retain the most important vim shortcuts in your working memory. It takes some time, but eventually you will use them without really thinking about the actual commands, rather just thinking in terms of the mnemonics you've made up for yourself.

Here is an example of a minimal vim configuration that might be helpful in the beginning. Feel free to change it, or just pick out parts that seem useful.

Put this into your $HOME/.vimrc:

```
"This breaks compatibility with vi, saying that we want to use the
benefits of vim
set nocompatible

" Enable syntax highlighting
syntax on

" Increase the command history to be very big
set history=10000

" Indent based on the previous line
set autoindent

" Make it so searches wrap around at the end of the file
set wrapscan

" Show the current mode in the command line
set showmode

" Displays partial commands in the last line
set showcmd

" Highlight searches
set hlsearch

" Use case insensitive search
set ignorecase
" Don't use case insensitive search use when using capital letters
set smartcase

" Display the cursor position at the bottom
set ruler
```

Vim bindings in other software

Should you start enjoying and preferring the way vim works, it is worth mentioning that many text editors and IDEs have options and plugins to switch to a vim input mode. There are even web browsers with vim-style inputs!

If you're curious or would like a review of the vim material in this chapter, you can find a video tutorial that covers some of the most important parts of this chapter (and even some extra vim features!) here: https://www.youtube.com/watch?v=ggSyF1SVFr4

Editing a file you don't have permissions for

Regardless of which editor you use, sometimes you'll want to edit a file that your user doesn't have write permissions for. For example, if you're a regular user and you want to edit /etc/hosts – a file owned by root, and writable only by root – you'll need to either become root or use the sudo command. See *Chapter 7, Users and Groups*, for more details.

While a command like sudo $EDITOR /etc/hosts can be used to edit files as root, a better approach is to use sudoedit to execute your editing command as root:

- sudoedit /etc/hosts
- EDITOR=nano sudoedit /etc/hosts
- EDITOR=vi sudoedit /etc/hosts

The first example will use whatever editor you've got set in your EDITOR environment variable, while the other two commands pass in (or override) the EDITOR environment variable as part of the command.

Setting your preferred editor

Linux and in fact all Unix-like systems allow you to set your preferred editor via the EDITOR environment variable. Most command-line software that launches an editor for certain tasks, like git when you make a commit or visudo editing your sudoers file, will use this variable to know which editor to open. You can set this EDITOR variable to a path to any editor you like, even graphical ones (provided your system has a graphical user interface installed):

```
bash-3.2$ echo $EDITOR
nano
bash-3.2$ export EDITOR=vim
```

Note that the interactive shell command above will only work until the current shell session is closed; to persist this setting in the Bash shell, I'd add it to my ~/.bashrc file. See *Chapter 4, Using Shell History* for more details.

Conclusion

In this chapter, you learned how to edit text files on the command line. First, we introduced the easiest way to get started (nano), and then we showed you how to start graduating to a skillset that will pay dividends for the duration of your career: vi/vim and their keybindings, which you'll find supported in an incredibly wide variety of software.

Use the cheat sheets in this chapter to get started with command-line editing, but know that after a day or two of practice, you'll be ready to learn additional shortcuts and commands in vim. That's best done through a combination of vimtutor, online cheat sheets, and YouTube videos. We also really like the book *Practical Vim*, 2nd Edition, by Drew Neil.

Becoming comfortable with command-line text editing is one of the surest ways to look and feel like a professional when you're working. Don't neglect this skillset!

Learn more on Discord

To join the Discord community for this book – where you can share feedback, ask questions to the author, and learn about new releases – follow the QR code below:

```
https://packt.link/SecNet
```

7

Users and Groups

In this chapter, we'll be taking a look at two of the building blocks that Linux uses to manage resources and maintain security: users and groups. After learning the basics and covering a very special user, root, we'll show you how the concept of Linux user groups adds a convenient layer on top of the user abstraction.

Once we've covered the necessary theory, you'll jump directly into the practical commands you need to create and modify users and groups. And, in a stunning triumph that will pay dividends if it ever comes up in an interview, you'll see for yourself *what a Linux user is actually made of* (hint: it's just three lines of plaintext).

By the end of this chapter, you'll:

- Understand what users are and what they're used for
- Understand the distinction between root and normal users, and how to switch between them when you need to
- Know how to create and modify users and groups
- Take a deeper dive into user metadata, and see what a Linux user is actually made of

What is a user?

A user, in the context of a Unix system, is simply a named entity that can do things on the system. Users can launch and own processes, own files and directories and have various permissions on them, and be allowed or prevented from doing things or using resources on the system. Practically, a user is who you log in as, what your processes run as, or who owns your files.

The word "user" is obviously a metaphor for a real person with a user account, a password, and so on. But most "users" on real systems don't actually represent specific humans. They're machine accounts, meant to group resources like processes and files for the purposes of security or organization.

But there's a much more important distinction than whether or not an account is intended to be used interactively by a human operator. There are exactly two types of users, and before we jump into practical user-management skills, we need to talk about that distinction.

Root versus everybody else

The world can be a harsh place, and sometimes it's dangerous to run a command. For example, fdisk can wipe the partitions of a disk or otherwise modify hardware. iptables can open a network port and let an attacker exploit a vulnerability. Even using an innocuous echo command to send a value to the wrong place on a filesystem can change the operating system's configuration in subtle and terrible ways.

To guard against this, the Unix-like environment that your command-line interface is running in has some built-in guardrails. There is a "superuser" called root in every Unix system. As a result, the basic security model is as follows:

- First, there is root. This user is the equivalent of the system administrator on other systems and is the user with the highest number of permissions. root can do almost anything.
- Then, there's everybody else. Non-root users have limited permissions – they can't launch processes or edit files that could affect the whole system, but they can launch their own (unprivileged) applications and edit their own files.

To guard against problems, only the root user can execute commands that change important aspects of your system. Because even seemingly innocuous commands can cause potential havoc if they're run with the right arguments, you may find yourself needing root privileges just to edit a text file.

sudo

Because it would be an inconvenience to have to log in as a separate user every time you want to do something potentially dangerous on a system, there's the sudo command. Prefixing a command with sudo, which stands for "substitute user (and) do," lets you perform that command *as the root user*. When that command finishes executing and exits, your next command is interpreted as coming from your regular (non-root) user again.

You can see this behavior for yourself by running two commands. First, run the whoami command, which is a command that prints out the current user:

```
whoami
```

In this case. I'm logged in as the "dave" user, so this command prints out:

```
dave
```

Now, prepend "sudo" to that same command:

```
sudo whoami
```

Even though you're still logged in as a non-root user, your *effective* user ID has changed for the duration of a single command, because of sudo:

```
root
```

Let's look at a more practical example where we want to run a single action as root, but then continue running other commands as our regular user:

```
sudo systemctl start nginx
<go back to doing regular-user stuff>
```

That first command starts the nginx web server (presuming the nginx package is installed), which is something that only root can do. Any commands after that are executed as your regular user again.

This is a common workflow that ensures safety – you spend most of your time working as a regular user, incapable of borking the entire system in a single command. When you need root powers, you invoke them by prepending *only those commands that require it* with root. It's a nice psychological barrier to accidentally breaking things on a system.

You'll see this pattern used for various potentially dangerous things on a system, such as editing system-level configuration files, creating directories outside of your user's home directory (covered later in this chapter), and more:

- `sudo mkdir /var/log/foobar`
- `sudo vim /etc/hosts`
- `sudo mount /dev/sdb1`

You can use sudo to get a long-lived root shell session if you plan on running many commands as root (or if you're troubleshooting something that runs as root, or simulating the environment that a cloud-init script would be executing in):

```
sudo -i
```

This will get you an *interactive* shell session as the root user. Be careful with this! There's nothing stopping you from destroying the system with a mistake or a poorly typed command.

While sudo defaults to replace the current user with the root user, you can also change that to another user, via the –u option. For example:

```
sudo -u myuser vim /home/myuser/.bashrc
```

This will open /home/myuser/.bashrc in vim as the user myuser.

Which user (or group) is allowed to do what exactly can be defined in /etc/sudo.conf. You should never edit this file directly; use the visudo command to modify the file.

What is a group?

Groups are an additional primitive that allows a set of users to share permissions. Groups are often used to get the functionality of a permission set or profile. For example, on Linux, there's often a group called sudoers, and on macOS, you'll encounter a group called wheel. By convention, users who are members of the sudoers or wheel groups on these systems are allowed to use sudo to execute commands as root. This is functionally the same thing as adding a user to the Administrators group in Windows.

You can extrapolate that if groups are useful for managing who is allowed to run the sudo command, they might be useful for grouping together users and managing other kinds of permissions, too.

Mini project: user and group management

For example, imagine that we want to allow every user who is a software developer at our company to read a given file – let's call it document.txt. We can simply create a developers group and add all of our developer users to that group.

Then, when we're setting ownership and permissions for document.txt, we can reference the developers group instead of trying to keep track of every single user who might be a member of that group individually.

Creating a user

On a Linux system that has the adduser command installed, you can use it to *interactively* create a user named dave. If you don't, the package is usually named useradd (see *Chapter 9, Managing Installed Software* for more details on installing packages).

Running the command with a username as the only argument will give you a wizard-style user creation process. Notice that we're using sudo here, since only root can add or delete users:

```
$ sudo adduser steve
Adding user `steve' ...
Adding new group `steve' (1000) ...
Adding new user `steve' (1000) with group `steve' ...
Creating home directory `/home/steve' ...
Copying files from `/etc/skel' ...
New password:
Retype new password:
passwd: password updated successfully
Changing the user information for steve
Enter the new value, or press ENTER for the default
Full Name []: Steve
Room Number []:
Work Phone []:
Home Phone []:
Other []:
Is the information correct? [Y/n] y
```

We've bolded the parts that required user interaction on our part – namely, setting the password, the full name, and the confirmation that we want to create this user on the system.

This is a nice way to add one or two users, but what if you're working on a Linux test server that needs individual accounts for your 300 largest customers? You'll want the non-interactive useradd command instead, which lets you specify user attributes as arguments to a single command. This makes user changes easy to script (see our note about scriptability later in this chapter):

```
useradd --home-dir /home/dave --create-home --shell /bin/zsh -g dave -G
   sudoers dave
```

That command also:

- Sets and creates the user's home directory (`--home-dir` and `--create-home`)
- Sets a custom shell (`--shell`)
- Sets the user's primary group to dave (although this could also be something like employees) with the `-g` option
- Adds a supplementary group membership to the sudoers group (you can pass multiple comma-separated group names here)

And that's it – if the command exits successfully, your new user has been created!

But we're not done yet – this user is going to be working on the new, top-secret tutorialinux application, so let's create a group for that project and add our new user to it.

Create a group

To create a new group called tutorialinux, you'll use the groupadd command:

```
groupadd tutorialinux
```

This creates a new group on the system, adding a line to the /etc/group configuration file, which is the record of all groups that exist on a Unix system. You can validate that the group was created by "grepping" (searching) for the group name in that file:

```
# grep tutorialinux /etc/group
tutorialinux:x:1001:
```

You can see that a group with the name tutorialinux now exists, with **Group ID (GID)** of 1001.

We're not going to dive deeply into what the x character here means; it's enough to know that this file is made up of one line for every group, with colon-separated values. You'll only ever care about the group name (first column), group ID (third column), and members (last column, which is empty in this example).

Modifying a Linux user

Just as useradd allows you to set user metadata to your heart's content during user creation, usermod and gpasswd allow you to modify all aspects of an existing user. Let's add the dave user we created earlier to the new tutorialinux group, so he can work on project files that only group members can see or modify.

Adding a Linux user to a group

To change the primary group of the user: `sudo usermod -g groupname username`

That's not exactly what we want here, though: the dave user should continue to be in the eponymous dave group; it's just that we want dave to *also* be a member of the tutorialinux group. To add a user to a group *without* making it that user's primary group, use the -aG options ("**add to additional groups**"):

```
sudo usermod -aG tutorialinux dave
```

If you inspect /etc/group again, you can see that the dave user is now a member of three groups: dave, sudoers, and tutorialinux:

```
grep dave /etc/group

sudoers:x:27:dave
dave:x:1000:
tutorialinux:x:1001:dave
```

Using the commands you learned in the previous chapter to modify file ownership and permissions, you can now control the access that all members of the tutorialinux group have to certain files and directories.

Now, when a specific user is done working on the tutorialinux project, you can clean up and revoke their access without having to modify individual file and directory permissions.

Removing a user from a group

To remove a user from a group, we can use the gpasswd command like this:

```
gpasswd -delete username groupname
```

Removing a Linux user

To remove a Linux user entirely, use the userdel command:

```
userdel -r account_name
```

If you want to preserve that user's home directory, omit the (-r / --remove) flag.

Remove a Linux group

There's also a groupdel command for groups that are no longer needed:

```
groupdel groupname
```

Advanced: what is a user, really?

Users and groups are one place where something quite wonderful about Unix and Linux can be seen clearly: there's very little magic here.

A Linux user is really just a **User ID (UID)**, which is a simple numerical representation of a user (an unsigned 32-bit integer). The root user's UID is 0. All other users have a UID larger than 0. The same goes for groups.

This information is not stored in some secret location, in some binary format, or some proprietary data structure that only the operating system can work with: users and groups are defined in plain-text files, which are traditionally modified using the few simple commands we've covered here.

That simplicity and lack of magic means that mere mortals (such as a panicked developer with just a faded memory of this chapter) can quickly find out the state of users and groups on a running system, troubleshooting application errors that may come from an incorrectly prepared host environment that's missing a necessary application user. It also comes in handy during the "systems engineering" portions of developer interviews.

So, in the interest of cementing your intuition about how this stuff works, here are a few more useful facts about what's going on under the hood as we create and manage users and groups.

User metadata / attributes

Users defined only by a number aren't particularly useful – not without some additional metadata to spice things up. For example, an account that I use for my day-to-day work on a Linux or macOS machine, which happens to have UID 502, might also have:

- A friendly login name (dave)
- Its own group (the dave group)
- Various group memberships (staff, developer, and wheel)
- A login shell (bash, zsh, and so on)
- A home directory (/Users/dave/ on macOS, or /home/dave/ on Linux)

If you're curious, you can get information about your current user by running the id command:

```
# id
uid=0(root) gid=0(root) groups=0(root)
```

By default, a few files define and contain all this extra user information:

- /etc/passwd contains a username, UID, GID, home directory, and login shell, all on one colon-delimited line per user:

```
root@localhost:~# cat /etc/passwd

root:x:0:0:root:/root:/bin/bash
daemon:x:1:1:daemon:/usr/sbin:/usr/sbin/nologin
bin:x:2:2:bin:/bin:/usr/sbin/nologin
sys:x:3:3:sys:/dev:/usr/sbin/nologin
sync:x:4:65534:sync:/bin:/bin/sync
```

- /etc/shadow contains the user's hashed, salted passwords; it is readable only by the root user:

```
root@localhost:~# cat /etc/shadow

root:$6$SPevRPxD94AYwtmF$IOp9k15dnaN8FW8RUpDDQlifLPp9pJ3btgJcMfI
QEs1kT.ZNjDfX66XBOcPOBZzkRcGOb3Rwq6qTsDQ0jiZNh/:19251:0:99999:7:::
daemon:*:19251:0:99999:7:::
bin:*:19251:0:99999:7:::
sys:*:19251:0:99999:7:::
sync:*:19251:0:99999:7:::
```

- /etc/group – the equivalent of /etc/passwd, but for groups instead of users. You saw (and used) this file earlier in the chapter.

Optionally, a home directory like /home/dave:

```
# /etc/passwd username:password:UID:GID:comment:home:shell
```

 WARNING: While it makes sense to know what these files contain, you should NEVER edit any of these files manually. Use the tools we used in the previous sections to create, remove, or modify system users and groups.

Hopefully, this quick theoretical overview of the moving parts – or more accurately, the static plaintext files – that make up users and groups was enlightening. Not only do we want to make sure that you've got an intuition for how this works, but we hope that this section stresses how *simple* this really is under the covers. There's no magic here! You can feel confident that you're not missing something the next time you're troubleshooting why an application won't start, or why a user doesn't have permission to view a certain file with specific group ownership permissions.

A note on scriptability

Earlier, we alluded to preferring automatable tools like useradd, instead of interactive wizard-based tools like adduser – even if those automatable tools are a bit more complex or hard to learn. Or perhaps you're asking, "Why not just use a graphical tool, instead of these hard-to-remember CLI commands?"

One of the things we want to teach you during the course of this book is to generally prefer non-interactive commands.

Because these commands don't rely on real-time user input when they run, they are scriptable: creating a hundred users is almost as easy as creating one. This really comes in handy when you're dealing with real-life problems like building Docker images, repeatedly preparing production environments, or writing cloud-init setup scripts for your cloud instances.

As a developer, this should ring true: automating things makes them more repeatable, safe, and fast. By learning commands that are non-interactive, you retain the power to use that command as part of a larger piece of automation, instead of having steps that require error-prone, time-consuming, and risky manual intervention.

Conclusion

You just learned the basics of how Linux uses the abstractions of users and groups to manage and control processes, files, and other resources on a system. Just as importantly, you learned the basic commands you need to create and manage users and groups on a real system. You learned about the important difference between the root user and all of the other normal users on a system.

Then, we walked through a practical exercise where you created a user, added a group to the system, modified that user, and then cleaned up all the resources you created.

Finally, we went beyond the day-to-day commands to show you that there's no magic behind the scenes here: it's all just plaintext files that define users and groups on a Unix system. This is a good thing; it's going to make your life as a developer easy, whether you're:

- Creating a Docker image to run your application as a specific non-root user.
- Setting up a long-running cloud instance with logins and a shared group for your data science team.
- Trying to minimize the blast radius of a mistake in your own local test environment.

- Troubleshooting user- and group-based errors on applications, for example, on a web application that needs root-user powers to open a secret file or do privileged actions on a system.

In the next chapter, we'll use all of this knowledge to dive deeply into how the Unix security model works, by looking at ownership and permissions.

Learn more on Discord

To join the Discord community for this book – where you can share feedback, ask questions to the author, and learn about new releases – follow the QR code below:

`https://packt.link/SecNet`

8
Ownership and Permissions

In this chapter, you'll learn how users and groups are combined with ownership and permissions to create the basic Linux security model. This combination of primitives is used to control access to just about everything on a Linux system – processes, files, network sockets, devices, and more.

First, you'll get a tour of all the important file information you get from a long listing (with an emphasis on permissions, naturally). Then we'll cover the common permissions that you'll encounter on production Linux systems, and finally, we'll show you all the Linux commands you'll use to set and modify permissions on files. Together, we'll do the following:

- Decipher the output of a long listing
- Learn about file attributes
- Understand how ownership and permissions work
- Understand a common sticking point, the "octal" permission format
- Learn practical commands for changing ownership and permissions

Deciphering a long listing

Let's dive into this topic by way of a long listing.

Sometimes, when you're navigating around a system, seeing only file and directory names isn't enough. When you want more information about the files you're seeing, use ls with its "long" option: ls -l.

Here is an example of its output when run on the /lib directory of a system. Open a terminal and type ls -l /lib/:

```
# ls -l /lib/
total 56
drwxr-xr-x 10 root root 4096 Mar  8 02:12 aarch64-linux-gnu
drwxr-xr-x  5 root root 4096 Mar  8 02:12 apt
drwxr-xr-x  3 root root 4096 Mar  8 02:08 dpkg
drwxr-xr-x  2 root root 4096 Mar  8 02:12 init
lrwxrwxrwx  1 root root   39 Jul  6  2022 ld-linux-aarch64.so.1 ->
aarch64-linux-gnu/ld-linux-aarch64.so.1
drwxr-xr-x  3 root root 4096 Mar  4  2022 locale
drwxr-xr-x  3 root root 4096 Mar  8 02:12 lsb
drwxr-xr-x  3 root root 4096 Aug 29  2021 mime
-rw-r--r--  1 root root  386 Feb 16  2023 os-release
drwxr-xr-x  2 root root 4096 Mar  8 02:12 sysctl.d
drwxr-xr-x  3 root root 4096 Apr 18  2022 systemd
drwxr-xr-x 16 root root 4096 Jan 17  2022 terminfo
drwxr-xr-x  2 root root 4096 Mar  8 02:12 tmpfiles.d
drwxr-xr-x  3 root root 4096 Mar  8 02:12 udev
drwxr-xr-x  3 root root 4096 Mar  8 02:12 usrmerge
```

We see a lot of interesting information here – let's step through it, field by field.

File attributes

The first field displays a file's attributes: file type and permissions. In other words, this field shows us which type of file we're looking at, and what its file permissions are. The default lists this information in symbolic mode, in contrast to numeric mode, which you can view with -n.

File type

```
-rw-r--r--  1 root root  386 Feb 16  2023 os-release
```

The first character here indicates the file type. In the listing above, the - character indicates a regular file. Lines starting with l indicate a *symbolic link*, which is simply a special file that has no content of its own, and just points to another location on the filesystem. You can think of it as a Windows shortcut or a macOS file alias.

Other common file types are d, indicating a directory, or c, which indicates that you're looking at a character file – you'll mainly find the latter in /dev, representing hardware input devices such as keyboards. For more on file types, see the *Filesystem* section of *Chapter 5, Introducing Files*.

Permissions

```
-rw-r--r--   1 root root   386 Feb 16  2023 os-release
```

These are the "permission bits," which determine which users and groups on the system are allowed to read, write, and execute this file. We'll dive deeper into this in the *Permissions* section of this chapter.

Number of hardlinks

```
-rw-r--r--   1 root root   386 Feb 16  2023 os-release
```

The next field indicates the number of hard links. Hard links are special pointers linking file names to an actual file. So in most situations, this will be 1 for files. In contrast to a symbolic link ("symlink"), which points to a filepath, a hardlink points to an actual file. If you move the file that a symlink points to, this makes the symlink invalid; a hardlink will keep pointing to a file even if that file is moved around, renamed, or otherwise modified.

You may have noticed that while most files have only one link pointing to them, directories have wildly varying numbers of links in this column. This is because each file and directory inside of that directory creates another link reference to it. Even an empty directory starts with two links, "." (the shortcut for "this directory") and ".." (the shortcut for "the directory above this one").

User ownership

```
-rw-r--r--   1 root root   386 Feb 16  2023 os-release
```

The third field shows which user owns the file; all files in our example are owned by root. While you see a username in this example, running ls in numeric mode – ls -ln – will also show a numeric user ID instead of the friendly username you see here.

Group ownership

```
-rw-r--r--   1 root root   386 Feb 16  2023 os-release
```

The following field shows the owning group, which also happens to be root in the example listing above.

File size

```
-rw-r--r--  1 root root  386 Feb 16  2023 os-release
```

As you might have guessed, the next field displays the file size. When no additional flags are specified, it is displayed in bytes. To make it more readable the -h ("human-readable") flag can be used.

If you're paying attention, you'll have noticed that directories all seem to have the same file size, 4096:

```
drwxr-xr-x 1 root root 4096 Apr 18  2022 systemd
```

Files can take up as much or as little space as they need, but directory storage is allocated in discrete filesystem blocks. Because the smallest blocksize on most filesystems is 4096, directories will report their size as 4096.

This rabbit hole goes deeper, but we don't think the information will be useful enough in your day-to-day work as a software engineer to warrant including it here. If you're still curious and want to go deeper, start reading about "Linux inodes."

Modification time

```
-rw-r--r--  1 root root  386 Feb 16  2023 os-release
```

Next, we see the modification timestamp of the file – the last time this file was changed.

Filename

```
-rw-r--r--  1 root root  386 Feb 16  2023 os-release
```

Finally, we come to the filename, which is the only thing you'd see if you were doing a regular listing instead of a long listing (ls instead of ls -l). This will usually just be a plain file or directory name, except in the case of a symbolic link, or symlink – in that case, you'll see the symlink name, and the file path that it links to.

Ownership

To change the owner of files or directories, use the chown (change owner) command. The syntax is chown user:group path where user is the name of the owning user and group is the name of the group, while path is the full or relative part to the file or directory.

You can omit the colon and the group to just change the owning user and leave group ownership alone. Of course, the user attempting to change permissions on a file needs to have permission to do so, so in most situations this command will be run as the root user.

In the following command snippet, you see a long listing of a file owned by root, which subsequently has its owner changed using the chown command:

```
bash-3.2$ ls -l mysecret.txt
-rw-r--r-- 1 root staff 0 Apr 12 15:39 mysecret.txt
bash-3.2$ sudo chown dave mysecret.txt
bash-3.2$ ls -l mysecret.txt
-rw-r--r-- 1 dave staff 0 Apr 12 15:39 mysecret.txt
```

Permissions

Here's a single file from our ls -l file listing earlier. I've tweaked the permissions to make this example more illustrative:

```
rwxr-xr-x 1 root root  386 Aug  2 13:14 os-release
```

Specifically, look at the permission bits:

```
rwxr-xr-x
```

They are displayed in three groups of three here. Imagine them separated into three groups, to make it easier:

```
rwx r-x r-x
```

Each of these triplets represents read (r), write (w), and execute (x) permissions for a specific set of users, based on the user and group ownership information for that file. If you see a - character in place of a letter, that action (for the set of users it applies to) is not permitted. Let's look at them in more detail:

1. The first three bits represent the permissions of the file owner. In this case, the file's owner (root) can read, write, and execute the file – rwx.

2. The second three bits represent permissions for the group owner of the file, which in this case is also root. The permissions here are r-x, or read and execute (no writing!). But because root is also the user-owner of the file, those (more permissive) permissions take precedence; root can write to this file. The reason you often see permissions like this is because a group owner is *required* to be set on files, and if you don't want to share a file with other groups, you can just use the owner's group here. The group permissions on a file are usually less permissive than the owner permissions.

3. The last three bits represent the permissions that all other system users have for this file ("the world"). This is almost always the most restrictive set of permissions, because most files don't need to be shared with anyone outside of the owner (and sometimes a separate group owner). In this case, we're looking at a shared library file that needs to be accessible by all system users, so the permissions are r-x (read and execute, no writing allowed).

Numeric/octal

"Read," "write," and "execute" are terms that make permissions easy to understand, but there is another important way that permissions are represented in Linux and Unix: octal.

As a developer, you're probably familiar with non-decimal number systems – octal is simply a base-8 system (instead of the base-10 system – decimal – that we usually use as humans, and in contrast to the base-2 system – binary – that computers use).

Because there are only eight possible states for each three-bit permission combination, octal is a perfectly efficient system for representing them.

Think of our 9 bits, again divided into 3-bit chunks. Each 3-bit permissions-chunk can represent an octal number, which requires three bits to represent. These 9 bits give us exactly the amount of room that we need to represent three octal numbers – one for user permissions, one for group permissions, and one for other/world permissions.

Octal	Binary	Meaning
0	0	**No** permissions (–)
1	1	**Execute** permission (–x)
2	10	**Write** permission (-w-)
3	11	**Write and execute** permissions (-wx)
4	100	**Read** permission (r–)
5	101	**Read and execute** permissions (r-x)
6	110	**Read and write** permissions (rw-)
7	111	**Read, write, and execute** permissions (rwx)

Table 8.1: Octal permissions

You'll notice that this is laid out so that octal addition works – adding "read" (4) and "execute" (1) together gives you "read and execute" (5).

This may seem strange and arbitrary (and it is!), but you'll get the hang of it quickly. You'll mostly be using 7 (all), 6 (read/write), 5 (read/execute), 4 (read), and 0 (no permissions) while working.

Common permissions

The most common permissions you'll see are:

- `-rw-r--r--` (644): Owner can read and write; all others can only read.
- `-rwxr-xr-x` (755): Owner can do everything; all others can read/execute the file. This is a common one for executable files like scripts and binaries, and the default permission for directories.
- `-rw------` (600): Only the owner can read and write, no one else can do anything with it. This is common for secret keys, files that contain passwords, and other sensitive information. SSH, for example, won't use keys that are group- or world-readable until you change their permissions to make them secret.

Changing ownership (chown) and permissions (chmod)

You'll use two commands to change ownership and permissions on files: `chown` and `chmod`.

Chown

chown (change owner) is used to change the owner and group of a file. It's used in the following way:

```
chown [OPTION]... [OWNER][:[GROUP]] FILE...
```

For example, imagine we have this file:

```
$ ls -lh testfile
-rw-r--r-- 1 dave dave 10 Aug 14 16:18 testfile
```

Change owner

Let's change the owner to `chris` (presuming there's a `chris` user on the system):

```
$ chown chris testfile
$ ls -lh testfile
-rw-r--r-- 1 chris dave 10 Aug 14 16:18 testfile
```

Change owner and group

We've changed the owner, but if we wanted to change the group, too, we could have run:

```
$ chown chris:staff testfile
$ ls -lh testfile
-rw-r--r-- 1 chris staff 10 Aug 14 16:18 testfile
```

Recursively change owner and group

One common task is changing the owner and group for all files in a given directory. You can do this with the -R or --recursive option:

```
$ chown -R dave:staff /home/dave
```

This will recursively set ownership for /home/dave/ and every file and directory inside it.

Chmod

chmod (change mode) is used to change the permissions of a file. You can use regular or octal permissions here:

chmod [OPTION]... MODE[,MODE]... FILE...

chmod [OPTION]... OCTAL-MODE FILE...

Your options can be given in the form: ugo{+,-}rwx

1. ugo (user, group, other – assumed to be all three if you don't specify).
2. + to add permissions, - to remove them.
3. rwx (read, write, execute – any or all of these letters).

For example, to add execute permissions for the user who owns the file:

```
$ chmod u+x testfile
$ /tmp ls -lh testfile
-rwxr--r-- 1 dave dave 10 Aug 14 16:18 testfile
```

To add write and execute permissions for the group and all other users:

```
$ chmod go+wx testfile
$ /tmp ls -lh testfile
-rwxrwxrwx 1 dave dave 10 Aug 14 16:18 testfile
```

Oops, we actually wanted to remove all permissions for others:

```
$ chmod o-rwx testfile
$ /tmp ls -lh testfile
-rwxrwx--- 1 dave dave 10 Aug 14 16:18 testfile
```

Octal format for permissions can be set just like you'd expect:

```
$ chmod 744 testfile
$ /tmp ls -lh testfile
-rwxr--r-- 1 dave dave 10 Aug 14 16:18 testfile
```

Actually, let's make that file read-only:

```
$ chmod 400 testfile
$ /tmp ls -lh testfile
-r-------- 1 dave dave 10 Aug 14 16:18 testfile
```

Using a reference

Both chown and chmod allow us to use a --reference argument, with which we can pass a file from which ownership or permissions will be copied.

Conclusion

In this chapter, we covered everything you need to know to solve the most common Linux permissions problems: you learned how to view permissions on files and how to modify them. More importantly, we showed you how to reason about permissions and how they tie in with Linux users and groups, which is where many people stumble.

Make sure you have a strong grasp of the material in this chapter; a huge percentage of the troubleshooting you'll have to do during your career will revolve around file ownership and permission problems. Thankfully, most of these problems arise from a simple lack of understanding, which you no longer have. Go forth and troubleshoot!

Learn more on Discord

To join the Discord community for this book – where you can share feedback, ask questions to the author, and learn about new releases – follow the QR code below:

`https://packt.link/SecNet`

9

Managing Installed Software

As you work in various Linux or Unix environments, you'll need to add or remove software. This is usually done via package managers, although occasionally you'll have to use other methods in a pinch.

You're likely familiar with tools that manage libraries in your programming environment – npm, gem, pip, go get, maven, gradle, and so on. These package managers all operate on the same principles as the ones found in Linux and Unix.

Software **package managers** abstract away the many configuration and binary files that make up a piece of software and let you work with a single, neat "package" instead. This should feel familiar if you're coming from Windows (.exe or .msi installers) or macOS (.dmg installers).

Additionally, most Linux package managers add a layer of security to the process, by:

- Using secure transport (TLS) for your download.
- Using cryptographic signing on the packages themselves, to prove that the authors are at least who they say they are (whether you implicitly trust them or not).

Various Linux distributions also pioneered the idea of searchable package repositories that help users find software to download, which inspired the Apple and Microsoft "App Stores" that exist today.

In this chapter, we'll cover the following:

- What package managers are
- The most common package managers you'll see
- The most important package management operations and the individual commands you'll need to execute them, "translated" across package managers – this is 90% of what you'll need to know in practice

- A popular procedure for downloading and executing custom install scripts
- A quick practical introduction to locally building and installing software yourself

If you're looking for instructions on installing software in Docker, please check out *Chapter 15, Containerizing Applications with Docker* instead.

First things first: as a developer, you'll reach for package management commands when you want to do a few common things:

- Install new software packages, for example, dependencies that your application expects to be available in its execution environment.
- Check for installed packages (for example, "Is the nginx web server already installed on this system?").
- Update the currently installed set of packages, to make sure you've got the latest versions of everything. This is common for addressing vulnerabilities that are discovered, or ensuring you've got all the latest features of a piece of software.
- Remove a package – that is, uninstall it from the system.

Let's jump into how to achieve these practical goals and see the practical commands that you'll be using.

Working with software packages

Before we dive into practical commands, you should know that the exact commands you'll use will differ based on the flavor of Unix (or distribution of Linux) that you're using. Different Linux distributions use different package managers, and although their syntaxes diverge *just* enough to be annoying, they all work in an almost identical fashion. Common package managers include:

- homebrew (macOS)
- apt (reliably found on Ubuntu and Debian-based systems, even minimal ones that don't have aptitude installed)
- pacman (Arch)
- apk (Alpine)

In the rest of the practical sections that follow, we'll introduce the high-level goal we want to achieve (such as "install a specific package"), and then show you the exact commands that accomplish that task, using the popular package managers we just named.

Update your local cache of repository state

Before installing or deleting packages, you'll want to make sure that your local package cache (your system's record of the packages available on the internet) is up to date.

For example, if you're trying to install the nginx web server, but the last time someone updated the local package cache was a month ago, you might unintentionally install an outdated version from last month, instead of the new release from this week.

To update the cache, find your package manager in the list below and run the corresponding command:

Package manager	Commands
homebrew	brew update
apt	apt update
pacman	pacman -Sy
apk	apk update

Your local cache of available packages will be updated, and then you can move on to the exciting work of finding and installing a package.

Search for a package

Not all packages have the same name as the software they contain. Firefox may be available in the firefox package, but you might be disappointed if you try to install ag (package name: silversearcher-ag). Search for a description of the package you're considering installing with the following package manager commands:

Package manager	Commands
homebrew	brew search $PACKAGENAME
apt	apt-cache search $PACKAGENAME
pacman	pacman -Ss $PACKAGENAME
apk	apk search $PACKAGENAME

This is a good way to confirm you're getting what you expect but it can also be used to spread out your search and look for general software related to your problem. For example, on Ubuntu, I can search for grep-like tools with apt-cache search grep. Any package containing grep in the name or description will be shown.

Install a package

Finally, the main event! Now that our repository cache is up to date *and* we know exactly which package we want to install, let's run an `install` command:

Package manager	Commands
homebrew	`brew install $PACKAGENAME`
apt	`apt install $PACKAGENAME`
pacman	`pacman -Sy $PACKAGENAME`
apk	`apk add $PACKAGENAME`

If your package manager prompts you for confirmation, respond to the prompt and your package will be installed (along with any other packages it depends on).

Because some of these commands prompt for confirmation before installing a package, these can block a script. When you're automating tasks with scripts, and you need to install a package, make sure to read the appropriate package manager man page for how to install packages in a noninteractive way. This is often done via an environment variable or an extra argument to the command.

Upgrade all packages that have available updates

On a long-running system, you'll want to occasionally upgrade the installed packages to their latest versions. This fixes known vulnerabilities, gets you the newest features, and keeps different systems from having their state drift apart just because they were provisioned a few months before or after another system:

Package manager	Commands
homebrew	`brew upgrade`
apt	`apt dist-upgrade`
pacman	`pacman -Syu`
apk	`apk upgrade`

These commands will also prompt for confirmation, so if you're using them in scripts, the same advice about adding an option to make them noninteractive applies. For example, `apt -y dist-upgrade` will not wait for manual confirmation, and will just perform the upgrade.

Remove a package (and any dependencies, provided other packages don't need them)

Sometimes you want to uninstall a package: maybe you were just trying it out, your application requirements have changed, or it's known to be vulnerable without a fix in sight. All package managers have a command for removing an installed package:

Package manager	Commands
homebrew	`brew remove $PACKAGENAME`
apt	`apt remove $PACKAGENAME`
pacman	`pacman -Rs $PACKAGENAME`
apk	`apk del $PACKAGENAME`

One thing you may need to do before or after removing a package is verify that a package is even installed. Let's see how to do that now.

Query installed packages

If you need to list all packages that are currently installed on a system, you can do that with a single command:

Package manager	Commands
homebrew	`brew list`
apt	`dpkg -l`
pacman	`pacman -Qi`
apk	`apk info`

Because this list is often hundreds or thousands of packages long, it's a bit unwieldy. Narrow down the output by piping it into a search command like grep, to find just what you're looking for:

```
dpkg -l | grep silversearcher
ii  silversearcher-ag 2.2.0+git20200805-1 arm64 very fast grep-like
program, alternative to ack-grep
```

If you're confused by how we're using that pipe to feed the output of dpkg into the grep command, see *Chapter 1, How the Command Line Works* for the basics of chaining together commands with the pipe character (|). We'll also take a much deeper dive into this mechanic in the upcoming *Chapter 11, Pipes and Redirection*.

Now that we've covered the basic package management commands that you'll be using 90% of the time, it's time to demonstrate a few patterns you'll use when there is no pre-built package available for the software you want to install.

Caution required — curl | bash

Sometimes you won't find a pre-built package for the software you need. And that's okay! Many online sources – even trustworthy and popular ones like homebrew on macOS – recommend a command-line install process that looks like this:

```
curl $SOMEURL | bash
```

This uses the `curl` command to download content from the web, and then uses that content as the input (|, the pipe character, which we covered in *Chapter 1, How the Command Line Works*) for running Bash. When you do this, you're essentially running a script on the web instead of as a local file. This can be an extremely convenient way of installing software, but please make *absolutely* sure that it's coming from a trustworthy source.

We recommend always at least *looking* at the script source, which you can see in the browser by visiting the script URL for this command (represented in the example below as `$SOMEURL`), or by splitting the single `curl $URL | bash` command into multiple commands, so that you can:

- Download the script.
- Read through it in a local text editor to verify that it's not doing anything malicious, and optionally edit the script to suit your requirements.
- Run the script, now that you've verified it does only what you want it to do.

To split something like this `curl $URL | bash` pattern into multiple commands, you'd take the following steps:

```
# Download the installer and name the resulting file installer.sh
curl $SOMEURL -o installer.sh
# Read and optionally modify the script using a text editor like vim
vim installer.sh
# Make the script executable and run it
chmod +x installer.sh
./installer.sh
```

By splitting this into multiple steps instead of just downloading an untrusted script and running it immediately, we give ourselves time to review the code we're about to execute and verify that it's safe. The end result is the same (the install script runs), but this approach gives us much more control and requires less blind trust.

There's another way to get software installed on a system, even if there's no pre-written install script available.

Compiling third-party software from source

This is the most manual, and most time-honored, way to install software on a system – manual compilation and installation! It doesn't have the many advantages of a package manager, like speed, repeatability, ease of managing the installed software, and cryptographic validation of the software binary you're installing.

But in a pinch, it's still the most reliable way to get something installed, with no real outside dependencies except for the basic software tools (compiler, linker, and make script) that you're already familiar with as a developer.

You'll find yourself manually compiling and installing software when:

- There is no pre-packaged version of the software in the package manager you have available. For example, If you're using a minimal container distribution (such as, Alpine), you might not find what you need in the package manager. In that case, you can compile your own binary from source, and get it into your container image that way.
- You need to add your own (or other custom) software to a Docker container.
- You need the absolute latest, bleeding-edge version of a piece of software, for which a packaged version doesn't yet exist. This can be the case for slower-moving projects that don't always have new packages available, or for situations where a hotfix for a critical vulnerability needs to be rolled out *immediately*, before the hotfix has made its way through the packaging process.

This process involves a few steps, with slight variations depending on the software.

Usually, this involves:

1. `curl` or `wget` to download the compressed software archive.
2. `tar zxf downloadname` or `unzip downloadname` to unarchive and decompress the source code directory you just downloaded.
3. Changing directory into the source directory you downloaded and reading any included `README` files. This is where you'll be informed of the exact process you need to follow to build the software, as well as any deviations from the norms we're describing here.
4. Running `./configure`, followed by `make`, followed by `sudo make install` to build and install the binary.

As with other ways of installing software, either manually or through a package manager, keep in mind that `configure` and `make` execute arbitrary code *by design*. This means that running `make install` as root will result in all of this arbitrary code running as root. This should worry you. Make sure to verify that the software's source code is trustworthy and that you are downloading it from a trustworthy source.

Example: compiling and installing htop

To run through a real example of this, we're going to download, compile, and install htop, which is a small, extremely useful system monitoring tool (similar, but superior, to the built-in top command). For the record, this is easily available via almost every Linux distribution's package manager, but we're going to pretend that it's a hard-to-find, custom program that is not widely distributed through package managers.

The system we're doing this on is an Ubuntu 22.04 Linux server, so if you want to follow along without having to do any troubleshooting of your own, use that.

First, we check for the latest release from the official GitHub repository here: https://github.com/htop-dev/htop/releases — at the time of this writing, that's version 3.2.2.

Now you'll want to make a directory for this build, just to keep things neat — I recommend something in the /tmp directory, which holds temporary files and has its contents deleted every time the system starts up:

```
mkdir /tmp/htopbuild && cd /tmp/htopbuild
```

That way, we can delete everything once the build is complete, to prevent cluttering our system with junk files from old builds. Now we're ready to get started.

Install prerequisites

First, we need to install the basic C development toolchain (compiler, linker, make, and other tooling — all the stuff you need to compile C code on Linux). On Ubuntu, this is accomplished by installing a *metapackage* — a package that is a kind of alias for multiple other packages — called build-essential:

```
sudo apt install build-essential
```

We'll also install a few other tools that we'll use: wget to download files from the web and the ncurses dev library, which htop uses for a responsive command-line interface:

```
sudo apt install wget libncurses-dev
```

Download, verify, and unarchive the source code

First, we're going to download the source code and verify its cryptographic signature to make sure it's a genuine release signed with the developer's key:

```
wget https://github.com/htop-dev/htop/releases/download/3.2.2/htop-3.2.2.tar.xz
```

That gets us the compressed, archived source code directory, which we'll be compiling into a binary.

Let's now ensure that we have a developer-sanctioned release by checking the signature, which is just a sha256 hash of the source code.

Download the file containing the expected hash for this release and print it to the terminal:

```
wget https://github.com/htop-dev/htop/releases/download/3.2.2/htop-
3.2.2.tar.xz.sha256
cat htop-3.2.2.tar.xz.sha256
```

Provided you're working with the same version as we are in this example, you'll see this hash:

```
bac9e9ab7198256b8802d2e3b327a54804dc2a19b77a5f103645b11c12473dc8  htop-
3.2.2.tar.xz
```

Now hash the source code we downloaded to verify that the hashes match, using the sha256sum tool:

```
sha256sum htop-3.2.2.tar.xz
bac9e9ab7198256b8802d2e3b327a54804dc2a19b77a5f103645b11c12473dc8  htop-
3.2.2.tar.xz
```

Wonderful! We now know that the software we have is the same as the official release that we meant to download. Let's unarchive the source code directory and step inside it:

```
tar xf htop-3.2.2.tar.xz
cd htop-3.2.2
```

If you're interested, now is the time to read the Readme file (general information about the program) and the INSTALL file (instructions for how to build and install the program).

Now we're ready to start configuring and compiling this piece of software!

Configure and compile htop

Inside the source code directory, it's time to run the ./configure script. This script ensures that we've got any dependencies required for compilation (shared libraries, tooling, and so on) installed, and configures things for the compilation we're about to do:

```
./configure
```

This will produce output while the script runs, checking various dependencies and ensuring that your environment looks like it has everything needed for compilation.

If this script produces errors, read them carefully: usually, it will clearly tell you what's wrong – a missing library or a problematic operating system setting. After fixing any problems it alerts you about, re-run it. When it has run successfully to completion, you're ready to compile the htop binary:

```
make
```

This will again produce reams of output while the compile script runs. If you're totally new to makefiles, they are an extremely useful automation tool used widely by developers. Here's an excellent tutorial: https://makefiletutorial.com/

Once the compilation is complete, we can install the htop binary we just created (it'll be in the main source directory, named htop). Usually, there's an automated way to do this:

```
sudo make install
```

sudo is required because you're moving the compiled binary into a protected (root-owned) location. After that, you can verify that htop is installed and working by typing:

```
htop
```

You should see a beautiful terminal-based GUI (thanks to the ncurses library) showing you your system's current CPU load, memory utilization, and process list.

For programs that don't ship with a full-featured install command, you can rely on the fact that there's no magic in Linux and simply install the binary by moving it into the /user/local/bin/ directory, where locally compiled binaries belong:

```
mv htop /usr/local/bin/
```

Having seen how straightforward this process can be, you now have all the knowledge you need to go forth and compile!

Conclusion

In this chapter, you learned the basics of managing the software that's installed in your Linux environment. First, we looked at how to accomplish this the easy way: software management via the package managers you're most likely to encounter. Although this first approach should cover 90% of your needs, you then learned about the procedures you'll need to apply to the last 10% of situations – careful vetting, followed by using custom install scripts or manual compilation and installation.

Hopefully you followed along with the practical compilation example and tried out the htop system monitor. Thankfully, htop is available via package managers everywhere – it's a really useful tool that a lot of system administrators find invaluable on long-running production systems.

You should now be comfortable with the high-level concepts and practical commands you'll need to effectively use many Unix and Linux systems, in both development and production environments.

Learn more on Discord

To join the Discord community for this book – where you can share feedback, ask questions to the author, and learn about new releases – follow the QR code below:

https://packt.link/SecNet

10

Configuring Software

Sooner or later, everyone has to configure software on a Linux system. And while there are many ways to do that, there is thankfully a general pattern that you can follow to get the results you want. On Linux, this is especially common; because much of the standard tooling in Linux follows the "small, sharp tools" philosophy, the tendency is toward lots of small, powerful programs that provide flexibility by supporting extensive configuration.

In this chapter, you'll learn about the configuration hierarchy that well-designed programs tend to use. Whether you just need to check a manual page to find a command-line argument for a single command or whether you want to set an environment variable that applies to all commands you run in your shell, you'll see how to do it.

From there, we'll show you the general configuration hierarchy that almost all Unix software uses, so that you'll always know where to check if a program isn't quite behaving how you expect based on the configuration you've given it.

Finally, you'll see how this configuration translates to programs managed through systemd, the most popular service management tool on Linux.

To summarize, this chapter will cover the following topics:

- The configuration hierarchy
- Command-line arguments
- Environment variables
- Configuration files
- Configuration in Docker

Configuration hierarchy

One of the first things that you'll do when running programs on Linux is to tweak them to your specific needs. In fact, you've already done that: by passing arguments to commands like ls, grep, and others, you have changed how these programs behave.

You probably have an intuitive feeling about how this should work because you've been around software your whole life. For example, it might seem natural to you that passing command-line arguments would override program defaults: ls -1 gives you output that's different from the default output of ls.

Let's now dive into this intuition a bit more rigorously and see if we can map out some heuristics for how configuration *generally* works in a Unix environment. One of the norms that most standard Unix command-line programs conform to is a specific configuration hierarchy, where earlier values are overridden by later values. If you've written software that takes user configuration, you may have created a priority hierarchy like this before:

1. Set configurable values to built-in defaults.
2. Check for values passed via configuration files, overriding those defaults.
3. Check for environment variables (people may refer to these as env vars), overriding configuration files and earlier values.
4. Check for command-line interface arguments (you may hear these referred to as CLI args), and update values as necessary, overriding earlier values.

Each successive level is closer to the user running the software at a specific moment, and so each successive level takes priority over the previous one.

For example, if your software detects conflicting values in the config file and the CLI arguments that the program was launched with, it should prefer the value in the command-line arguments. In other words, **the values found closer to the program's invocation "shadow"** (in the sense of obscuring or replacing) **the values further away from execution**. The CLI argument value replaces the configuration file value because the configuration file is further away from the point of invocation than the arguments passed to the program when it's started. That should make intuitive sense: you can't depend on software if it ignores your command-line flags in favor of program defaults. ls -1 shouldn't give you the same output as ls.

Most software on Linux follows this hierarchy when there are multiple ways to configure that software. Keep in mind that not all software uses all the configuration paths we'll show as examples here, and not all software respects this configuration order exactly.

Let's look at this hierarchy again, but this time, connecting it to practical, specific examples for the **nginx** web server program. You'll likely get to work with nginx at some point in your career, since it's one of the most popular web servers in the world, used to front all kinds of dynamic web applications. Let's see how each part of the priority hierarchy we just covered maps to practical nginx configuration:

1. **Built-in defaults**: The hardcoded nginx default for the user that it executes as after starting up is nobody.

2. **Global configuration files** can change this for all nginx processes, so it's common to find a global nginx configuration file at /etc/nginx/nginx.conf with the value "user www;" which instructs nginx to run as the www user instead.

3. **User-level configuration files** are typically "dot-files" (files named with a leading . character, which excludes them from regular ls listings) in the User's /home directory. For example, /home/dave/.bashrc is a place for user-specific bash configuration. nginx is a long-running process that doesn't usually run as a regular Linux user, but it does have something like this: individual sites are often configured in their own, separate configuration files at /etc/nginx/conf.d/yourwebsite.conf. These usually inherit values from the global configuration from the previous level.

4. **Environment variables.** nginx gets timezone information from an environment variable named TZ.

5. **Command-line arguments** are specified when software is run, either manually or in an automated way (for example via cron, or unit files). Make sure to look at these possible external sources of command-line arguments when debugging a problem – they're frequent culprits when you see a disparity between program behavior and the configuration files. nginx takes various command-line arguments that modify its behavior: from overriding the configuration files it will use to preventing it from acting as a web server entirely and instead signaling an already-running nginx process to stop or reload.

Now that you've seen both the theoretical and practical aspects of how this configuration hierarchy interacts with all the programs you run on Linux, and all the programs you might *write* for it, let's go through the configuration hierarchy step by step to take a closer look at each level. We'll start with the most direct and powerful form of configuration, which overrides everything else: passing command-line arguments at the moment in which you invoke a program.

Command-line arguments

You're already familiar with the most common way to configure programs: with command-line arguments. These configure a program at the moment it's invoked as a shell command.

To find valid command-line arguments for a program, start with the man (manual) page for your command. Except on the most minimal systems, Unix software ships with manual pages that document most programs, explain available flags, and – usually at the end – list other kinds of configuration methods, like configuration files.

Let's look at the beginning of the man page content for the find command:

```
man find
FIND(1)
General Commands Manual
FIND(1)


NAME
     find – walk a file hierarchy

SYNOPSIS
     find [-H | -L | -P] [-EXdsx] [-f path] path ... [expression]
     find [-H | -L | -P] [-EXdsx] -f path [path ...] [expression]


DESCRIPTION
     The find utility recursively descends the directory tree for each
path listed, evaluating an expression (composed of the "primaries" and
"operands" listed
     below) in terms of each file in the tree.


     The options are as follows:


     -E      Interpret regular expressions followed by -regex and -iregex
primaries as extended (modern) regular expressions rather than basic
regular expressions
             (BRE's).  The re_format(7) manual page fully describes both
formats.


     -H      Cause the file information and file type (see stat(2))
returned for each symbolic link specified on the command line to be those
of the file
```

```
              referenced by the link, not the link itself.  If the
    referenced file does not exist, the file information and type will be for
    the link itself.  File
                 information of all symbolic links not on the command line is
    that of the link itself.
```

You can see that most of this manual page documents the various command-line arguments that are available when running find. You've used plenty of command-line arguments since *Chapter 1*, so this should all feel familiar.

Let's look at the next, slightly more distant kind of configuration: environment variables.

Environment variables

While a command-line argument is powerful, it applies only to the single program invocation that it's a part of. When you type ls -l, only that one ls command will have the long-form output. But what if you want a configuration value to persist over multiple invocations of a command? This is useful if, for example, you're writing a script that will install packages at a few different points, and you want to set a configuration option *once* instead of having to add it over and over again as a command-line argument every single time you run the package installation command. That's where environment variables come in.

As a developer writing any kind of software, you are likely aware of environment variables: shell values that are analogous to variables in any other programming language. These differ from command-line arguments because they operate one level higher. Environment variables give you more leverage: once you set a configuration variable in the shell, it applies to all program invocations made in that shell session. Set it once, and a program that looks for the environment variable will respect it every time it's run, until the variable changes or you end the shell session.

Note

We'll dive deeper into environment variables in *Chapter 12, Automating Tasks with Shell Scripts*, but this section covers the basics.

Most standard Unix environments use environment variables as a means to specify common configurations that are relevant to many different programs, not just one. For example, environment variables keep track of where the User's /home directory can be found ($HOME), what the current working directory is ($PWD), which shell should be used by default ($SHELL), where to look for the executable files that correspond to commands received via the CLI ($PATH), and so on.

Feel free to inspect them right now; you can see the value of a specific environment variable by printing it out with the echo command:

```
$ echo $SHELL
/bin/zsh
```

Or you can use the env command to see all of the environment variables currently set:

```
$ env
...
# many lines of output, one for each of your environment variables
...
```

To set an environment variable in your current shell, simply use = for assignment (ensure that there are no spaces around the equals sign):

```
MYVAR=fruitloops
```

You've set it for your current shell:

```
$ echo $MYVAR
fruitloops
```

To persist this variable for any subshells you spawn (for example, when you run a script), use the export builtin:

```
export MYVAR=fruitloops
```

You'll learn more in *Chapter 12*, *Automating Tasks with Shell Scripts*, but the above command is the extent of what you'll need to pass environment variable configuration to most programs you interact with.

Back to the find example: if you scroll down far enough on the find man page, which we looked at in the previous section, you'll see a section titled ENVIRONMENT:

```
ENVIRONMENT
     The LANG, LC_ALL, LC_COLLATE, LC_CTYPE, LC_MESSAGES and LC_TIME
environment variables affect the execution of the find utility as
described in environ(7).
```

This is a different level of configuration – instead of being passed as command arguments at runtime, these are the configuration directives that can be read from shell environment variables.

Why should a program treat environment variables differently from arguments? Let's think it through: the command-line argument –H is incredibly specific because it is defined at the command invocation level. As a result, it applies only to the command being run at that instant.

On the other hand, environment variables are less specific. They're defined at the shell level and, therefore, are available to all commands run from that shell.

Let's keep walking up the configuration hierarchy: if a value isn't set at runtime in a command-line argument, or as an environment variable in the shell session that a program is launched from, where does configuration come from?

Configuration files

The next place a program looks for configuration is in its configuration files. *Where* a program looks for configuration can vary wildly, but there are a few standard places to look.

System-level configuration in /etc/

First, the /etc/ directory is a good place to start. You've seen this directory before, in *Chapter 5, Introducing Files*. /etc/programname – where programname is a stand-in for the name of the program you're interested in configuring – is a common choice of directory for software to keep system-wide configuration. For many programs, that's enough. For example, the nginx web server is a system-level program: different users aren't commonly running their own instances of web servers on a single machine, so a system-wide configuration is all that's needed.

That said, configuration for large or complex programs can still be broken up inside of the /etc/ programname directory. Nginx is a good example of this; its main configuration file is at /etc/ nginx.conf, with additional config files being sourced from additional files in the /etc/nginx/ conf.d/ directory.

User-level configuration in ~/.config

For programs that have significant per-user configuration – think text editors, development tooling, games, and more – the ~/.config directory inside a user's home directory is used. Recall from *Chapter 1, How the Command Line Works* that ~ is a shorthand for "the current user's home directory," and that directories whose names start with a period character (".") are omitted from ls output unless you pass the -a flag. The ~/.config directory is part of the XDG base directory standard, which you can get an overview of here: https://wiki.archlinux.org/title/ XDG_Base_Directory.

As an example, my neovim configuration is meaningfully different from other developers' configuration, yet a single neovim binary on a system can support hundreds of developers working on the same machine simultaneously because each developer's invocation of neovim uses their user-specific configuration files kept in ~/.config/nvim/. And that's good!

You can imagine the pandemonium that would ensue if there was only a single system-wide place to configure this program in /etc/ – either each developer would have to set countless environment variables before running the neovim editor or invoke the editor command with countless command-line flags.

Now that you've taken a walk through the classical configuration sources for Unix programs, let's look at one Linux-specific complication that you should know about: how configuration via environment files and CLI arguments is managed for programs controlled through systemd.

systemd units

In most Linux distributions – aside from Docker containers – systemd runs the show. We've already covered the basics of systemd in this book (see *Chapter 3, Service Management with systemd*), and in this section, we'll take a quick look at how systemd manages configuration for programs.

First, a quick review, in case *Chapter 3* seems awfully distant: in a systemd-managed Linux environment, services are packaged into systemd unit files, which wrap and control the actual executable binary, its arguments, the commands used to launch, restart, and stop the unit, and much more.

There are many systemd unit types, as we've already covered, but we're interested in the service unit type here.

We've already covered the fact that unit files can exist in several different directories, depending on their purpose, but your own custom systemd units will usually live in /etc/systemd/system.

To understand how a systemd unit lets you affect the layers of the configuration hierarchy that we've covered in this chapter, let's create a systemd-managed service by writing our own systemd unit for an imaginary program called yourprogram.

Create your own service

As a developer, you may need to wrap a program you're writing into a service, which can be more easily managed than a manually (interactively) invoked program. That's perfectly useful on its own, but in this chapter, we're digging into the extra control that systemd units give you over how and where your program is configured. Let's walk through the process of creating a service by wrapping a binary with a systemd unit file.

First, ensure that you have an executable file copied to a place that is in the default $PATH: /usr/local/bin/yourprogram. If you want to get the most out of this, use a manually compiled program like the htop binary you created in the previous *Chapter 9, Managing Installed Software*, and replace the imaginary yourprogram with htop.

Now, create the following systemd unit file at /etc/systemd/system/yourprogram.service:

```
[Unit]
Description=Your program description.
After=network-online.target

[Service]
Type=exec
ExecStart=/usr/local/bin/yourprogram -clioption=1 -clioption2
EnvironmentFile=-/etc/yourprogram/prod_defaults
Restart=on-failure

[Install]
WantedBy=multi-user.target
```

Can you find the two configuration-related lines in this unit file?

You can see that the ExecStart line specifies how the program is invoked when someone starts this systemd service. We're using the systemd unit file to pass command-line arguments to the program to make sure that anytime someone starts the service, the program is run with exactly the options we want. Anytime someone runs systemctl start yourprogram, we have ensured that yourprogram will be called with -clioption=1 and -clioption2.

Second, the EnvironmentFile line specifies a file path for systemd to check, where it can expect environment variables relevant to this program to be set. This file will be parsed by the shell that systemd uses to run the binary; it should contain shell variable assignments like:

```
# yourprogram environment variables
ENV=production
DB_HOST=localhost
DB_PORT=5432
```

Have systemd re-read its config files to make sure it sees the new service Unit you've defined:

```
$ sudo systemd daemon-reload
```

Now you can manage this like any other systemd service:

```
systemctl start yourprogram
```

```
systemctl status yourprogram
```

```
systemctl stop yourprogram
```

```
systemctl enable yourprogram
```

```
systemctl disable yourprogram
```

You know that every time you start this service, your environment file at /etc/yourprogram/ prod_defaults will be used to source environment variables, and the ExecStart line will pass the CLI options you've specified.

We've shown you an extremely simple service here, just so you can get your head around how systemd is used to control program configuration, but there are *many* other configuration directives you can pass here. Spend some time reading the systemd unit documentation (https:// www.freedesktop.org/software/systemd/man/latest/systemd.unit.html#%5BUnit%5D%20 Section%20Options) if you have a more complex service on your hands.

Quick note: configuration in Docker

Earlier in this chapter, we mentioned that Docker is often the exception when it comes to configuration. Because Docker containers are a much more minimal environment, they don't have a lot of the extra binaries, services, and configuration files that you'll find in a traditional Unix system. But because much of the software that software developers create now runs in containers, as opposed to traditional, full operating system environments, we want to cover some basics here to make sure you've got an intuition for how configuration is different in Docker containers. We'll dig much deeper into Docker containers in general in *Chapter 15, Containerizing Applications with Docker*.

In a container environment – whether it's Docker or another container runtime – you're dealing with a dramatically smaller environment. There are very few installed programs and utilities, a dramatically stripped-down init in place of systemd, and a much smaller filesystem that doesn't have many of the directories we've mentioned here.

The principle of the configuration hierarchy still holds, though. Most containerized applications expect to get their configuration either from:

- A config file somewhere on the container filesystem, often dynamically created by a container scheduler just before the container is started
- Environment variables, passed in by the container scheduler or the operator launching it
- Command-line arguments

Even though this is a simplified version of the configuration hierarchy, you'll notice that it's basically identical to the one we explored in full, non-container Linux systems.

We'll dive a bit deeper into containers in *Chapter 15, Containerizing Applications with Docker*.

Conclusion

This chapter gave you an overview of the Linux configuration hierarchy and how it applies to the programs you'll use (and write) every day. You learned about command-line arguments, environment variables, and all the other things that fit into the larger hierarchy that programs pull configuration from.

If you followed along, you even created a systemd service that wraps a program and allows you to manage its configuration in a more uniform way.

Learn more on Discord

To join the Discord community for this book – where you can share feedback, ask questions to the author, and learn about new releases – follow the QR code below:

```
https://packt.link/SecNet
```

11
Pipes and Redirection

In this chapter, you're going to learn how to harness one of the most powerful computing concepts in existence: pipes! Pipes can be used to connect commands, building up complex, customized flows that accomplish a specific task. By the end of the chapter, you'll be able to understand (or compose) something like this:

```
history | awk '{print $2}' | sort | uniq -c | sort -rn | head -n 10
```

In case you're curious, this prints out a top-10 list of your most commonly used shell commands; on my machine, it produces this output:

```
1000 git
 115 ls
 102 go
  83 gpo (an alias I've set up for pushing a local git branch to the
origin)
  68 make
  65 cd
  59 docker
  42 vagrant
  35 GOOS=linux
  30 echo
```

To really understand pipes, you need to first understand file descriptors and input/output redirection, so that's where we'll start. Some of the information in this chapter is quite dense; just take your time and try out all the examples to make sure you understand everything. The time you invest in learning these concepts now will save you many hours throughout your career.

In this chapter, we'll cover the following topics:

- File descriptors
- Connecting commands together with pipes (|)
- The CLI tools you need to know
- Practical pipe patterns
- Inspecting file descriptors

File descriptors

You're probably familiar with file handles (also known as *file descriptors*) from your software engineering experience. If not, we recommend you check out *Chapter 5, Introducing Files*. In short, if your program needs to read or write a file on the operating system, opening that file gives you a "file handle" to it – a pointer, or reference, to that file object.

Because the operating system mediates all access to system resources like files, it tracks which file handles, or descriptors, your program is actively referencing.

But even if a process doesn't touch a single file on the operating system, it's got some file handles open. In Unix-like operating systems, every process has at least three file descriptors:

- `stdin`: standard input - or, `fd 0` ("file descriptor zero")
- `stdout`: standard output - or, `fd 1` ("file descriptor one")
- `stderr`: standard error - or, `fd 2` ("file descriptor two")

These first three file descriptors function as standard communication channels to (and from) a process. As a result, they exist in the same order for every process created on the system. The first always points to a file which will be used to read in input. The second points to a file that will be used for writing output. And the third references a file that will receive error output.

Optionally, after those first three standard file descriptors, there can be any number of other file descriptors/handles, based on what the program is doing. Your process could have:

- Files it's working with
- Sockets it's reading from or writing to (think Unix or TCP sockets being written to for networking)
- Devices like keyboards or disks it needs to use

What do these file descriptors reference?

You now know, from the perspective of a process, what these file descriptors are used for:

- 0 (STDIN): get input from here
- 1 (STDOUT): put regular output here
- 2 (STDERR): put error output here

But if we zoom outside of a single process, which files are these file descriptors actually pointing to? Where does input come from, and where do output and errors get written to?

Let's use a Bash shell process as an example: by default, it takes input (STDIN) from your terminal (which is represented by a file on the filesystem). Bash prints output and errors to the same terminal. In essence, your entire shell session is happening via read and write operations to a single file. You'll learn much more about Bash in the next chapter, *Automating Tasks with Shell Scripts*.

Let's look at this kind of input and output redirection in more detail.

Input and output redirection (or, playing with file descriptors for fun and profit)

This knowledge comes in handy quite often during real-life development tasks: every time you want to avoid typing lots of input and take it from a file instead, or when you want to log the output of a program, and many more situations. When you create a process, you can control where its three standard file descriptors point, with powerful results.

Input redirection: <

The < (less-than) symbol lets you control where a process gets its input from. For example, you're used to giving input to Bash with your keyboard, one command at a time. Let's try giving Bash input from a file, instead!

Assume I have a file named commands.txt with the following content (I'm using cat here to print out my example file):

```
# cat commands.txt
pwd
echo "hello there, friends"
echo $SHELL
cd /tmp
pwd
```

These are valid shell commands, as far as Bash is concerned, so I'm going to launch a new Bash process and use this file as standard input:

```
# bash < commands.txt
/tmp/gopsinspect
hello there, friends
/bin/bash
/tmp
```

Instead of prompting me for input and waiting until I give it, Bash reads and executes one line at a time: it reads input from the file until it comes across a newline (\n) character, and just as if you'd hit the *RETURN* key, it executes the command.

In this example, the program's standard output is still going back to our terminal, where we can read it. Let's change that now.

Output redirection: >

We want to redirect STDOUT (file descriptor 1) to a file instead of a terminal, logging the output of each command instead of printing it out to the terminal in real time:

```
# bash < commands.txt > output.log
```

Notice that there is no visible output in the terminal now – because the > character has redirected output to output.log. Use cat to print out the log file and confirm that it contains the expected output:

```
# cat output.log
/tmp/gopsinspect
hello there, friends
/bin/bash
/tmp
```

Interestingly, you'll notice that because file descriptor 1 is standard output, writing > is the same as writing 1>. You'll rarely see a 1 used, because it's assumed that standard output is being redirected. In other words:

```
date > mydate.log
is equivalent to writing
date 1> mydate.log
```

Use >> to append output without overwriting

In the previous example, we created a log file by redirecting command output with >. If you run the example a few times, you'll notice that the log file doesn't grow at all. Each time you redirect output to a file with > filename, anything in that file will be overwritten.

To avoid that – as in the case of a long-lived log file that collects output from more than a single process or command – use >> (append). This will simply append to your output file, instead of overwriting its entire contents each time.

We'll cover Bash scripts in more detail in a later chapter, but for now, here's a quick script that writes a timestamp of the current time to a log file once per second:

```
while true; do
    date >> /tmp/date.log
    sleep 1
done
```

In this example script, we create an infinite loop (while true; do [...] done) which runs the date command. It redirects the output of this command to the /tmp/date.log file using >>, which appends the output to the file (> would overwrite the file each time). Then, the script sleeps for one second, and starts again from the beginning.

Running the date command once produces the following output:

```
→  ~ date
Sat Jan  6 16:39:37 EST 2024
```

Running this script, on the other hand, does nothing visible at first, because the output is being redirected to a file. Here's what it looks like when I paste this little script into my terminal, let it run for a bit, kill it with *Ctrl + C*, and then print out the contents of the file it created:

```
→  ~ while true; do
    date >> /tmp/date.log
    sleep 1
done
^C%
→  ~ cat /tmp/date.log
Sat Jan  6 16:44:01 EST 2024
Sat Jan  6 16:44:02 EST 2024
```

```
Sat Jan  6 16:44:03 EST 2024
[ ... ]
Sat Jan  6 16:44:08 EST 2024
```

You'll use this kind of simple output redirection in all kinds of everyday situations, like creating an ad hoc log file for a quick debug script you throw together.

Error redirection with 2>

Many command-line programs that have a lot of expected output will also output occasional errors – think of a find command that encounters occasional "permission denied" errors for directories you're not allowed to peek inside.

Although these kinds of errors are minor and expected, you don't want them mixed in with everything else, polluting your output. This becomes especially important when you're not using command-line tools interactively, but rather writing small scripts or larger programs that process the output of the commands you're running.

You've seen how to redirect Standard Input (fd 0) and Standard Output (fd 1). Let's look at how to redirect Standard Error (fd 2) using the 2> (redirect file descriptor 2) syntax:

```
find /etc/ -name php.ini > /tmp/phpinis.log 2>/dev/null
```

This command searches for any files named php.ini inside the /etc directory tree. The files it finds (find's STDOUT) are written to /tmp/phpinis.log, and any errors it encounters are ignored by sending them to a special file called /dev/null.

> **Tip**
>
> /dev/null is a special file-like object that returns zeros when you try to read from it and ignores anything written to it – it's used as a kind of garbage dump for output that engineers want to silence or ignore. You'll see it used quite often in scripts.

Now that you've seen input and output redirection, let's look at pipes, which put both of those concepts together: they redirect the output of one command to the input of another.

Connecting commands together with pipes (|)

You've learned how to redirect each of the three standard file descriptors to various locations and seen why that's often useful. But what if, instead of just redirecting input and output to and from various files, you wanted to connect *multiple programs* together?

On the command line, you can use the pipe character (|) to connect the output of one program to the input of another program. This is an extremely powerful paradigm that is heavily used in Unix and Linux to create custom sorting, filtering, and processing commands:

```
echo -e "some text \n treasure found \n some more text" | grep treasure
```

If you paste this into your shell, you'll see treasure found printed out. Here's what happened:

1. The first command, echo, runs and produces the output you see between double quotes (the newline characters make this a 3-line string).

2. The pipe character streams that output (file descriptor 1) to the input of the next command (file descriptor 0), grep. grep's input is now hooked up to the output of the previous command.

3. The grep command looks at each newline-delimited line in turn and finds a match for treasure on the second line. grep prints that second line to its standard output.

Multi-pipe commands

Here's the – fairly extreme – example you saw at the beginning of the chapter:

```
history | awk '{print $2}' | sort | uniq -c | sort -rn | head -n 10 > /
tmp/top10commands
```

Each pipe in this complex command simply takes the output of the previous command (STDOUT) and uses it as the input (STDIN) for the next command.

Piping the output of one command into the input of another is what enables these kinds of flows, filtering and sorting the data streaming between these commands without actually having to write any custom software. Just because there's no program called top10commands doesn't mean you can't quickly cobble one together with existing, standard commands like this.

Reading (and building) complex multi-pipe commands

No matter how complex or magical some of the piped-together commands you encounter will seem, they were all built the same way: one command at a time. Whether you're trying to read a complex series of commands like this or creating one of your own, the process is the same:

1. Take the first command and make sure you understand what it does, at a basic level. Scan the man page or other documentation if you aren't familiar with it.
2. Run the command and inspect its output.
3. Add the pipe and the command following it.
4. Repeat from *step 1* until you've made it all the way through the commands.

You'll see that even the scariest shell/pipe monstrosities become manageable when you apply this process. Always remember that you're just dealing with a data stream, which flows through the pipes from command to command, being shaped, modified, filtered, redirected, and transformed along the way.

We'll discuss this more in *Chapter 12, Automating Tasks with Shell Scripts*, but try to be respectful of other programmers who must read your code: limit your statements to two or three pipes, and use well-named variables to store intermediate results for easy reading if your memory constraints allow it.

Now that you've seen how the primitives of file descriptors are exposed as easy-to-use input and output redirection, let's look at some real-world examples of useful program combinations that rely on this composability that's built into Unix.

The CLI tools you need to know

Before we jump into the kinds of wild combinations that you saw at the beginning of the chapter, let's look at some of the most common Unix helper tools that are used to filter, sort, and glue together these data streams you'll be creating on the command line.

cut

cut takes a delimiter (-d) and splits input on that delimiter, like String.Split() or String. Fields() in many programming languages. You then select which field (list element) you want to output with -f, for example, f1 for the first field.

If you feed cut more than one line of input, it will repeat that same operation on all lines:

```
echo "this is a space-delimited line" | cut -d " " -f4
space-delimited
```

You can see how using different delimiters for cut would work, too; in the following example, we cut on the hyphen character instead of a space:

```
→  ~ echo "this is a space-delimited line" | cut -d "-" -f1
this is a space
→  ~ echo "this is a space-delimited line" | cut -d "-" -f2
delimited line
```

You can see that this changes the number of fields available as well – two in this case, since there's only one hyphen in the text. Trying to print the fourth field with -f4, as in the previous example, will just give you an empty line.

To get friendly names for all users with root in their names on an macOS machine, you can use the following:

```
# grep root /etc/passwd | cut -d ":" -f5
System Administrator
System Services
CVMS Root
```

sort

sort does a per-line sorting, alphabetical or numeric.

Reverse-sorting with -r is often useful when dealing with numeric data (-n). You'll often want -rn together (see Top X in the Practical pipe patterns section of this chapter).

The -h flag can be very useful for sorting by human-readable output of many other commands, like this:

```
# du -h | sort -rh
1.6M    .
1.3M    ./.git
1.2M    ./.git/objects
 60K    ./.git/hooks
 28K    ./.git/objects/d8
```

uniq

Removes duplicate lines. This command needs sorted data to work the way you expect, otherwise it only checks whether each line is a duplicate of the previous line:

```
# cat /tmp/uniq
one
two
one
one
one
seven
one
```

Default behavior; probably not what you want:

```
# uniq /tmp/uniq
one
two
one
seven
one
```

uniq skips occurrences when they follow each other but leaves them when they're separated by other text. Now the same thing, with sorted data:

```
# sort /tmp/uniq | uniq
one
seven
two
```

Counting

uniq also has a useful "count" option, accessible with -c. The same caveat about sorted input is worth restating here – for example, a file with the following content:

```
arch
alpine
arch
arch
```

Will produce the following output when run through `uniq -c`:

```
$ uniq -c /tmp/sort1.txt
    1 arch
    1 alpine
    2 arch
```

This is not what most users expect: there are 3 occurrences of arch in the file, but uniq shows two separate counts for the same word. To get the behavior you expect (uniq should return output that doesn't contain any duplicate lines), your input must be sorted.

This is annoying for beginners, but very much in line with the Unix philosophy: tools should be small and sharp and shouldn't duplicate functionality from each other. If you write a sorting tool, it should only sort, and if you write a uniquifying tool, it is allowed to depend on sorting from another tool to ensure extremely conservative (and consistent) memory usage.

Here, we sort before using uniq, which gets us the output we expect:

```
$ sort /tmp/sort1.txt | uniq -c
    1 alpine
    3 arch
```

You'll notice that this sorts in ascending order, which isn't what you want for the top-X list of commands you saw at the beginning of the chapter. To solve this, we do a "reverse numeric" sort (-rn) of this numbered list (since each line now starts with a number, thanks to uniq -c, this is easy to do). Here's an example of this in action, on a file with many more duplicates:

```
$ sort /tmp/sortme.txt | uniq -c | sort -rn
    6 ubuntu
    4 alpine
    3 gentoo
    2 yellow dog
    2 arch
    1 suse
    1 mandrake
```

wc

With this command you can measure the word, line, character, and byte input counts. You can also count space-delimited words with -w:

```
# echo "foo bar baz" | wc -w
      3
```

Line-counting is extremely common in the following format:

```
# wc -l < /etc/passwd
    123
```

head

Head returns the first lines of a stream or file – 10 lines by default. Specify how many lines you want with -n:

```
# head -n 2 /etc/passwd
##
# User Database
```

tail

This is the opposite of head: it returns lines from the end of the file or stream. It takes -n just like head.

tail can also be used interactively for following along with a log file, even as that file has new data streamed/written to it. You'll see it used a lot like this during troubleshooting:

```
tail -f /var/log/ngnix/access.log
```

tee

Sometimes, one copy of the data from standard input just isn't enough. tee copies standard input to standard output, while also making a copy in a file. As a software developer, I really like tee for two specific cases.

First, for debugging and logging: when I'm running scripts or programs that generate output, tee can be used to both display the output on the screen and log it to a file for later analysis. We're using the echo command here, but you'd likely be calling your own program before the first pipe here:

```
# echo "Hello" | tee /tmp/greetings.txt
Hello

# cat /tmp/greetings.txt
Hello
```

The second use case where tee comes in handy is for copying data from a pipeline like the ones we're learning to construct in this chapter. You can use tee to intercept this flow at any point in the pipe, and save/inspect the intermediate results without disrupting the pipeline.

Here's the "top 10 commands" example from earlier, but with `tee` inserted before limiting the results to just 10. This saves the full results in a temp file before we truncate them:

```
history | awk '{print $2}' | sort | uniq -c | sort -rn | tee /tmp/all_
commands.txt | head -n 10
```

Now if you want to see all of the commands, not just the top 10, you can just use `cat` or `less` to inspect the /tmp/all_commands.txt file.

awk

awk is often just used for dealing with columns of data, but it's actually a whole language.

For example, you can grab the second column from each line in the following way:

```
# echo "two columns" | awk '{print $2}'
columns
```

sed

sed is a stream editor with tons of options. Most commonly, it's used for character replacement in streams or files.

Imagine we have a file like this:

```
# cat /tmp/sensitive.txt
Nopasswords
not_a_password_either
sillypasswordtimes
password
ok this works
```

If we want to redact ONLY the line that has `password`, and nothing else, on it:

```
sed 's/^password$/REDACTED/' /tmp/sensitive.txt
nopasswords
not_a_password_either
sillypasswordtimes
REDACTED
ok this works
```

This example uses a file rather than an input stream coming from another command. By default, this will not modify the original file. If you *do* want to modify the input file, use the `-i` (in-place) option.

Now that you've been introduced to pipes and have seen some of the most common command-line tools, let's put those building blocks together and learn several practical patterns that you can use to make your daily command-line life a bit easier.

Practical pipe patterns

As mentioned before, longer multi-pipe commands are built iteratively – one command at a time. However, there are some useful patterns that you'll see re-used frequently.

"Top X", with count

This pattern sorts the input by the number of occurrences, in descending order. You saw this in the original example from this chapter, which displayed the most frequently used shell commands from Bash's history file.

Here's the pattern:

```
some_input | sort | uniq -c | sort -rn | head -n 3
```

We can note the following details about this pattern:

- The input is sorted alphabetically, and then run through uniq -c, which needs sorted input to work on.

- uniq -c eliminates duplicates, but adds a count (-c) of how many duplicates it found for each entry.

- sort is run again, this time as a reverse-numeric (-r and -n) sort which sorts the unique counts from the input and outputs the lines in reverse (highest number first) sorted order.

- head takes that top ranking and cuts it down to three lines (-n 3), giving you the top three strings from the original input, along with how often they occurred.

This pattern can come in handy when you need to know the most common browser user-agents hitting your website, the IP addresses of the worst offenders who are trying to probe and exploit your website, or any other situation where a sorted, ranked list is useful.

curl | bash

The curl | bash pattern is a common shortcut used in Linux to download and execute scripts directly from the internet. This method combines two powerful command-line tools: curl, which fetches the content from a URL, and bash, the shell interpreter, which executes the downloaded script. This pattern is a significant time-saver, allowing developers to quickly deploy applications or run scripts without manually downloading and then executing them.

As an example, let's install the Pi-hole adblocking DNS server using this pattern:

```
curl -sSL https://install.pi-hole.net | bash
```

Let's break this down, step by step:

1. `curl -sSL https://install.pi-hole.net`: This fetches the Pi-hole installation script, which is hosted at this URL. We pass two options:

    - `-sS`: Silent mode gives you the raw response from the server, but shows errors should they occur.
    - `-L`: Follow redirects.

2. `|`: The pipe symbol passes the output of the previous command (`curl`) as input to the next command (`bash`).

3. `bash`: Executes the script fetched by `curl`.

This is a tremendously useful pattern for automating things like code deployments or local environment installation/configuration. However, take special care that the script you download and execute is not malicious. Blindly running scripts from the internet is extremely bad practice.

Security considerations for curl | sudo | bash

Anytime you trust a third party to run code on your machine, you're trading some security for convenience. In that sense, using `curl | sudo | bash` to install something via a script hosted on a trusted server is not much different from using a package manager. Most package managers (except for `nix`) don't have a particularly impressive security design either, but they generally give you a reasonable set of security features. You're giving all of these security features up when you `curl | sudo | bash` an install script:

- There's no package that can be checksummed and cryptographically signed to make sure you got the correct and official version.

- There's no restriction on – or enforcement of – which servers you download from, and you don't know how secure those servers are: you have no way to identify a compromised server hosting malicious install scripts.

- The scripts themselves are just code being run as the root user on your machine, so they can do anything *you* can on your machine, for better or worse. To be fair, many popular package managers also have this problem.

For all of these reasons, please heed our warning to split `curl` into its own step and read through the downloaded install script before running `sudo bash` to execute it. The main things to look out for are:

- Ensure the server/domain you're downloading the script from is trustworthy; this should be a reputable developer's website or a trusted third-party code hosting platform.

- Ensure you use HTTPS for the `curl` download (i.e., the URL should start with `https://`).

- Read through the script carefully, to see which commands it runs and where it pulls additional code or executables from. If it downloads additional scripts or executables, have a look at those too.

I think we've established that `curl` | `sudo` | `bash` is not a particularly secure method of installing software. Following these guidelines can help you be a bit safer if you – like most of us – give into temptation one day and follow this installation method for a specific piece of software (for example, `homebrew` on macOS).

Let's look at another common pattern now: filtering and searching with grep.

Filtering and searching with grep

When you run commands that produce a lot of output, it's generally best practice to filter the output down to just what you need. The most common tool for this is called grep, and you can think of it as a highly configurable text search or string-matching function. Here's an example of what filtering might look like.

Imagine that you need to find a Linux process's working directory. The `lsof` tool can accomplish this:

```
→  ~  lsof -p 3243 | grep cwd
vagrant 3243 dcohen   cwd      DIR                1,4       192
51689680 /Users/dcohen/code/my_vagrant_testenv
```

Here's a quick description of what's happening:

1. I'm getting a listing of open file handles for a specific process (PID 3243), using `lsof`.

2. I'm then passing the results (|) to the grep utility and using that to search the results for the string `cwd`. There's only one line of results that contains the string `cwd`, so that's the only line that grep prints to the terminal.

This pattern is useful anytime you have a *lot* of data as input, but you only need a subset of that data that can be identified by a specific string. grep operates on lines of input text, so it's hugely helpful for picking out data like:

- Loglines containing the IP address you are following
- Occurrences of a username in a piped data stream
- Lines that match a pattern (grep is regular-expression aware and can take string patterns in addition to literal search strings)

grep is a large and powerful tool that you'll have occasion to use almost every day. For more information, check out the manpage for grep by typing man grep.

You've already seen grep used on files in this book (for example, grep searchstring hello. txt), but it's also an invaluable filtering component in piped commands. Let's look at a practical example now.

grep and tail for log monitoring

When you're looking at production logs to try to figure out what's wrong, you'll often only want to see loglines containing certain keywords or search strings. To do that, you'd run something like:

```
tail -f /var/log/webapp/too_many_logs.log | grep "yourSearchRegex"
```

This pattern continuously monitors the log file for new entries whose content matches "your-SearchRegex", so you can see only the logs you need for the task at hand.

find and xargs for bulk file operations

xargs is a powerful utility that gives you the power of iteration (in other words, a "for" loop) inside of a single command. By default, xargs takes each (space, tab, newline, and end-of-file delimited) chunk of input it receives and executes the specified program using that chunk as input. For example, if you need to search for specific file content across ONLY the files returned by a certain find query, you can run this command:

```
find . -type f -name "*\.txt" | xargs grep "search_term"
```

This command finds all files whose names end with .txt and then uses xargs to apply the grep command to each file individually. This pattern is handy for searching or modifying multiple files at once. Please be forewarned that xargs is a powerful – and *large* – program, capable of doing many things (including string interpolation into the command it executes). We can't cover it all here, so please read the manpage and scour the internet for examples if you're in a situation where this kind of functionality would save the day.

sort, uniq, and reverse numerical sort for data analysis

This is a useful pattern that you saw applied at the beginning of the chapter, where I used it to filter a large command history to get a list of the "top X most popular commands run on this system." The core pattern is this:

```
(input stream) | sort | uniq -c | sort -rn
```

Useful for analyzing data, this pattern sorts the data from the input stream, deduplicates it while counting unique occurrences, and then performs a reverse numerical sort to give you the deduplicated data, with the most common lines first.

This is commonly truncated with | `head -n $NUMBER` to get only the top $NUMBER of results:

```
history | awk '{print $2}' | sort | uniq -c | sort -rn | head -n 10
```

Here, we use history to fetch the entire shell command history. This gives us a series of lines like:

```
    12  brew install --cask emacs
```

We're only interested in the top-level command (in this case, brew), so we use awk to fetch the second column.

Then we sort so that duplicates of the same command occur next to each other in the stream. Then we remove those duplicates with uniq, adding a count of occurrences to each remaining one. Now we sort again – this time using -rn for a reverse numerical sort, which gives us the "top X" effect. Finally, we take the first 10 lines with head.

This prints out the aforementioned top-10 list of your most-used shell commands; on my machine, it produces this:

```
1000 git
 115 ls
 102 go
  83 gpo (an alias I've set up for pushing a local git branch to the
origin)
  68 make
  65 cd
  59 docker
  42 vagrant
  35 GOOS=linux
  30 echo
```

awk and sort for reformatting data and field-based processing

awk is more than a program; it's a stream-processing language. If you work with data streams on Unix system, then spending a few days learning the basics can save you weeks of time over your career. That said, just using $# syntax to reference whitespace-delimited columns in each line of the data stream is a good start.

Let's look at an example given a data stream like the following:

```
Foo bar baz
Some data is nice
```

When the awk interpreter sees $1, it interprets this to mean "the first column" or in this case Foo in line 1 and Some in line 2. $2 is the second column (bar, data), and so on. This is an incredibly common feature to use when working with data that's just a bit too complex for simple cut commands:

```
cat file.txt | awk '{print $2, $1}'
```

This would produce output like:

```
bar Foo
data Some
```

In this case, it prints out column 2 before column 1 for each file, and ignores all other data in each line. This is often used for reformatting and organizing data based on specific fields.

sed and tee for editing and backup

sed stands for **Stream EDitor** and is used when you want to transform a data stream. You do this ten times a day in your text editor when you find/replace a symbol. The following command is essentially the command-line version of that functionality: it transforms all occurrences of old in file.txt into the string new and writes the resulting stream to a new file, file.txt.changed. It does this without making changes to the original file.txt file:

```
sed 's/old/new/g' file.txt | tee file.txt.changed
```

Although editing file content is an easy demonstration of this concept, sed is tremendously useful for transforming stream data as it zips from the output of one command to the input of the next:

```
(input stream) | sed 's/old/new/g' | (next command)
```

ps, grep, awk, xargs, and kill for process management

Although pgrep is a good utility for sending signals to all processes whose name matches a pattern, sometimes it's just not available on your system. You can cobble together similar functionality (and get much more specific with what you want to target, not just the name) by using this set of piped-together commands:

```
ps aux | grep "process_name" | awk '{print $2}' | xargs kill
```

ps starts you off with a list of running processes, which grep filters to just those containing the pattern you're searching for. awk gets the second column (the process ID) for each matching line, and then feeds all matched lines to xargs (our quasi for loop), which executes kill on each PID. This sends a SIGTERM to each matching process and (hopefully) halts it.

tar and gzip for backup and compression

Although many utilities have flags that let you do both, chaining together archiving and compression is another use case that makes sense. This gives you the added flexibility of adding additional chained commands. For example, if you want to add encryption, that's just a single additional piped command away:

```
tar cvf - /path/to/directory | gzip > backup.tar.gz
```

This creates a compressed archive of a directory, commonly used for file backup and storage. You can see larger commands using this kind of pattern:

```
ssh user@mysql-server "mysqldump --add-drop-table database_name | gzip
-9c" | gzip -d | mysql
```

This is an especially fun example that logs into a database server using SSH, dumps out a database, compresses that data stream, shuttles it back to the local machine over SSH, decompresses it again, and finally dumps it into the local MySQL server.

Your aim shouldn't necessarily be to write commands as complex as this one (or some of the others you've seen here), but if you know how to put something like this together in a pinch, it can get you out of some extremely tight spots as a developer. We hope this section has demonstrated that understanding the input and output redirection primitives that Unix systems expose to you – via <, >, >>, |, and file descriptors in general – is basically a superpower. Use it wisely.

Advanced: inspecting file descriptors

On Linux, you can easily *see* where a process's file descriptors are pointing. We're going to use the slightly magical /proc virtual filesystem to do just that.

Procfs (the proc virtual filesystem) is a Linux-only abstraction that represents kernel and process state as files. The data inside of these files comes straight from the operating system kernel, and only exists while you're reading them. Just listing the /proc directory will show you many files; here's a selection of some of the more important ones, taken from the Arch Linux wiki:

```
/proc/cpuinfo - information about CPU
/proc/meminfo - information about the physical memory
/proc/vmstats - information about the virtual memory
/proc/mounts - information about the mounts
/proc/filesystems - information about filesystems that have been compiled
into the kernel and whose kernel modules are currently loaded
/proc/uptime - current system uptime
/proc/cmdline - kernel command line
```

What's most interesting to us with regard to file descriptors is something not shown in the listing above: /proc contains a directory for every single process running on the machine, named after each **process ID (PID)**.

In a process's /proc directory, that process's file descriptors are represented as symbolic links in a directory called fd. When you do a long listing on this /proc/$PID/fd directory, you'll see that l is the first character in the long listing, which denotes a special link file, as you'll recall from *Chapter 5, Introducing Files*.

Practically speaking, /proc/1/ is the init process's proc directory, and you can view init's file descriptors by doing a long listing on /proc/1/fd.

Let's look at the file descriptors for an interactive Bash shell process running on my machine, which ps aux | grep bash tells me is PID 9:

```
root@server:/# ls -alh /proc/9/fd
total 0
dr-x------ 2 root root  0 Sep  1 19:16 .
dr-xr-xr-x 9 root root  0 Sep  1 19:16 ..
lrwx------ 1 root root 64 Sep  1 19:16 0 -> /dev/pts/1
lrwx------ 1 root root 64 Sep  1 19:16 1 -> /dev/pts/1
lrwx------ 1 root root 64 Sep  1 19:16 2 -> /dev/pts/1
lrwx------ 1 root root 64 Sep  5 00:46 255 -> /dev/pts/1
```

You'll notice that it's an interactive shell session: its standard input is coming from a virtual terminal (/dev/pts/1), and its standard error and output are going back to that same terminal. That checks out.

Let's look at a text editor like vim, which behaves a lot like a terminal – input and output happen via a terminal. However, there's an added complication, which is that text editors usually keep one or more files open for writing. What does that look like?

In this example, I'm running the vim text editor, and editing a file in the /tmp directory. Let's find the process ID for vim, so we know which /proc directory to look inside:

```
root@server:/# ps aux | grep vim
root        453  0.0  0.1  17232  9216 pts/1      S+    15:57    0:00 vim /tmp/
hello.txt
root        458  0.0  0.0   2884  1536 pts/0      S+    15:58    0:00 grep
--color=auto vim
```

There it is; process 453. Don't be misled by the grep command which also includes vim in its command arguments. Now that we have the PID, let's look at vim's file descriptors:

```
root@server:/# ls -l /proc/453/fd
total 0
lrwx------ 1 root root 64 Jan  7 15:58 0 -> /dev/pts/1
lrwx------ 1 root root 64 Jan  7 15:58 1 -> /dev/pts/1
lrwx------ 1 root root 64 Jan  7 15:58 2 -> /dev/pts/1
lrwx------ 1 root root 64 Jan  7 15:58 3 -> /tmp/.hello.txt.swp
```

We can see that stdin (0), stdout (1), and stderr (2) are all pointing to a terminal device, just like a shell. And we also see that the editor has a file open, with file descriptor 3 linked to the file that vim is editing. When a process opens additional files, new file descriptors are created, and you can view them here.

Beyond being interesting for its own sake, this can come in handy when programs are behaving erratically due to bugs, or when you're trying to trace what a potentially malicious program is doing. procfs is quite interesting and useful if you invest a bit of time in learning it: just type man proc to get started, or read the Arch Linux Wiki page for a gentler introduction at https://wiki. archlinux.org/title/Procfs.

Conclusion

In this chapter, we put together all of the previous skills and theory we've covered to unlock one of the most powerful features of Unix and Linux systems: streaming data through multiple commands using pipes and input/output redirection.

We started by showing you how the operating system exposes primitives like file descriptors, and then started looking at practical uses of input and output redirection. Then, we covered pipes, which are arguably one of the most useful features of Linux and other Unix operating systems. After covering the necessary theory and showing you some useful examples, we dove deep into the most common helper tools that people use to slice and dice the data streams that they build up using pipes. Finally, we showed you some of the most common and useful patterns and program-combinations that people use in the real world.

What's in this chapter is the foundation for much of the advanced command-line usage you'll encounter and use in your day-to-day work. You've now been exposed to some of the basic theory, tools, and patterns that you'll see in the wild, which will make it easy to dive in and start building custom commands for common development, troubleshooting, and automation use cases.

To grow your skills, use what you've seen in this chapter in your day-to-day work! Use it as a reference for patterns to try, and keep learning new tools and commands that you can add to your own custom recipes and use to filter or otherwise manipulate data on the command line. You'll feel like a wizard in no time.

Learn more on Discord

To join the Discord community for this book – where you can share feedback, ask questions to the author, and learn about new releases – follow the QR code below:

```
https://packt.link/SecNet
```

12

Automating Tasks with Shell Scripts

Sometimes, you'll find yourself repeating the same few commands over and over, perhaps with slight variations. You reach the point of frustration, and say, "That's it; I'm scripting this." Being a CLI wizard, you do the following:

1. Run `tail -n 20 ~/.bash_history > myscript.sh` to create a file that contains the last 20 Bash commands you ran.

2. Then run `bash myscript.sh` to execute it.

Although this isn't the recommended procedure (we'll get to that in this chapter), it's a perfectly valid way to create and run a Bash script.

This chapter is a Bash scripting crash course. Like any programming crash course, it is completely useless unless you actually follow along, type in all the code yourself, and run it in your own Linux environment. In addition to showing you the subset of Bash's syntax which is considered modern and best-practice, we'll give you plenty of tips from our hard-earned experience over the years, calling out common pitfalls and sharp edges.

Bash isn't our favorite language, but sometimes it's exactly the right tool for the problem you face. We'll try to give you an understanding of this as well.

In this chapter, we will cover the following:

- Bash scripting basics
- Bash versus other shells
- Shebangs and executable text files
- Testing
- Conditionals

Why you need Bash scripting basics

Shell scripts are an indispensable tool for any developer; even if you're not writing scripts on a weekly basis, you'll be reading them. In this chapter, we'll cover the basics you need to know so that you feel comfortable when, for example:

- You're confronted by a shell script that someone wrote a few years ago, for example "Can you check to see if we can reuse the automation scripts that Steve wrote before he left for Google?"

- You see an opportunity to write your own shell script, when you have a job that existing shell programs already solve (filtering, searching, sorting output, and feeding one program's output into another one).

- You want to control precisely what goes into each Docker layer as you build up an image.

- You need to coordinate other software in the context of a Linux server's operating system: startup ordering, error checking, aborting early between programs, and so on.

There are innumerable use cases where a shell script is *just* the right size and shape for your problem space. After this chapter, you'll have the skills you need to write that custom script.

Basics

Bash can be learned like any other programming language. It's got an environment (Unix or Linux), a kind of standard library (any CLI-driven program installed on the system), variables, control flow (loops, testing, and iteration), interpolation, a few built-in data structures (arrays, strings, and booleans – sort of), and more.

This entire book assumes that you're a software developer and, therefore, know how to program, so rather than teach you about these standard programming-language features, we'll simply show you what they look like in Bash, along with some advice on idiomatic use (or common misuse).

Variables

Like any programming language, Bash has variables that can either be empty or set to a value. Unset variables are simply "empty," and Bash will happily use them without panicking unless you set the -u (error on unset variables) option via set -u.

Setting

To set a variable, use the equals sign.

`FOOBAR=nice` will set the `FOOBAR` variable to the value `nice`.

There are no types in Bash – it's about as untyped as a programming language can get.

A variable symbol itself can contain letters, numbers, and underscores, but may not start with a number.

It is common practice to use uppercase variable names for environment variables and lowercase ones inside of Bash scripts. These variable names typically use underscores to separate individual words. When using numbers inside of variable names, avoid starting with digits. Bash forbids this. As with other languages, it's a good practice for names to indicate what a variable is used for and whether it is a constant, or use a plural name for an array:

- Illegal: `%foo&bar=bad`
- Illegal: `2foo_bar=bad`
- Legal but bad: `foo_BAR123=still_very_bad`
- Good environment variable: `PORT=443`
- Good: `local_var=512`
- Good environment variable: `FOO_BAR123=good`
- Good local array var: `words=(foo bar baz)`

Getting

To use a variable, reference it with the $ character:

```
$ echo $FOOBAR
nice
```

Bash versus other shells

A huge variety of shell programs exist for Unix-like environments; you could argue that one of the major reasons for Unix's popularity is the fact that it's always been an environment with essentially no barriers to scripting and automation.

This chapter teaches you how to write your own scripts in Bash. Much of what you'll learn here will also work on other shells (for example, `ksh` and other common minimal shells that you'll find at `/bin/sh`), but we're focused on Bash here.

If you're writing a shell script, Bash strikes the perfect balance between wide availability and a language feature set that's large enough to make it comfortable to write small programs.

Shebangs and executable text files, aka scripts

In Unix-like systems, a "script" is just an executable plaintext file. The operating system (often called "the kernel" in Linux) looks at the very first line to determine which interpreter to feed the file's content into.

That first line is the so-called "shebang" (or hashbang), and it consists of a hash and an exclamation mark (#!) character, followed by the path to the interpreter that is used to execute the file's code. Here's an example shebang line:

```
#!/usr/bin/env bash
```

When the kernels of Unix-like systems run a file with the executable bit set, they'll take a look at the first bytes. This might contain a magic number. This number can be part of binary files or some human-readable character, like in the shebang. The kernel uses this information to know whether there is a proper way to execute it. This, for example, prevents situations where the kernel would try to execute an image file and crash. Depending on the system, the kernel or the shell will make sure that the command following is executed. The env program will run the command and take the PATH environment variable into account to find and execute bash.

While a hash denotes a comment in most scripting languages and would, therefore, be ignored by the interpreter, this special comment at the beginning of a file tells the operating system which command to run to interpret the rest of the file. Here are some common examples you'll see:

- #!/bin/sh: use this specific shell program at this specific filesystem location
- #!/usr/bin/python3: use this specific Python binary
- #!/usr/bin/env python: use the env program to figure out which Python binary to use in this environment (different systems may have different versions of the same program installed, at different paths)

While you will see all of these variants, the best option is to always use /usr/bin/env for portability. /bin/sh is the exception here, since every POSIX-compatible system is required to have a POSIX-compatible shell in this location.

Common Bash settings (options/arguments)

Since the shebang line is executed as a command, arguments may also be passed. And while it can be a good idea to keep things simple, a common theme is to pass extra arguments to shells, especially to Bash, which is often used for large scripts because it has extra features compared to the smaller shells usually found at /bin/sh.

In Bash scripts, you will often see the -e, -u, -x, -o pipefail arguments passed. You may find these arguments in the shebang line itself:

```
#!/usr/bin/env bash -euxo pipefail
```

Or, as the next statement, using the set command in Bash, which sets arguments or options:

```
#!/usr/bin/env bash

set -eu -o pipefail
```

Setting these options makes Bash behave a bit more like the programming languages you're used to, by:

- Exiting immediately if any component of a command pipeline fails, and
- Treating unset variables as fatal errors.

Here's a breakdown of the documentation for these options, along with a useful debug option (-x) as a bonus:

- -o pipefail: When using pipes, this will make sure that errors happening in the pipeline will be passed on. If more than one error happens, the rightmost will be used.
- -e: If there is an error or a command fails, this will make sure that the shell script exits immediately.
- -u: throw an error if any unset variables are used.

For debugging, -x is useful:

- -x: This will enable tracing. This means that each command will be written to standard error before executing it.

All arguments, except –o pipefail, can be found in most Unix shells. For more information on the options that Bash contains, see its manual page: https://manpages.org/bash.

/usr/bin/env

Here's something to keep in mind: /bin/sh is a standardized path in POSIX leading to any POSIX-compatible shell. You can count on it to be there on ANY Linux or Unix system. Typically, this is not bash, but a more minimal shell, offering just enough functionality to satisfy the POSIX standard, which allows you to write very portable shell scripts. For all other shells and interpreters your script might need, it's best practice to use the #!/usr/bin/env prefix for any other case. This makes sure that the correct path from PATH is used, and it will prevent a "command not found" error when the binary isn't located in /usr/bin/.

There are various scenarios in which /usr/bin/bash or /bin/bash wouldn't be the right path. For example:

- A package manager or company-specific configuration scripts will often install the inter-preter in a different place than it would be on your development system.

- Someone installing software manually, for example, to work around or reproduce a bug, often places the resulting binary in /usr/local.

- Virtual environments of various scripting languages will put binaries into a subdirectory of each source code project/repository.

- People installing the interpreter without root permissions, for example, in their home directory.

- People using a version manager for the interpreter (rvm, nvm, and so on).

- Various Unix-like operating systems and some Linux distributions don't install third-party packages into /usr/.

While many people can't imagine their script ever ending up in such a non-standard place, chances are good that you'll run into this eventually. Instead of risking your software breaking in these cases, it's a good idea to simply get into the habit of writing /usr/bin/env bash (or whatever interpreter your code is written for) in your scripts. This prevents someone else – or your very tired future self, woken up by a pager at 3 in the morning – from having to notice, troubleshoot, find, or make such changes on source files when they break due to a minor change in the environment.

Special characters and escaping

One special character you should use often is the hash symbol (#), which makes everything on the line following the symbol a comment that the interpreter ignores.

Other characters have special meaning in Bash, and they need to be escaped with a forward slash (\) when you use them as part of a variable's value. Here are some of them:

- Quotes (" and ')
- Brackets and parentheses ({, }, [,], and (,))
- Carets (< and >)
- Tilde: ~
- Asterisk (the "glob character" in Bash): *
- Ampersand: &
- Question mark: ?
- Common operators: !, =, |, and so on

Escape them like you do in most other programming languages:

```
$ FOO="jaa\$\'"
```

Command substitution

One of the benefits and major use cases of shell scripting is that any command is easily accessible. A very common example of this is command substitution. This is useful when you want to use the output of one or more commands. You can do this with command substitution:

```
echo "Right now, it's $(date)"
```

This executes those commands – in this case, just date, but it could also be a complex expression that you've piped together. Another way to do the same is to use backticks. The following example will have the same output:

```
echo "Right now, it's `date`"
```

Testing

The testing commands shown here are usually used along with if/else control flow statements. Both the string testing function ([[) and the arithmetic testing function ((() return 0 if the test evaluates to a true value, or 1 if the test evaluates to false. This is due to the 0 exit code of commands indicating success, and it is different from other programming languages you might know that typically evaluate a zero value as false. There is no native boolean data type in Bash; the integers 0 and 1 are used in boolean contexts like this one. Sometimes, the variables true and false are initialized and used throughout a script.

Testing operators

Here are some basic boolean operators that you can use to construct statements in Bash – essentially, what you're used to from other languages:

- ! – not (negation)
- && – and
- || – or

These operators can be used with both string and arithmetic test types:

- == – is equal to
- != is not equal to

[[file and string testing]]

The [[compound command allows you to perform (and combine) "string" comparisons. As mentioned before, Bash doesn't have the kind of strict data types that you're used to from other programming languages, so we're calling them "string" or "string-like" comparisons because that's a familiar concept to software developers.

If the user's home directory does not exist, create it:

```
if [[ ! -d $HOME ]]; then
    echo "Creating home directory: ${HOME}..."
    mkdir -p $HOME
    echo "done"
fi
```

That ! character is a Bash negation, so you can read the first line of this example as if NOT (test) is-a-directory $HOME, then....

Here's a slightly more complicated example. If the user's home directory does not exist, OR if the ALWAYSCREATE variable is set to yes, create the home directory:

```
ALWAYSCREATE=yes

if ! [[ -d $HOME ]] || [[ $ALWAYSCREATE == yes ]]; then
    echo "Creating home directory: ${HOME}..."
    mkdir -p $HOME
    echo "done"
fi
```

Useful operators for string testing

- -z is unset (used for variables)
- -n is non-zero (set – used for variables)
- =~ is a left operand that matches a regular expression (right operand), for example [[foobar =~ f*bar]]

Useful operators for file testing

- -d: a directory
- -e: exists
- -f: a regular file

- -S: a socket file
- -w: writable, from the perspective of this Bash process

((arithmetic testing))

Arithmetic evaluated in a ((test will set the test's exit value to 1 if the expression evaluates to 0; otherwise, it will return an exit status of 0. This makes testing quite intuitive, using operators you already know from virtually every other programming language:

- > and >= – greater-than and greater-than or equal-to
- < and <= – less-than and less-than or equal-to
- == – test equality

(($SOME_NUMBER == 24)) is a fairly straightforward arithmetic test. Let's see how it behaves.

For the number 24:

```
→ SOME_NUMBER=24
→ (( $SOME_NUMBER == 24 ))
→ echo $?
0
```

The "echo $?" command prints out the exit status of the previous command, which lets us see what the arithmetic test actually evaluated to. For other values, including non-numeric ones:

```
→ SOME_NUMBER=foobar
→ (( $SOME_NUMBER == 24 ))
→ echo $?
1
```

If $SOME_NUMBER is unset (for example, [[-z $SOME_NUMBER]]):

```
→ unset SOME_NUMBER
→ (( $SOME_NUMBER == 24 ))
zsh: bad math expression: operand expected at `== 24 '
```

So, to review:

- (($SOME_NUMBER == 24)) will evaluate to 0 if the SOME_NUMBER variable is set to 24.
- If $SOME_NUMBER is set to a value OTHER THAN 24 (including a non-numeric value), it will evaluate to 1.

- If $SOME_NUMBER is *unset*, you'll get an error because your arithmetic test doesn't have a left operand to use for the comparison.

Conditionals: if/then/else

A Bash if statement is usually found in this form:

```
if [[ $TEST ]]; then $STATEMENTS else $OTHER_STATEMENTS fi
```

Remember a few things about this form before we look at examples:

- if and fi begin and terminate the if block, respectively.
- ; delimits statements in Bash; add one right after the test.
- [[and]] delimit your test expression.
- The else clause is optional.

Here's what the if statement looks like in Bash:

```
if [[ -e "example.txt" ]]; then
    echo "The file exists!"
```

ifelse

If you want to tack an else clause onto this structure, you can!

```
if [[ -e "example.txt" ]]; then
    echo "The file exists!"
else
    echo "The file does not exist!"
fi
```

Loops

Bash loops come in the general format for / do / done. They also support break and continue statements, which break out of the loop and skip to the next iteration, respectively.

C-style loops

Bash supports C-style loops, with an initializer expression, a conditional expression, and a counting expression:

```
for (( i=0; i<=9; i++ ))
do
  echo "Loop var i is currently $i"
done
```

for...in

Let's talk about iteration with for...in loops. Try running the following in your shell:

```
for i in 1 2 3 4 5
do
  echo $i
done
```

Here's a loop with some control flow inside:

```
for os in FreeBSD Linux NetBSD "macOS" DragonflyBSD
do
  echo "Checking out ${os}..."
  if [[ "$os" == 'NetBSD' ]]; then
    echo "(I'm pretty sure this would run on my toaster, actually)"
  fi
  sleep 1
done
```

While

Another common control structure you might be familiar with from other programming languages is the while loop. In Bash, this works very similarly. To break out of a loop, the break statement can be used.

The following script will read the lines.txt file line by line until it encounters the STOP line. The last line also shows how you can pipe a file into a loop. The read command will take care of processing the file line by line:

```
file="lines.txt"

while read line; do
    if [[ $line == "STOP" ]]; then
        echo "Encountered STOP. Exiting loop."
        break
    fi

    echo "Processing: $line"
    # Additional commands to process $line can be added here.
done < "$file"
```

Variable exporting

Exporting a variable by prefixing it with export ensures that any subshells spawned from your script's process will also have access to that variable's value. It's a way of ensuring that a variable is propagated down to any future sub-scopes (or sub-namespaces) of your current shell's variable scope or namespace.

Set a variable in your shell:

```
MYDIR=$HOME
```

Create and run this script (warning: this will fail!):

```
#!/usr/bin/env bash

LISTING=$(ls "${MYDIR}/Documents")
echo $LISTING
```

You'll see an error, `ls: /Documents: No such file or directory`, because running this script spawned a subshell that did not have access to unexported variables in its parent shell (the shell that spawned it, in other words your interactive shell). Letting subshells access your variables must be done explicitly, via the export keyword:

```
export MYDIR=$HOME
```

Rerun the example script now that you've exported the variable, and you'll see that it can now access the MYDIR variable.

Functions

We generally recommend that by the time you find yourself needing Bash functions, you will have found another language to write your growing program in. However, sometimes Bash is still the right language for a problem, and we want to show you the absolute basics, with a strong bias toward how we recommend using them.

Define a function by using the function keyword:

```
function my_great_function {
  $EXPRESSIONS
}
```

Call functions by simply invoking their name:

```
my_great_function
```

Prefer local variables

Bash works with a more-or-less global scope – more accurately, per (sub)shell. Many modern programming languages give you a separate function scope to work with, so function state doesn't pollute global state after a function exits.

Using local variables in your functions will protect you from this, and we recommend you use them:

```bash
#!/usr/bin/env bash

important_var=somevalue

function local_var_example() {
    local important_var="changed this locally, don't worry"
    echo "local_var_example: ${important_var}"
}

function bad_example() {
    important_var="this is mutating the global var because I'm bad, and I
should feel bad."
    echo "bad_example: ${important_var}"
}


echo "before functions: ${important_var}"
local_var_example
echo
echo "after local_var_example: ${important_var}"
echo
bad_example
echo "after bad_example: ${important_var}"

exit 0
```

Run this code yourself and see the difference that using local vars makes.

Input and output redirection

When you run scripts, you'll often want to redirect their output:

- To another program (via a pipe – | – see *Chapter 11, Pipes and Redirection*, for more details)
- To a regular file (like a log file)
- To a special location like /dev/null, which can act as a kind of black hole for data you don't need

Aside from pipes, here are the most common input/output redirection tricks you'll see in the wild.

<: input redirection

This is often used to grab input from a file, instead of from the shell spawning a process:

```
grep foobar < stuff.txt
```

> and >>: output redirection

The > symbol will stream output to wherever you point it, overwriting anything that's already there if it's a regular file:

```
ps aux | grep foo > /var/log/foo_overwrite.log
```

Every time you run this, the output of ps aux | grep foo will be written to /var/log/foo_overwrite.log, overwriting any existing file content.

Using >> instead will *append* to the output file, leaving any existing content intact. This is usually what you want for log files:

```
echo $(date && cat /proc/stat) >> /var/log/kernelstate.log
```

Use 2>&1 to redirect STDERR and STDOUT

Sometimes, you want to redirect both standard output and standard error to a file:

```
consul agent -dev >> /var/log/consul.log 2>&1 &
```

This command runs Hashicorp's Consul in dev-mode and backgrounds the process (the & symbol at the end), redirecting standard output to a log file. 2>&1 tells Bash to "redirect file descriptor 2 (STDERR) to the same place as 1 (STDOUT)" – in this case, that's /var/log/consul.log.

You already know about file descriptors – STDIN, STDOUT, and STDERR. What if you only want to redirect a standard error to a *different* file than a standard output?

Variable interpolation syntax – ${}

To accomplish what's known as "string interpolation" in most programming languages – substituting part of a string with the value of a variable – you want Bash's variable interpolation, ${}. Try it yourself:

```
MYNAME=dave
echo "I can't do that, ${MYNAME}."
```

There are other ways to interpolate variables in Bash, but this is our favorite way, since it has the lowest chance of breaking your program due to unexpectedly-shaped input (spaces, special characters, and so on).

If you are going to use a variable as a string-like value, use this syntax – even if that variable is by itself and doesn't really need to be interpolated into another string:

```
NAME="${MYNAME}"
```

This will prevent many strange bugs and behaviors with Bash, so it's a good habit to get into.

Note

When working with variable interpolation, you'll almost always want to run Bash with the -u option (either by calling it with -u, or by using set -euo pipefail at the beginning of your scripts, as we recommend). This will prevent you from having to check for zero values before you use a variable.

Limitations of shell scripts

Bash has innumerable features, many of which we're not covering here. If you need to dig deeper into the Bash language and environment, there are many books and tons of free resources on the web. The Bash manpage (man bash) is a good start too, now that you're oriented.

We expect you to encounter many Bash scripts over the course of your career. However, it's very likely that you'll spend more time reading and deciphering existing scripts than writing large new Bash programs. Bash is an amazing fit for small problems and system tasks that lend themselves to being solved with existing software, which just needs to be tied together into a solution. It's often a *terrible* fit for large problems that extend beyond tying together standard Linux and Unix programs.

With Bash, we find that:

- Small is better than large
- Clear is better than clever
- Safe is better than sorry

It's not uncommon to replace Bash scripts with tools written in a different programming language (often Python) as they grow. That's not a dig against Bash! It's perfect at filling the niche that it occupies, which is why it's been so widespread for so long. If you occasionally stop to ask yourself, "Is a Bash script still the right solution for this problem?" you'll be just fine.

Conclusion

This chapter was a no-punches-pulled, drink-from-the-fire-hydrant Bash scripting crash course. It's dense, but it covers all the basics you need to become an effective Bash scripter. Work through it more than once if you have to. In addition to the syntax, we covered what we think are best practices that make writing readable, maintainable real-world scripts easier (or at least possible).

Practice, practice, practice – preferably on real-world problems you have, not just toy examples. There's no faster way to get good.

Citations

- *Bash Test and Comparison Functions*. Used for [[and ((option tables. Accessed Sept 25, 2022 `https://developer.ibm.com/tutorials/l-bash-test/`.

Learn more on Discord

To join the Discord community for this book – where you can share feedback, ask questions to the author, and learn about new releases – follow the QR code below:

`https://packt.link/SecNet`

13

Secure Remote Access with SSH

The **Secure Shell Protocol (SSH)** is a Swiss Army knife – a do-everything tool – for creating secure connections and tunneling data through them. During your career, you'll use SSH for a bit of everything:

- Securely logging in to a remote system
- Cloning your private Git repository
- Transferring files from your laptop to a server, or between servers
- Mapping a web service behind a VPN to a local port on your laptop so that someone on your home network can use it
- Various other tasks that involve tunneling traffic or sending files through multiple network connections

In this chapter, we'll give you everything you need to be comfortable with the basics. You'll learn how public key cryptography works, which is essential to being able to reason about these kinds of tools and their usage. You'll create SSH keys and use them to log in to a remote server. To cement the basics, we've even created a small project for you, where you'll set up key-based logins for a remote host that you work with often.

For those times when you inevitably have issues when using SSH, we've collected some of the most common SSH errors we see in the wild. You'll learn what the most common error messages indicate, and how to use SSH's built-in "debug" option to troubleshoot your way out of them.

In this chapter, we'll cover the following topics:

- A primer in public key cryptography
- Message encryption
- Message signing
- SSH keys
- Converting SSH2 keys to the OpenSSH format
- File transfer
- SSH tunneling
- The configuration file

Let's jump right in with the very basics of what you need to understand about public key cryptography so that the rest of this chapter doesn't just sound like obscure black magic to you.

Public key cryptography primer

Depending on what path your career has taken, you may have already come across the topic of public key cryptography. While cryptography is its own field, and this is not a book about cryptography, it *is* important to have an understanding of the basics. Thankfully, the core concepts are very simple and will get you far. We'll make this section as short as possible, and then dive right into the commands you need to configure and use secure access with SSH.

Public key cryptography is a system that uses two separate keys, called the public key and the private key. Together, these make up what is called a key pair. As the names imply, the public key is a key that can be shared with everyone, while the private key is supposed to remain private at all costs.

Message encryption

Once you've created a key pair, any message that has been encrypted using that key pair's public key can be decrypted with the corresponding private key.

Imagine a person named Alice, who wants to send Bob an encrypted message. To do this, Alice downloads Bob's public key and uses it to encrypt the message. Alice then sends the encrypted message to Bob. As he owns the matching private key, Bob will be able to decrypt and read the message. Even if someone else sees the encrypted message, they won't be able to decrypt and read it because only Bob has the private key.

For this reason, it is important to *never* share your private key with a third party. Doing so would be a breach of security.

Message signing

There is another way to use these two keys: they can be used to sign a message. "Signing" a message is a way to cryptographically prove that a message was really written by the person owning the key. This makes use of the fact that while a message encrypted with the public key can be decrypted with the private key, the reverse is also true – a message *encrypted* with the private key can be *decrypted* using the public key.

When Alice wants to sign a message, the private key can be used to encrypt the message (or a cryptographically secure hash of the message). Everyone who possesses Alice's public key can use it to decrypt the message and, if it works, knows that it must have been encrypted with Alice's private key.

Both mechanisms, encryption and signing, are often used together. Additionally, signatures themselves are frequently used to ensure security (by verifying authorship) when you're downloading software, for example, through package managers or app stores.

It's worth noting that these core public-key encryption and signing mechanisms are used for everything from encrypting emails to securing HTTPS web traffic to thousands of other things in the modern world. In other words, Alice and Bob don't have to be people; they can be computers, services, and so on.

Now that you've seen the basic cryptographic building blocks that SSH takes advantage of to secure your remote access, you're ready to make practical use of all of this fancy technology!

SSH keys

One of the first things you are likely to do when it comes to SSH is create your very own key pair. This will allow you to authenticate to an SSH server. A classic command for creating a key pair is this:

```
ssh-keygen -t ed25519 -C 'John Doe <john.doe@example.org>'
```

This will create an ed25519 (a modern elliptic curve cryptography algorithm) key pair using John Doe <john.doe@example.org> as a comment. Comments are like the comments you know from programming languages, in that they can be any string of text and won't interfere with anything on a functional level. In the case of SSH, this comment will be appended to your public key, making it easier to distinguish keys when they are uploaded to a server, for example, in an authorized_keys file. Later in this chapter, we'll dive deeper into the authorized_keys files and how to use them to set up seamless, secure access to remote servers.

After you run this command, OpenSSH will ask you a few questions about where to store the key files it creates and what password you'd like to use to encrypt the private key. Since this will be the key used to access remote systems, make sure to set a strong password.

 Note

By default, keys will be placed in your ~/.ssh directory.

Now that you've created a key pair, it's time to reiterate the most important practical point: never, ever share the private key. Doing so would allow a third party to impersonate you. No service should ever ask you to share your private key. The public key, which is supposed to be shared and is safe to make public, will contain a .pub suffix, so you can tell the difference.

Thankfully, the contents of these files look very different, so if you ever get confused, you can peek at them to see which is which:

- The public key is in the format of `<algorithm> <key> <comment>`.
- The private key starts with a line like `-----BEGIN OPENSSH PRIVATE KEY-----`, followed by the key and a similar ending line.

Be careful never to overwrite these key files, and ensure that you have stored both of them in a secure backup. Again, your password manager is a good choice for this. Many password managers even have a specific option to store private key files or generic text.

Exceptions to these rules

For personal use – on your laptop, for example – you'll always want to encrypt your private key (by specifying a password during key creation), and then never share it, as mentioned before.

However, there are some situations where it's okay to break these rules – specifically when setting up keys for automated systems to use. If you want your build server to authenticate to GitHub before checking out your code base, you'd likely use a key pair whose private key is *not* encrypted (unless you want to have to manually type in that password every time your build service runs).

Machine-to-machine authentication and encryption are great reasons to use cryptographic key pairs. Just be sure to always make dedicated, single-purpose key pairs for jobs like these, and do not reuse or share those key pairs across machines or services.

Logging in and authenticating

Logging in to a remote system using SSH-based authentication looks similar to this:

```
ssh user@example.org
```

user is the username that you want to log in as, and example.org is a stand-in for any remote system you'd like to connect to. This is often just an IP address, as opposed to a fully qualified domain name.

If you're logging in with an SSH key, or you need to specify a specific key (identity, or -i), it'll look like this:

```
ssh -i ~/.ssh/id_ecdsa user@example.org
```

When accessing an SSH server that you have never connected to before, you will be presented with the fingerprint of the remote server. This allows you to make sure that the server you are talking to is indeed the one you intend to connect to and that no man-in-the-middle attack is taking place. You should make sure this is correct.

Once you type yes and mark that fingerprint as trusted, it will be saved to a file. Should it ever change – for example, if someone sets up a malicious server at the same IP address that your trusted server was using before – you will be notified by your SSH client, and authentication will not be possible.

After you mark the server as trusted, your local client and the server will negotiate which form of authentication to use. OpenSSH offers a wide variety of options, with the two most common ones involving a password or a key pair. Depending on which is chosen, OpenSSH will ask you to enter the password (or the password to decrypt your private key). Once the authentication step succeeds, you will be logged in.

Practical project: Set up a key-based login to a remote server

Presuming you have access to a long-running Linux server that you want to allow key-based login on, follow these steps.

Step 1: Open your terminal on the SSH client (not the server)

You'll be using your local command-line environment for the rest of these steps.

Step 2: Generate the key pair

If you've already set up a key pair because you were following along earlier in this chapter, good for you! You can skip this step.

If you don't yet have an SSH key pair, create one by typing the following command and hitting *Enter*:

```
ssh-keygen -t ed25519

# ensure that the public key is not world-readable
chmod 600 ~/.ssh/id_ed25519
```

As mentioned before, we strongly recommend adding a passphrase for extra security.

Step 3: Copy the public key to your server

After generating the keys, you'll need to place the public key on your server. The public key usually has the extension .pub and by default will be located in your ~/.ssh directory.

You can manually copy it to the remote user's authorized_keys file (a file that contains all authorized public keys for that user, one key per line), or you can condense all of those actions into a single command using the ssh-copy-id program:

```
ssh-copy-id username@example.org
```

Replace username with your user on the remote server and remote_server_address with the server's IP address or domain name.

This command will ask for your user password on the remote server. After entering it, the public key will be appended to the ~/.ssh/authorized_keys file of the remote user's home directory. This allows you to log in and execute commands on the remote machine without being prompted for a password.

Step 4: Test it out!

Now try logging in to the server:

```
ssh username@example.org
```

If everything worked, you should be logged in without being asked for a password (unless you set up a passphrase for your SSH key). Instead of using a small password string that might be guessed by an attacker, you're now using a *much* more secure cryptographic key to authenticate yourself.

Welcome to the wonderful world of secure, password-free SSH access!

Converting SSH2 keys to the OpenSSH format

When not using a Unix-based operating system, you'll often come across the SSH2 public key format. PuTTY is probably the most famous software using this format and many people using Windows use it to connect via SSH. To connect to an **SSH File Transfer Protocol (SFTP)** server, Git repository, or other system that uses the OpenSSH key format, you need to convert an SSH2 public key into the OpenSSH format. Here is how to convert it.

What we are trying to achieve

We start with an SSH2-formatted public key that looks like this:

```
---- BEGIN SSH2 PUBLIC KEY ----
Comment: "rsa-key-20160402"
AAAAB3NzaC1yc2EAAAABJQAAAgEAiL0jjDdFqK/kYThqKt7THrjABTPWvXmB3URI
pGKCP/jZlSuCUP3Oc+IxuFeXSIMvVIYeW2PZAjXQGTn60XzPHr+M0NoGcPAvzZf2
u57aX3YKaL93cZSBHR97H+XhcYdrm7ATwfjMDgfgj7+VTvW4nI46Z+qjxmYifc8u
VELolg1TDHWY789ggcdvy92oGjB0VUgMEywrOP+LS0DgG4dmkoUBWGP9dvYcPZDU
F4q0XY9ZHhvyPWEZ3o2vETTrEJr9QHYwgjmFfJn2VFNnD/4qeDDHOmSlDgEOfQcZ
Im+XUOn9eVsv//dAPSY/yMJXf8d0ZSm+VS29QShMjA4R+7yh5WhsIhouBRno2PpE
VVb37Xwe3V6U3o9UnQ3ADtL75DbrZ5beNWcmKzlJ7jVX5QzHSBAnePbBx/fyeP/f
144xPtJWB3jW/kXjtPyWjpzGndaPQ0WgXkbf8fvIuB3NJTTcZ7PeIKnLaMIzT5XN
CR+xobvdC8J9d6k84/q/laJKF3G8KbRGPNwnoVg1cwWFez+dzqo2ypcTtv/20yAm
z86EvuohZoWrtoWvkZLCoyxdqO93ymEjgHAn2bsIWyOODtXovxAJqPgk3dxM1f9P
AEQwc1bG+Z/Gc1Fd8DncgxyhKSQzLsfWroTnIn8wsnmhPJtaZWNuT5BJa8GhnzX0
9g6nhbk=
---- END SSH2 PUBLIC KEY ----
```

The goal is to convert it to an OpenSSH public key like the following:

```
ssh-rsa AAAAB3NzaC1yc2EAAAABJQAAAgEAiL0jjDdFqK/
kYThqKt7THrjABTPWvXmB3URIpGK
CP/
jZlSuCUP3Oc+IxuFeXSIMvVIYeW2PZAjXQGTn60XzPHr+M0NoGcPAvzZf2u57aX3YKaL93cZSBHR
97H+XhcYdrm7ATwfjMDgfgj7+VTvW4nI46Z+qjxmYifc8uVELolg1TDHWY789ggcdvy92oG
jB0VUgMEywrOP+LS0DgG4dmkoUBWGP9dvYcPZDUF4q0XY9ZHhvyPWEZ3o2vETTrEJr9QHYwgjmFf
Jn2VFNnD/4qeDDHOmSlDgEOfQcZIm+XUOn9eVsv//dAPSY/
yMJXf8d0ZSm+VS29QShMjA4R+7yh5Wh
```

```
sIhouBRno2PpEVVb37Xwe3V6U3o9UnQ3ADtL75DbrZ5beNWcmKz1J7jVX5QzHSBAnePbBx/
fyeP/
f144xPtJWB3jW/kXjtPyWjpzGndaPQ0WgXkbf8fvIuB3NJTTcZ7PeIKnLaMIzT5XNCR+xobvdC8
J9d6k84/q/
laJKF3G8KbRGPNwnoVg1cwWFez+dzqo2ypcTtv/20yAmz86EvuohZoWrtoWvkZLCoyxdqO93ymE
jgHAn2bsIWyOODtXovxAJqPgk3dxM1f9PAEQwc1bG+Z/Gc1Fd8DncgxyhKSQzLsfWroTn
In8wsnmhPJtaZWNuT5BJa8GhnzX09g6nhbk=
```

How to convert the SSH2-formatted key to OpenSSH

The ssh-keygen command, which we used to create a new key, can also convert it with this very simple command:

```
ssh-keygen -i -f ssh2.pub > openssh.pub
```

The command above will take the key from the file ssh2.pub and write it to openssh.pub.

If you just want to look at the OpenSSH key material or have it ready for copying and pasting, then you don't have to worry about piping stdout into a file (the same command as above, without the last part):

```
ssh-keygen -i -f ssh2.pub
```

This will simply display the public key in the OpenSSH format.

A more practical example of this might be converting and appending a coworker's key to a server's authorized_keys file. This can be achieved using the following command:

```
ssh-keygen -i -f coworker.pub >> ~/.ssh/authorized_keys
```

After this, a coworker using the relevant private key will be able to log in to the system as the user who runs this command.

The other direction: Converting SSH2 keys to the OpenSSH format

The opposite – converting OpenSSH to SSH2 keys – is also possible. Simply use the -e (for export) flag, instead of -i (for import):

```
ssh-keygen -e -f openssh.pub > ssh2.pub
```

SSH-agent

When you're frequently logging in to servers using SSH keys, it can be annoying to have to retype your private key password over and over, every time you connect (or reconnect) to a host. SSH-Agent allows you to store an identity (private key) for a local session – in other words, it lets you decrypt your private key once, and then keep it in memory until you log out or start a new shell session. This means that you add an identity (key pair) once, and get to use it over and over again without re-decrypting your private key.

Note

The SSH Agent doesn't always run in your local shell session – various IDEs, window managers, desktop managers, and password managers can also run an agent for you. You'll know this is the case when you only have to enter the password for an identity once.

To add a key to the agent, just use the `ssh-add` command – the argument is the path to your private key for that identity:

```
ssh-add ~/.ssh/id_ecdsa
```

We recommend that you make it a habit to use the -t option, which adds a time limit to how long your keys are kept decrypted in memory. The following command is the same as the one above, except it sets a time limit of 30 seconds, after which the agent will delete the keys from memory:

```
ssh-add -t 30 ~/.ssh/id_ecdsa
```

To show which keys have been added to the agent, use the following command:

```
ssh-add -L
```

To remove all identities from the SSH agent, use -D:

```
ssh-add -D
```

> **Note**
>
> If you've added more than three identities to the agent, you may still have to specify
> `-i $YOUR_IDENTITY` when logging in via SSH. This is because most servers are con-
> figured to reject logins after three incorrect attempts, and SSH will try each of the
> keys stored in the agent, one by one, when logging in. If the first key doesn't work,
> it'll try the second one, and so on. If the server aborts the login attempt after three
> tries, you'll never get to the fourth key in your agent.

You can enable agent forwarding when using SSH to log in to remote machines with -A; however, you should do so sparingly and carefully, for reasons we'll explain:

```
ssh -A user@remotehost
```

After logging in to remotehost with this command, SSH will forward your keys to that host so you can use them to jump to additional hosts from there. The reason we recommend doing this sparingly is that it allows a compromised host to see your private keys, which we've hopefully taught you should always stay private, preferably on your machine or, during your wildest moments, in your password manager. In other words, if remotehost has been hacked, then your SSH keys are now compromised.

One final note about security: some Linux desktop environments like GNOME/MATE will keep your SSH key in memory indefinitely when you use and decrypt it once. This happens by default and is a security risk you should be aware of.

Common SSH errors and the -v (verbose) argument

The -v flag in the SSH command enables verbose mode, which prints out a detailed, step-by-step log of the connection process. This feature is particularly useful for diagnosing common issues such as authentication failures, connection timeouts, and key mismatches. Use it like this:

```
ssh -v username@example.org
```

You'll receive step-by-step information about each stage of the SSH handshake and connection, making it easier to identify and resolve any issues that may arise.

Here are some of the frequent errors that you might encounter, which verbose output can help you diagnose:

- **Permission Denied (public key/password)**: This indicates that the server rejected your login attempt. The verbose log will show you which keys were tried, helping you to pinpoint whether the correct key was used or even offered. This is an *incredibly* common issue when you have more than three key pairs stored on the client, and the server only allows three tries.

- **Connection Timed Out**: If the connection is taking too long, you might have a network issue or an incorrect IP address or port. The -v flag will show where the process gets stuck, helping you understand whether the client even reached the server.

- **Connection Refused**: This usually means that SSH isn't running (or reachable) on the target port on the server. The verbose output will clearly indicate that the connection attempt was rejected, helping you focus on firewall rules or SSH server settings.

- **Host Key Verification Failed**: The server's key doesn't match the one saved in your system's known_hosts file. The –v flag will show the mismatched keys, at which point you can focus on figuring out **why** (for example, is there a new server at this IP address or hostname?).

- **Could not resolve hostname**: Often related to DNS or network issues.

- **No Route to Host**: This suggests network issues, maybe involving firewalls or incorrect routing.

- **Too Many Authentication Failures**: The maximum number of authentication attempts has been reached. The verbose mode will show all the methods tried, which may include unwanted or unexpected key offers.

- **Key Load Errors**: These usually indicate a problem with the format or permissions of your SSH key. The -v flag will identify which key the SSH client is trying to load, allowing you to check for formatting or permission issues.

Using the –v flag will help you understand what exactly is going wrong and how you might be able to fix it. At the very least, it will help you start looking in the right direction.

File transfer

In the sections below we will explore the sftp and scp commands for file transfer. Going through a few examples using these commands will help you understand how you can handle files in most situations. That said, we will also cover file transfer without SFTP or SCP, in case they are disabled on the server.

SFTP

While OpenSSH is frequently used as a way to log in to remote systems, it also allows for file transfer independently of a login session. This is usually accomplished via the SFTP subsystem. Though SFTP resembles **File Transfer Protocol (FTP)**, it is actually a completely custom protocol. Like FTP, SFTP allows authenticated users to transfer files to and from remote servers. Unlike FTP, which is insecure, SFTP's authentication and file transfers are secure and fully encrypted.

There are many FTP clients that also support SFTP. One famous example is Filezilla, which has an excellent graphical user interface. However, since this is a book about the Linux command line, we will give you a basic overview of how to use SFTP on the command line.

Authentication is nearly identical to ssh:

```
sftp user@example.org
```

After this, you'll be presented with an FTP-style interface. It accepts simpler/modified versions of some shell commands that we have already gone over in previous chapters, and also introduces some new ones. Here are the most common commands:

- help: lists all commands and gives a short summary
- ls: lists the contents of a remote directory
- lls: lists the contents of a local directory
- cd: changes the remote directory
- lcd: changes the local directory
- pwd: displays the remote directory you are in
- lpwd: displays the local directory you are in
- get: downloads a file from the remote server
- put: uploads a file to the remote server
- chmod: changes the permissions of a remote file or directory
- chown: changes the owner of a remote file or directory
- quit, exit, bye: exits SFTP (*CTRL+D* also works)

SCP

The scp command is often a more practical way to upload and download files and directories than sftp. While it was historically independent of SFTP, today it uses the SFTP subsystem. It is meant to work as a replacement for the cp command, except that it allows copying to and from remote servers.

Commands are in the following format:

```
scp $SOURCE:filepath $DESTINATION:filepath
```

$SOURCE, $DESTINATION, or both can be remote systems; scp uses the SSH user@example.org syntax that you've already seen.

Here is what it looks like in practice:

```
scp user@example.org:/home/user/my_remote_file /home/user/my_local_file
```

This will do the following:

1. Connect to example.org.
2. Authenticate as user (prompting you for a password unless you're using SSH keys and the SSH agent).
3. Copy the file to the local path /home/user/my_local_file.

As you can see, the argument order is the same as for the Linux cp (copy) command.

Reversing the source and destination arguments – uploading a file, instead of downloading it – looks like you might expect:

```
scp /home/user/my_local_file user@example.org:/home/user/my_remote_file
```

Just like with cp, you can specify relative paths. The following command will copy the remote file to the current (local) directory:

```
scp user@example.org:/home/user/my_remote_file .
```

As with the cp command, it is also possible to recursively copy an entire directory using the -r (recurse, also -R on some systems) flag:

```
scp -r user@example.org:/home/user/directory local_directory
```

Clever examples

As with all commands and tools, ssh and scp can also be used in scripts; for example, you can use ssh to quickly back up a database:

```
ssh username@example.org "pg_dump databasename | gzip -c" > database_
backup.sql.gz
```

If you use clever shell hacks like this in a script, take care to alert on errors; otherwise, the process might just silently remain stuck when it runs into an issue. For development situations, this kind of command can really come in handy.

Without SFTP or SCP

In some rare situations, you'll find that SFTP has been disabled on a server and you can only log in to an interactive shell. You still want to transfer a file to the remote system, and while it might be possible to just open a file in an editor, this isn't always possible (for example, with whole directories or binary files). Here are a few tricks that you can use to still achieve your goal (they all make use of the Unix pipe in combination with an SSH session).

The simplest case is downloading a file from a remote server:

```
ssh user@example.org "cat /path/to/file" > local_target_file
```

This command will do the following:

1. Log in to the server.
2. Run the command cat /path/to/file on the remote server, which will result in the contents of that file being streamed to stdout.
3. stdout can then be locally piped into a file of our choice.

Like most well-behaved Unix software, errors and other possibly interfering output will be sent to STDERR, so you do not have to fear that a password prompt will get in the way and corrupt the file content being piped across your SSH tunnel, as an example.

Directory upload and .tar.gz compression

Let's do something different and upload a whole directory. Since this is potentially quite a lot of data, we will also compress it with the tar program. tar is a command that turns multiple files and/or directories into a single file (an "archive").

It's common to add a compression step after archiving – you've probably seen files with the tar. gz or tar.bz2 endings, for example. This means that the files have first been archived into a single file with tar, and then compressed using gzip or bzip2:

```
tar czf - /home/user/directory_to_upload | ssh user@example.org "tar -xvzf
-C /home/user/"
```

Here, we first archive /home/user/directory with tar, turning the result into a stream of bytes.

The - is the target file. In the case that you want to store it immediately instead of streaming it to another program, this would be something like /home/user/directory.tar.gz. As is customary with many Unix commands, a dash symbolizes that this should instead be written to stdout.

This resulting stream will then be piped into the ssh process, which uses it as input (stdin) for a tar command on the remote system, which decompresses and unarchives that stream, writing the resulting directory to /home/user/directory_to_upload.

Tunnels

SSH tunnelling is used to transport data over an SSH connection. In the following sections, we will look at two methods of tunnelling: local forwarding and proxying.

Local forwarding

SSH can create secure, encrypted tunnels to remote systems. This functionality is similar to what a VPN provides and can allow you to access services reachable from the remote system.

That's powerful functionality, and with SSH, it's actually simple to achieve. All you have to do is specify an additional argument, -L, with the destination and the local port to bind it to when establishing an SSH session.

Imagine a remote system running an HTTP server on port 8080. You want to access it on your laptop, on port 3000. Here is how to accomplish that with a simple command:

```
ssh -L 3000:localhost:8080 user@example.org
```

You can now open a browser and visit http://localhost:3000/ to access the web server as if you were opening that browser on the remote system and visiting http://localhost:8080.

Proxying

The same would be true if you wanted to access a server that you don't have access to, but the remote server does. Imagine app.example.org is where your web application runs. This web application connects to a database server like PostgreSQL at db.example.org, which is only accessible from the www.example.org internal network. Like most production databases, it's guarded by a firewall that prevents direct connections from outside.

From a network perspective, it looks like this:

```
(localhost) —-> (app.example.org) —-> (db.example.org)
```

You might want to use your local psql Postgres client to connect to that database. What you'd do is create a tunnel like this:

```
ssh -L 5000:db.example.org:5432 user@app.example.org
```

This will open a new SSH session to app.example.org, reach out to the DB server from there, and map db.example.org:5432 to localhost:5000.

Now, running psql --port=5000 --host=localhost dbname on your laptop will connect you to the Postgres database at db.example.org:5432, by bouncing through app.example.org to get access.

The configuration file

It is possible to specify host configuration in .ssh/config. This can be helpful in various situations, as it allows you to specify:

- Custom (friendly) names for hosts
- The default user to use
- The port
- Tunnels to open before connecting
- Identity files (keys)

Among many other things.

Note

If a server you connect to has a permanent IP address, it can make sense to specify it in your SSH config file to avoid relying on DNS or CDNs during a disaster recovery situation.

SSH configuration files aren't particularly complicated, so we'll show you an example here that uses many of the available features:

```
# Set Defaults for all hosts using the glob character (*)Host *
  ServerAliveInterval 30      # Check if the connection is alive every 30
seconds
  ForwardAgent yes            # Forward SSH agent to the remote host
  Compression yes             # Enable compression
  IdentityFile ~/.ssh/id_rsa # Default identity file

# Specific settings for host "example1.com"
Host example1
  HostName example1.com       # The real hostname to connect to
```

```
   User john                        # Default username for this host
   Port 22                          # SSH port (default is 22)
   IdentityFile ~/.ssh/id_ecdsa # Different identity file for this host


# Settings for another specific host "example2.com"
Host example2
   HostName example2.com
   User jane
   Port 22000                       # Different SSH port for this host
   IdentityFile ~/.ssh/id_ed25519


# Using a jump host to connect to a host behind a firewall
Host target-behind-fw
   HostName 192.168.0.2             # Private IP of the target host
   User alice
   Port 22
   ProxyJump jump-host              # Use 'jump-host' as a jump host


# Configuration for the jump host
Host jump-host
   HostName jump.example.com        # Public IP or domain of the jump host
   User jumpuser
   Port 22
   IdentityFile ~/.ssh/jump_key


# Using a SOCKS proxy to connect to a host
Host proxy-host
   HostName proxy-target.com        # The real hostname to connect to
   User proxyuser
   Port 22
   ProxyCommand nc -X 5 -x localhost:1080 %h %p  # Using SOCKS proxy on
localhost port 1080
```

Conclusion

OpenSSH is a very versatile tool, and we hope that the introduction you received in this chapter has motivated you to experiment and learn more. Just think of everything we've covered:

You've learned the basics of how public key cryptography works, which is essential to being able to reason about these kinds of tools and their usage. You saw how to create SSH keys and use them for remote shell sessions.

Hopefully, you got some practical experience, too, by following along and setting up key-based logins for a remote host that you work with often. If that remote host happens to be on **Amazon Web Services (AWS)** or another platform that uses .pem keys, you learned how to convert between key formats (that trick alone is sure to impress your coworkers).

Even if you didn't run into them yourself, we exposed you to some of the most common SSH errors we see people get stuck on in the wild, and how to track them down with the -v option.

We even covered SSH usage beyond remote interactive shell sessions – file transfers, tunneling network traffic, and setting up custom configurations for different servers. Surprisingly, there's even more that OpenSSH can do:

- Encrypt and sign files with ssh-keygen
- Add two-factor authentication via FIDO/U2F, storing your key on an external device
- Force certain commands to be run after login, which both limits the attack vector and allows SSH to be an interface to a service

The OpenSSH project provides excellent documentation on its manual pages and on its website. If you have a problem that requires secure connections between machines and you want technology that is battle-tested and proven, OpenSSH is worth checking out. Now go forth and encrypt!

Learn more on Discord

To join the Discord community for this book – where you can share feedback, ask questions to the author, and learn about new releases – follow the QR code below:

https://packt.link/SecNet

14
Version Control with Git

Git is a **distributed version control system (DVCS)** that, over the last two decades, has become the most widely used version control system in the world. Although it is very likely that you already know the basics of how to use Git, you might not be familiar with common command-line patterns, or some of its more rarely used (but powerful!) features. We'll cover those here. This chapter will also give you some background knowledge so that commonly used Git terms make more sense and commonly referenced concepts are clear.

Here's what you'll learn about:

- The basics of Git and distributed version control
- First-time Git setup
- Basic Git commands
- Common Git terminology
- Two powerful and slightly more advanced Git concepts: bisecting and rebasing
- Git best practices, especially around using commit messages effectively
- Useful Git shell aliases that will save you lots of typing
- GUI tools that you can use to interact with Git

Finally, the *Poor man's GitHub* section presents a small but legitimately useful project that you can do to practice and integrate the Linux skills you've learned up to this point. We hope you'll try it out: if you do, your comfort and skill on the command line will benefit tremendously.

Some background on Git

Git is a DVCS developed by Linus Torvalds, the creator of the Linux kernel. The origin of Git dates back to 2005 when the relationship between the Linux kernel community and a proprietary distributed version control system called *BitKeeper* broke down.

In response to this, Torvalds sought to create a free, open-source DVCS that would meet the needs of the Linux kernel development process. Within just a few days, he conceptualized and laid the foundation for Git.

Prioritizing performance, security, flexibility, and non-linear development (supporting thousands of parallel branches), Git quickly gained traction within the software development community. Its design, which emphasizes speed, data integrity, and support for distributed workflows, made it a favorite among developers, and it has since become the de facto standard for version control in the software industry.

What is a distributed version control system?

Traditional version control systems (like **concurrent versions system** (**CVS**) and others) use a central server that maintains a single, coherent repository state at all times. These systems let developers push and fetch code and allowed the use of branches, tags, and other familiar mechanisms. The important point is that these version control systems were designed with a central authority in mind.

Git and other DVCSs, like **Mercurial** and **Fossil**, use a different approach. Each developer has their own complete repository. Other developers, instead of going through a central server, pull from each others' repositories to fetch changes. In the case of the Linux project, there are hundreds of independent repositories in use by developers. Once a developer feels that the state of one of these repositories is ready, they will ask for the changes to be pulled into the main kernel. This is where the term **pull request** comes from.

While GitHub, GitLab, sourcehut, and others provide centralized hosting for Git, taking care of things like user authorization and providing many other features surrounding the development of software projects, Git works well without any of these and provides many mechanisms to do so. It is even possible to send and receive patches and groups of commits using email, without ever leaving the command line and Git. This allows for easy collaboration, even when a contributor has nothing but an email address to send a patch to.

Git basics

Here is a quick refresher on the most important Git command-line basics. These are provided as a reference, not as step-by-step instructions – although we've written them so that you can follow along if you want to practice.

First-time setup

First things first: if you're running Git for the first time on a machine, you may want to set a few global config options.

Set the default branch name to `main`:

```
git config --global init.defaultBranch main
```

Now configure your default name and email (attached to all of your commits):

```
git config --global user.email "you@example.com"
git config --global user.name "Your Name"
```

Now you can initialize a new Git repository.

Initialize a new Git repository

Create a directory and enter it:

```
mkdir my-repo
cd my-repo
```

Now tell Git you want to initialize this directory as a new Git repository:

```
git init
```

Make and see changes

Create a file with some simple content, and show the resulting change that Git detects:

```
echo "Hello World" >> README
git status
```

Stage and commit changes

Stage the change you made to be committed, and observe how the output of git status has changed:

```
git add README
git status
```

Show the staged content:

```
git diff --staged
```

Commit the staged changes:

```
git commit -m 'Add README file'
```

This is the short form of the commit command, which specifies the message (-m) directly. There is an interactive version of the commit command, which you'd get by running just git commit.

The interactive version of this command (without the -m option) will open the text editor specified in your shell's EDITOR environment variable, and once the file is saved and the editor exits – that is, when the $EDITOR command returns – the commit will be written.

Optional: add a remote Git repository

The following command will add a remote repository with the local name origin that Git can push to and pull from. This might look similar to the SSH login command that we covered in *Chapter 13*, *Secure Remote Access with SSH*, because that's exactly what Git will use in this case. Git also supports other protocols, such as HTTPS.

```
git remote add origin git@example.org:repo-path
```

This is just an example, but when you're working on a real repository – for example, one that exists on GitHub – you'll change the hostname and repo-path to match the repository you want to add. GitHub and other source-hosting tools all have clear documentation on how to do this for repositories hosted there.

Pushing and pulling

Push changes from your current branch to the remote Git repository:

```
git push -u origin HEAD
```

Pull changes from the remote branch:

```
git pull
```

Cloning a repository

Let's clone a remote repository – all of the code for a project-based Linux course I created:

```
git clone https://github.com/groovemonkey/hands_on_linux-self_hosted_
wordpress_for_linux_beginners
```

This will pull down the Git history for the codebase and set the origin of the remote repository to the URL specified. Then you can work on the codebase using all of the Git commands you've already learned in this chapter.

As before, you can check the status of the repository:

```
git status
```

While this command is typically used to check what was modified, it will also provide you with information on ongoing merges, show affected files during a merge conflict, and help you when bisecting code and in various other situations. It's worthwhile to check `git status` when you are not sure what is going on; chances are that you are in a special Git state that you either want to get out of or finish before continuing.

Now that we've covered the commands you'll use most often, let's get you comfortable with some of the terminology that often confuses people who are new to working with Git.

Terms you might come across

It can be very helpful to get a basic understanding of Git's vocabulary. Although it can be confusing when other software mixes these terms up, knowing what they mean in the Git world allows you to work a lot more confidently, for example, when troubleshooting and reading error messages.

Here is an overview of the most common terms and what they mean.

Repository

This is essentially a "project," the root directory of the code that is being managed and tracked by version control – the one containing the `.git` directory. A repository holds your source code and its history and changes.

Bare repository

This has a similar meaning, only that the code is not checked out. It matches what the `.git` directory contains. On servers hosting the repositories, such as GitHub, GitLab, sourcehut, or your company's Gogs or Gitea instances, these are usually in a directory named `project-name.git` containing only what you'd see in a checked-out (cloned) repository found in `project-name/.git`.

Branch

If you imagine the first commit as the seed of a new repository, a project is made up of various branches. There is a main branch (described below), and often one or more side branches, containing other directions a project is taking.

These might be major version branches, which have bug fixes applied to them but will never be merged back into the main branch. They could be experiments that may or may not ever be merged back into the main branch. Or, they could be new features or bug fix branches that are still in development but will be merged as soon as they're ready – the possibilities are endless.

Main/master branch

This is the default branch, which will be used when initializing or cloning a repository. Depending on the project, it usually contains either the latest (in development) or the latest stable code.

HEAD

This is the latest commit on a branch. It's also sometimes referred to as the "tip" of a branch. On the command line, HEAD is also commonly used in combination with relative commits.

For example, HEAD~2 references two commits back; therefore, the following command would show you the log up to two commits ago:

```
git log HEAD~2
```

In scripts and daily usage, it can also be used as an alternative to the current branch, because it is the tip of the current branch.

Tag

Unlike branches, tags are a way to mark specific commits, for example, to create (and later reference) a specific version of the codebase.

Shallow

Usually, "shallow" is used to describe checkouts that contain no – or very little – history. Shallow checkouts are used when Git is only used as a means to obtain code, rather than the full repository and its history. This, however, might prevent certain commands and tools that depend on more history from working.

Merging

Merging is the process of integrating code from one branch into another branch. This can happen in various scenarios, such as merging a feature branch into the main branch, pulling changes from a remote branch, retrieving code from the Git stash, and so on. These merges can happen in a fully automated way. Sometimes, as in the case of merge conflicts, a merge might need manual intervention.

Merge commit

This is a commit that results from code being merged. When merging code, that merge itself becomes a commit. When there is a merge conflict, this merge commit will have changes resolving that conflict. While technically possible, it's not a good idea to add any other changes (such as additional bug fixes) to such a commit. Merge commits should contain only the changes that are needed to make that specific merge work.

In the case of conflict-free merges that Git handles automatically, it's common to just commit them without any manual changes to the code or the message.

Merge conflict

When Git is not sure how to merge incoming code, this will result in a merge conflict that you need to manually resolve, usually with a merge tool. Such conflicts can occur when code is being pulled, when code is applied from the stash, when merging branches, or during any other activity that acts on your currently checked-out code. Merge conflicts need to be resolved and then committed. `git status` will usually tell you how to proceed.

Stash

Sometimes it is necessary to put changes away for later retrieval. Git provides a mechanism for this, called the stash. The stash is structured like a stack, making it easy to incrementally apply changes in order by `git stash` pop-ping from it.

Pull request

Git is a distributed version control system, which means that every developer has their own full repository and, therefore, can work independently of other developers working on the same project.

Imagine a developer, Steve, who makes some changes to the code in his repository. He wants another developer, Sarah, to integrate these changes into the codebase before an upcoming software release. Steve requests Sarah to pull these changes into her repository – as we saw earlier in the chapter, this is where the term "pull request" comes from.

Since many companies and projects do not use Git as a DVCS, preferring a central, authoritative code repository that all developers pull from and push to, the term "pull request" is now usually used to describe a request to add code to that authoritative repository (or sometimes just into the main branch of a repository).

Note

Because this concept deviates from Git's decentralized nature, there is no native Git word for it. Different products that implement this workflow (updating the authoritative, central version of the codebase) have different names for it: GitHub calls it a "pull request," while Launchpad calls it a "merge proposal" and GitLab calls it a "merge request."

Cherry-picking

Sometimes it makes sense to only obtain individual changes (commits) from a different branch. A typical example is bug fixes in a development branch, like a feature branch that should be added to a stable branch to be released. This can be done by cherry-picking. Unlike merges where the whole branch is merged, cherry-picking allows you to specify individual commits to add.

Bisecting

`git bisect` is a way to quickly find a commit causing a change, typically used to identify which commit introduced a certain bug. To do so, one specifies a known "bad" and a known "good" commit. The bad commit contains a bug and the good one is still fine. Git will now present you with commits that you can use to test for the bug. Here is an example:

```
git bisect start
git bisect bad
git bisect good a0634a0

Bisecting: 675 revisions left to test after this (roughly 10 steps)
```

The first line starts the bisect. In the second one, we tell Git that the current version is bad, so it contains the bug. Since we know that commit a0634a0 is still good, we specify that on the third line. Of course, this doesn't have to be a commit but can also be a tag or a branch. Git will then let us know how many versions will still have to be checked.

Now it's time to test the code for the bug we are trying to find. If it's present, we type in `git bisect bad`, otherwise, `git bisect good`. Rinse and repeat. Eventually, you will end up with the exact commit that introduced the bug.

If you want to get out of this mode and back to the state you were in before, typing `git bisect reset` will do so.

Depending on what you are trying to find, "good" and "bad" are not the best words and can be confusing when trying to find any other kind of behavior change. So it's possible to use "old" and "new" instead, to find the commit introducing the new behavior. Keep in mind it's not possible to mix these terms. It's either *good* and *bad*, or *old* and *new*.

There are also ways to speed this process up, such as specifying files or directories, if you know where the behavior was introduced. If you know that a change has to be related to the contents of some/directory or some/other/directory, you can narrow down your search like this:

```
git bisect start -- some/directory some/other/directory
```

Git will make sure to consider only commits that make changes to these paths.

There are even more ways to speed this process up, like specifying multiple good commits or even passing a test script that, depending on the exit code, will automatically find the commit. A look into man git-bisect is also helpful if you need to go through a lot of commits.

Rebasing

A git rebase is a common way to keep commit histories easy to follow by "replaying" (really, recreating) a given set of changes (like a feature branch) onto a new base commit, rather than the base commit where they really diverged.

Because development is usually distributed, you may have a "true" commit history like this:

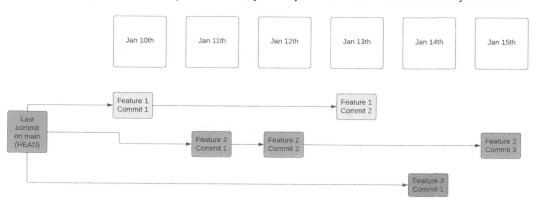

Figure 14.1: "real" commit history

Having multiple feature branch histories intermingled in the history is often more confusing than it is useful, so Git's rebase feature is used to streamline these feature commits as they are merged.

Feature 1 is merged first, so it uses the original base commit. The history now looks like this:

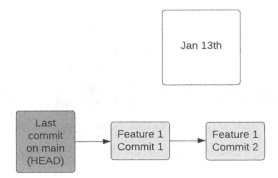

Figure 14.2: Feature 1 rebased/merged Jan 13th

Feature 3 is the next to be rebased and merged, so now the history looks like this:

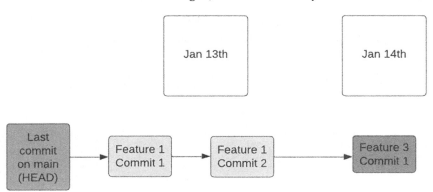

Figure 14.3: Feature 3 rebased/merged Jan 14th

Finally, Feature 2 is rebased, resulting in its base commit changing to the Jan. 14th Feature 3 commit. Now we have a nice, streamlined history like this:

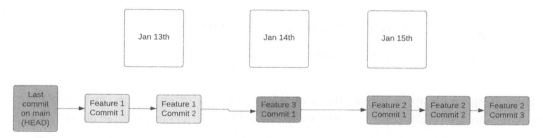

Figure 14.4: Feature 2 rebased/merged Jan 15th

GitHub and other centralized Git repository hosts have features that automate this process when merging, so you'll rarely have to rebase manually on the command line. However, here's the process for doing so:

1. Create a new branch and add a commit:

    ```
    git checkout -b dave/myfeature
    git commit -m "made some changes"
    ```

2. Presuming the base branch is named main, and some commits have been added since you started developing your branch, you can now "rebase on main":

    ```
    git rebase main
    ```

    This will modify the Git history to rebase your branch's commits on the latest main commit, as you saw in the graphic above. Because you're changing existing history, this may require force-pushing to the authoritative repository (such as the GitHub repository), which can cause other users to have conflicts. Please be aware of this when rebasing.

Now that we have identified some of the key terminology and concepts that you will come across when using Git, we can overview some good practices for writing effective commit messages.

Best practices for commit messages

As a general rule, "one change per commit, and one commit per change" is the way to keep your Git commits – and history – useful.

There are many situations where you might only work on one major change, but also add a few minor (unrelated) corrections and improvements to the code. These unrelated changes should generally be committed separately, though. It's a good idea to keep individual commits focused on the one specific thing you are trying to accomplish: a minor fix, fixing a typo, changing style, adding a (single) feature, and so on. Even if you end up making multiple interrelated changes at once, it might still make sense to split them up into multiple commits later. Committing more frequently can make this process a lot easier.

There are many reasons for this rule. One of the most practical reasons is that when your commits are small, individual changes can be easily cherry-picked or reverted should it become necessary (even if you never expected it while changing the code). Having small, tightly focused commits is also helpful when someone uses `git blame` to understand a change.

Good commit messages

Sometimes, vague suggestions, for example, "keep the commit message short when using `git commit`," can be confusing and hard to follow. For context, it makes sense to explain how Git is intended to be used. Git, being a DVCS, allows for patches to be sent as emails. As a result, commit messages themselves – in a way – take the form of emails. The first line is considered the subject line, giving a brief overview of what is done, followed by an empty line and a more verbose summary of what was changed.

Because this is a very open-ended schema, there are some commonly agreed-upon rules. Like all such rules, they may be overridden on a per-project or per-organization basis, but here is an overview of what many well-established open-source projects do:

- Keep the first line short. It should be a summary using 72 characters or less.
- Make the first line an imperative verb (such as Add..., Fix...).
- Capitalize the subject line.
- If you need more than that, add an empty line and a full summary.
- Use the body to explain *why* you have made this change. This can be very helpful for any future reader using `git blame`.

- Make sure to describe how you came to your conclusion/implementation, and why it is relevant. This is especially important for complex commits and for commits that might not immediately make sense to someone who is looking only at the code. This can be a tremendous help when tracking down bugs, removing obsolete code later, rewriting systems, or just getting into understanding the code.

- Consider whether some of what you're writing in your commit message might not be better added to code comments.

- Imagine a reviewer or future reader having no context at all. Make sure that the code changes can be easily understood.

With this advice in mind, you should be able to make clear and organized commit messages. Next, we will look at some further advice for easily and effectively using Git.

GUIs

While this book is strongly focused on building up your command-line skills, it's worth mentioning that there are some graphical tools available that can make interacting with Git easier for some use cases.

`tig` and `gitk` are two examples of graphical repository browsers, which give you a Git interface that's similar to what many IDEs provide. To try them out, simply navigate to a repository using `cd` and run `gitk` or `tig`. You'll likely have to install these tools via your package manager; many Unix flavors (including popular Linux distributions and macOS) don't have them installed by default.

Useful shell aliases

Here are a few useful shell aliases for common Git commands. Feel free to add these to your `~/.bash_aliases` file (presuming you're using Bash):

```
alias gpo='git push origin $(git branch | grep "*" | cut -d " " -f2)'
alias gp='git pull'
alias gs='git status'
alias gd='git diff'
alias gds='git diff --staged'
```

If you're typing in `git status` dozens of times each day, it can be a huge improvement to add an alias that enables you to type gs instead. Feel free to change these to something even more convenient – that's what customization is for!

Now let's zoom out a bit and see how we can practically apply all of this knowledge while building a small Linux server project: your very own private Git server.

Poor man's GitHub

In this section, we'll show you how to set up a remote Git repository for yourself. You only need an SSH account on the remote machine and a Git binary on your local machine (as in, the Git command itself). If Git is already installed on the remote machine, you won't even need root access.

This is a fun project that will make you comfortable with the basic OS-facing concepts involved with Git. This setup is not necessarily suggested for production use; rather, it will show you that there's absolutely no magic when it comes to Git. Like everything else in Linux, it's just files (in this case, remote files and an SSH tunnel).

Considerations

Depending on whether you have root access and whether you want to share the repository with others, you might want to consider creating a specific user for your shared Git service. This is completely optional.

We will use an SSH account for authentication, so if you share the Git repository, the person you share it with will have the same permissions as that user on the remote machine. It might make sense to create a separate user on the remote machine for this project (named git) if you don't fully trust your fellow programmers to have access to this account.

This project assumes you're comfortable setting up SSH and connecting to a server – if you're a bit rusty on the details, check out the previous chapter: *Chapter 13, Secure Remote Access with SSH*.

1. Connect to your server

Connect to the server, using the account you want your repository to belong to (such as git, or your own user):

```
ssh myuser@example.com
```

2. Install Git

First, check if Git is already installed by running:

```
git version
```

This should output the version of Git that is installed on your server. If you receive a message like command not found, then Git is not installed on your system.

To install Git, simply use your system's package manager to install the git package. On Ubuntu, you'd run:

```
apt-get install git
```

3. Initialize a repository

Now you can initialize a new bare repository. In this case, we will call it my-project. You can create this wherever you want. For the sake of simplicity, we will assume that it is your home directory:

```
git init --bare my-project.git
```

This will create a directory called my-project.git. It is not a file, but a directory structure that Git considers a repository. We won't go into detail here and it will probably be quite a while before you need to change something.

Believe it or not, that's actually all you need to do!

You can now disconnect from the server (*Ctrl+D* if you're connected via SSH).

4. Clone the repository

Despite it being completely empty, you can already clone the repository. After disconnecting from your server, run the following command from your local machine:

```
git clone myuser@example.com:my-project.git
```

As mentioned earlier, this assumes that you created the repository in the home directory of the myuser user. Starting after the example.com hostname (this might also just be your server's IP address if you haven't set up DNS), the path is relative to the user's home directory. If you want to specify a full (absolute) path, just start with a slash. In other words, using the command git clone myuser@example.com:/home/myuser/my-project.git would lead to the same directory being cloned.

Git will warn you that you cloned an empty repository. But since this is what we expect, there's no need to worry.

5. Edit the project and push your changes

We can now switch to the cloned directory and start working on the project:

```
cd my-project
echo "My personal project" >> README
git add README
git commit -m 'initial commit'
```

Now that we have our first commit, we can push it. The very first push has a minor caveat to be aware of: because the repository is still completely empty, it doesn't know any branches yet, not even the master branch. Git will tell you this if you only run git push. So just make sure to tell Git the branch when pushing to a new repository for the very first time:

```
git push origin master
```

That's it!

Now you or someone else with access to your SSH account can clone, push to, and pull from this repository. You can even set up hooks and do other fun things. Git is a very powerful tool with a huge variety of features. It can take a while to get used to them, so just consider this your starting point.

The possibilities are endless, and I'm always excited to hear about people using Git for interesting or unique use cases. Have fun!

Conclusion

In this chapter, you learned the basic concepts, commands, and workflows that you need to use Git effectively. Some of the often-used advanced features and terminology should be clearer to you now, and we passed on some advice for "soft" Git skills like writing good commit messages.

The shell aliases we showed you save us hundreds of keystrokes in a day of programming; we hope they are as useful to you as they have been to us, and that you'll use command aliases for all the hard-to-remember or hard-to-type commands you run daily.

We also hope that you followed along with the *Poor man's GitHub* project! Running the commands only takes a few minutes, but if you take an afternoon and really try it out (rent a Linux VM for a few hours, set up a remote repository there, and push some example commits), you'll get a feel for how powerful and effective your newfound Linux skills can be when they're combined to solve real-world problems.

Learn more on Discord

To join the Discord community for this book – where you can share feedback, ask questions to the author, and learn about new releases – follow the QR code below:

`https://packt.link/SecNet`

15

Containerizing Applications with Docker

Over the last decade, Docker containerization has become a kind of default packaging format for web applications and modern microservices. In a container, your program sits in a very lightweight, isolated shell of Linux filesystem, process, user, and network abstractions, safely separate from the host environment. Container images also happen to be incredibly portable – they're easy to shuffle around from a developer's laptop to a testing or staging environment to a production server. This solves many of the problems that have plagued software and infrastructure over the last several decades.

In some sense, containers are quite similar to the Linux packages you've learned how to install from repositories. A container image is, roughly, a compressed archive (such as, a `.tar.gz` file) of your application, along with all the configuration files and dependencies the application needs. That little package – an image – is executable by Docker. The revolutionary thing about such a container is that it neatly holds everything together in a single artifact and can run on any Linux system that has a container runtime (like Docker) installed.

This chapter could easily be a book on its own – Docker and Linux containers in general are fairly large subjects. However, like with everything else in this book, we're focusing on only the basic theory and practical skills that are necessary for you to be comfortable interacting with Docker-based infrastructure in your applications.

In this chapter, you'll learn about the following:

- The application development and operational problems that containers solve
- What containers are, and how they're similar to Linux packages

- The difference between Docker images and Docker containers

- All the practical basics for using Docker in your development workflow

- How to build your own container images with Dockerfiles (you'll containerize a real Python web application)

- Some more advanced topics like how virtual machines and containers are different, and how Linux creates container abstraction via namespacing

- Some hard-earned container tips, tricks, and best practices

Let's jump in.

How containers work as packages

Docker became standard tooling to package up software when the goal is to include a system that is known to be a working setup. A Docker container typically contains both the software you want to run as well as a whole, though frequently trimmed down, Linux system as its execution environment. This execution environment provides libraries and tools, as well as some other things, like basic system configuration, so that it can function as a standalone entity, independent of the system running the container. The primary goal is to make sure that the application can successfully be run on the developer's machine, production and test environments, and elsewhere, without having to take care of details, such as the operating system versions, installed libraries.

It is important to keep in mind that the operating system and libraries don't disappear. Bugs in libraries may still exist and any packaged dependencies should be updated for security and other reasons. However, the consumers of the packaged software, be it end users or your system operators, as well as any orchestration software, are now provided with a common package and don't need to take care about system dependencies. While the details of how the software is run and configured still depend on the software, the way it is executed (in a container) is somewhat standardized.

In summary, that means that any specific setup of the environment, such as installing dependencies, is now described as part of the Dockerfile, and once a working container image is created, short of specific configuration, the container is expected to run on any system capable of running Docker, or more broadly, **OCI** images.

 OCI (short for **Open Container Initiative**) provides standards to specify things like image format and the execution of Linux containers. Sometimes it used synonymously with Docker in the sense that a developer might use Docker to create the image, but the execution on an orchestrator might not use Docker at all.

There's no better way to get started than to install Docker on your machine and start trying some commands, so let's do that.

Prerequisite: Docker install

First, download and install Docker Desktop. You can find instructions for this at `https://docs.docker.com/get-docker/`.

There is also an excellent official tutorial for getting started at `https://docs.docker.com/get-started/`, but we recommend that you wait to read that until after you've gone through this chapter. We're going to cover some of the basics, but with less focus on specific command-line flags, and more focus on how you'll use these commands and workflows as an application developer.

Now that you've got Docker installed, let's jump into actually starting our first container!

Docker crash course

A **Docker image** is the "package" from our metaphor – it's a static artifact that is saved, stored, and moved around. It becomes a **container** when it's executed on a machine. This is important because you'll sometimes hear these terms used incorrectly: Docker images are the immutable base from which a container – a running, namespaced process – is launched. Images are the pre-built template from which live containers are generated at runtime.

Images are designed to be immutable: if you download an nginx web server image and run it, any changes you make to the resulting container don't affect the underlying image at all. This is the part that trips up most developers who are used to long-running virtual machines that are provisioned once and then started and stopped many times, preserving their internal state the whole time.

Docker containers are different. Ideally, they are designed to be ephemeral and stateless, while the images they're spawned from act as a long-lived blueprint that can be used to spawn an infinite number of containers across many different execution environments.

What follows is an example of a basic Docker workflow that's designed to get you acquainted with the most important Docker commands. Don't worry about memorizing the commands; we'll cover them in depth later in this chapter. For now, we'll just explain what's happening at each step, so you can get used to what you'll see on the screen at your next microservices gig.

First, let's start the nginx container (`docker run`) and interactively (`-it`) run the Bash shell (`/bin/bash`) inside of it:

```
→  ~ docker run -it nginx /bin/bash
```

This gets us a shell prompt for the unique container that was started from the `nginx` image. The container's Bash shell is now connected to our terminal:

```
root@e96107c9a58e:/#
```

Let's write a file called `test.txt` and verify that it exists:

```
root@e96107c9a58e:/# echo "I am immutable" >> test.txt
root@e96107c9a58e:/# cat test.txt
I am immutable
```

We can exit the shell with the usual command, `ctrl-d`:

```
root@e96107c9a58e:/#
exit
```

The container exits and we're now back in our regular shell. Here's where it gets confusing for most first-time Docker users: let's re-run the first command to start a container from the nginx Docker image again, and check on our file:

```
→  ~ docker run -it nginx /bin/bash
root@c3b4d95ab9e6:/# cat test.txt
cat: test.txt: No such file or directory
```

FILE A BUG REPORT! DOCKER IS BROKEN!

Actually, it's not. This is not the same container as the one you wrote the `test.txt` file in. If you were looking closely, you may have noticed that the hostname in the shell prompt was different on the second container. That's because each `docker run` command launches a new container from the specified image. Containers are designed to run, exit, and disappear forever.

The original container is actually still around:

```
→  ~ docker ps -a
CONTAINER ID    IMAGE            COMMAND                CREATED
STATUS                          PORTS                  NAMES
c3b4d95ab9e6    nginx            "/docker-entrypoint.…" 14 minutes ago
Exited (1) 6 minutes ago                               agitated_hofstadter
e96107c9a58e    nginx            "/docker-entrypoint.…" 14 minutes ago
Exited (0) 14 minutes ago                              nervous_gould
```

To get rid of them, you can use `docker rm` with the ID of the container you want to delete:

```
→  ~ docker rm c3b4d95ab9e6
```

```
c3b4d95ab9e6
```

It is possible to start a stopped container with `docker start`:

```
→  ~ docker start e96107c9a58e
e96107c9a58e
```

At which point, you would see the container running in your Docker process list:

```
→  ~ docker ps
CONTAINER ID    IMAGE      COMMAND             CREATED         STATUS
PORTS      NAMES
e96107c9a58e    nginx      "/docker-entrypoint.…"  18 minutes ago  Up 1
second    80/tcp    nervous_gould
```

Then you could use `docker exec` to execute a command inside that container, again starting and attaching to the Bash shell program with `-it`. From there, you can view the filesystem state (`test.txt`) that we modified:

```
→  ~ docker exec -it e96107c9a58e /bin/bash
root@e96107c9a58e:/# cat test.txt
I am immutable
```

However, keeping containers around for a long time – modifying their state and stopping and restarting them instead of always starting new containers from an image – is discouraged and leads back to many of the same bugs that Docker helped solve.

Let's avoid all of those mistakes and delete this running container forever by force-removing it:

```
→  ~ docker rm -f e96107c9a58e
e96107c9a58e
```

You could have also run `docker stop` followed by `docker rm`, but force-removing with `docker rm -f` will stop and remove a running container in one fell swoop.

You can see how Docker encourages immutable containers to keep the state from drifting away from the image, which is the "source of truth" for your application's initial environment. If you want to make changes to an image, you can't do so directly – images are immutable.

Changes should be *explicit* and *intentional*, which is important for creating and running reliable software. How do we do this? We start with the original image, make our changes in a controlled and reproducible way (not "SSH to the server and try running these commands"), and then save them by creating a new image. Enter the mighty Dockerfile.

Creating images with a Dockerfile

If you're ever tasked with building a new Docker image, or modifying an existing one – perhaps for a web application that you're developing – you'll be making heavy use of Dockerfiles (see the official Dockerfile documentation at `https://docs.docker.com/engine/reference/builder/`).

A large percentage of new software will already have an official (or at least open-source, third-party) Dockerfile available. Even if you need to do some customizing before you use these, a good place to look for examples is the documentation for the software or framework you use. These examples don't tend to break as easily as your own custom Dockerfile when major upgrades are released for the packaged software.

Also, some frameworks or development environments, for example, Spring Boot (Java), can generate Docker images as part of the build process.

So, even though there's a chance you'll never have to touch a Dockerfile yourself, it's unlikely, and you should have a basic idea of how they work.

Let's look at a very simple Dockerfile, from the open-source HTTP echo server project (`https://github.com/hashicorp/http-echo`). This creates a Docker image that packages a Go binary that acts as a simple web server:

```
FROM alpine

ADD "https://curl.haxx.se/ca/cacert.pem" "/etc/ssl/certs/ca-certificates.crt"
ADD "./pkg/linux_amd64/http-echo" "/"
RUN apk add curl
ENTRYPOINT ["/http-echo"]
```

Basically, this creates a new container image by:

1. Using the `alpine` Linux image as a base to build on.
2. Downloading some certificates and adding them to an image layer (essentially adding something to the resulting container's filesystem).
3. Copying the `http-echo` binary from the build directory into the container image.
4. Running an alpine package installation command to install the `curl` program.
5. Defining the executable or command that is run when a container started from this image is launched.

Each of these steps is invoked by a (capitalized) *Instruction* that the Dockerfile parser knows how to execute. This specific Dockerfile only uses a subset of the instructions available to you in a Dockerfile (FROM, ADD, RUN, and ENTRYPOINT).

Here's the full complement of instructions available to you when you're creating new Docker images via a Dockerfile:

- ARG: Declares a build-time argument; basically, a variable to be used later in the build.

- ENV: Environment vars to set during the build, which will persist in your running container environment (*not* just during the build!). Takes a key=value format.

- FROM: Base image.

- CMD: This provides a default command (or default ENTRYPOINT args) for the container to run when it's started. It can be overridden, but you should have one in your Dockerfile. Only one per Dockerfile is allowed – if there's more than one CMD, only the last one will count.

- ADD: A flexible instruction that copies files and directories, adding them to the image's filesystem. This can also be used to copy files from outside the image or from remote URLs (via HTTP), and to do complex things like expansion, decompression, unarchiving, and more. You saw it as a stand-in for the curl command in the sample Dockerfile above, to download a CA certificate file.

- COPY: Just copies files and directories – less complicated, magical, and powerful than ADD.

- LABEL: Adds image metadata, in a key=value format.

- EXPOSE: Informs consumers of this image about which network protocols and ports this container will be listening on.

- ENTRYPOINT: Tells the container what command to run when it starts. Use the *exec form* (ENTRYPOINT ["executable", "param1", "param2"]) to make sure your container can receive and respond to signals from outside the container process.

- RUN command arg1 arg2: Run command with arguments arg1 and arg2 in the image's shell:

  - RUN ["command", "arg1", "arg2, "argN"]: Same as above, but useful to avoid shell string munging.

  - Each RUN instruction executes in a new image layer (we're not diving into layers here but this can be helpful to know).

  - RUN --mount can be used to temporarily mount filesystems into the container during the build, without copying the files themselves into an image layer.

  - RUN --network and RUN --security also exist for managing network context and privileged containers, respectively.

- WORKDIR: Sets the working directory for instructions that follow in the Dockerfile. Equivalent to cd in Unix-like operating systems.

- SHELL: Override the default shell used to interpret commands during the Docker build. Commands must use the exec form.

- STOPSIGNAL: Set the system call signal that this container should interpret as the signal to exit. By default, this is SIGTERM, like any other Linux process.

- VOLUME: Define volumes that will be mounted in from the host.

- USER: Change (container) user to use for build commands, from this point forward (can be used multiple times to switch users during a build).

- ONBUILD: Define an instruction that's triggered when this image is used as the base for another build.

- HEALTHCHECK: Some health-checking functionality, which you likely won't use because your container scheduler has its own health-checking functionality.

We'll jump into a practical, end-to-end example of how to tie all of this together with a small project, but first let's revisit the commands we just used in a bit more depth.

Container commands

Now let's dive deeper into some of the more complicated, but important, commands and command invocations that you may run into when working with Docker.

docker run

Let's look at a more complex invocation of the docker run command we used earlier:

```
docker run --rm --name mywebcontainer -p 80:80 -v /tmp:/usr/share/nginx/
html:ro -d nginx
```

- --rm: Clean up (remove) this container when it exits.

- --name mywebcontainer: Give this container a friendly name – mywebcontainer.

- -p 80:80: Map port 80 of the host to port 80 in the container. The left port number is on the "outside" (the environment running the container), and the right port number represents the "inside" (container) port. For example, -p 4000:80 will map the container's port 80 to localhost:4000.

- -v /tmp:/usr/share/nginx/html:ro: Mount a volume – the host environment's /tmp directory will be mounted into the container at /usr/share/nginx/html; :ro ensures that this will be a read-only mount (mounted files can't be modified from inside the container).

- -d: Run the container in detached mode (in the background).
- nginx: The image to launch this container from.

If you want to see some HTML at http://localhost:80, you can add an index.html file to your /tmp directory:

```
cat <<EOF > /tmp/index.html
<!doctype html>
<h1>Hello World</h1>
<p>This is my container</p>
</html>
EOF
```

Because our /tmp directory is mapped to the container's /usr/share/nginx/html directory (where nginx will look for HTML files), nginx will immediately recognize and begin serving this file.

Volumes are the mechanism by which stateful applications can still be run using stateless containers.

docker image list

To see which images you've downloaded locally, you can run docker images (or docker image list, if you prefer).

The list may be long if you've been building and using lots of Docker images!

```
$ docker image list

REPOSITORY                                        TAG
IMAGE ID        CREATED        SIZE
nginx                                             latest
51086ed63d8c    10 days ago    142MB
vault                                             latest
22fdc6314051    2 months ago   207MB
golang                                            1.19-alpine
d0f5238dcb8b    2 months ago   352MB
```

docker ps

docker ps is a bit like the ps command in Linux. It lets you see which containers are running on your host, along with some context like their ID, which command they are running, their creation time and uptime, port mapping, and more.

Running the command

```
$ docker ps
```

will produce output like this:

```
CONTAINER ID    IMAGE           COMMAND              CREATED
STATUS                  PORTS               NAMES
2aca849eef73    nginx           "/docker-entrypoint.…"    About a minute ago
Up About a minute    0.0.0.0:80->80/tcp    mywebcontainer
```

docker exec

During the development of a container image, it's common to jump into a container and run commands. To start an interactive shell in a running container, use docker exec:

```
docker exec -it mywebcontainer /bin/bash
```

In the case of our previously started nginx container, this will spawn a Bash shell inside the container environment. Any state changes you make (file creation, kernel settings, and so on) will be lost when the container is stopped – the next docker run will simply spool up a new container from the same base image state.

docker stop

To stop a container, run docker stop $CONTAINERNAME – you can also use the container ID if it doesn't have a friendly name:

```
docker stop mywebcontainer
```

If the container was started with the --rm option, as our nginx container was, the container will be deleted and its state (if that state diverged from the base image) will be lost.

If the container was not started with --rm, its state remains on your filesystem and you can start the container again with docker start $CONTAINERNAME. Its state will be preserved.

Docker project: Python/Flask application container

We're going to containerize a small Python web service that uses the Flask web framework. This is an extremely common pattern, and Python lends itself well to containerization because packaging and dependency management are famously messy in a lot of Python projects. You'll create all the files yourself – try to use a command-line text editor for practice!

1. Set up the application

First, create a new directory and enter it:

```
mkdir dockerpy && cd dockerpy
```

Create the tiny Python web application. I'm using vim in this example, but use whichever editor you like:

```
vim echo_server.py
```

Paste the following text inside:

```python
from flask import Flask, request
import os


app = Flask(__name__)


@app.route('/')
def echo():
    return {
        "method": request.method,
        "headers": dict(request.headers),
        "args": request.args
    }


@app.route('/health')
def health():
    return {"status": "healthy"}


if __name__ == "__main__":
    env_port = os.environ.get("PORT", 8080)
    app.run(host='0.0.0.0', port=env_port)
```

That's the whole web application – it simply reads some of the information from an incoming request and uses that to push a response back to the client.

Save and exit the file (esc, :x).

Create a file named requirements.txt containing just the following line:

```
Flask>=3.0.0
```

Next, create your Dockerfile:

```
vim Dockerfile
```

Enter the following text:

```
# Use an official Python base image
FROM python:3.12-slim

# Set the working directory inside the container
WORKDIR /app

# Copy our list of dependencies into the container
COPY requirements.txt .

# Install Python dependencies
RUN pip install --no-cache-dir -r requirements.txt

# Copy the script into the container
COPY echo_server.py .

# Set a healthcheck to kill the container if it's not listening on the
internal port
HEALTHCHECK --interval=30s --timeout=5s \
  CMD curl --fail http://localhost:8080/health || exit 1

# Expose port for the application
EXPOSE 8080


ENV PORT=8080
CMD ["python", "echo_server.py"]
```

That's all you need for now. Your dockerpy directory should now contain three files:

- Dockerfile
- echo_server.py
- requirements.txt

2. Create the Docker image

Build a new Docker image with the `docker build` command. The `-t` is for "tagging" the container with a name:

```
docker build -t dockerpy .
```

Notice the `.` character at the end, which is telling Docker to use the current directory as its build context.

3. Start a container from your image

You've already used the `docker run` command earlier in this chapter. Use it to launch a container from your newly built image:

```
docker run --rm -d -p 8080:8080 --name my-dockerpy dockerpy
(the command will print out the ID of your new container)
```

There are a few new arguments here:

- `--rm` tells Docker to delete the container when it exits. This prevents old containers from hanging around on your filesystem, as you saw in the first examples in this chapter.
- `-d` tells Docker to daemonize the container. This keeps it from attaching to your terminal in the foreground.
- `-p` sets up a port mapping: the left side of the colon is the container port, while the right side is the host port that it'll be mapped to. If the container application were running on port 1234 and you wanted it to map to host port 80, this would read `-p 1234:80`.
- `--name` tags your container with a name so you can find it easily in the output of `docker ps`.

Now you've got your containerized application running, and can access it in a browser or on the command line. Let's use the `curl` command to connect to send a request to the web service:

```
curl localhost:8080
{"args":{},"headers":{"Accept":"*/*","Host":"localhost:8080","User-
Agent":"curl/8.1.2"},"method":"GET"}
```

For those who have suffered through impossible-to-recreate dependency nightmares (Python, Ruby, and others are famous for this), this should be a revelation. All of the complexity that you used to have to drag around with your application – from local dev environments to CI and testing, to staging, and finally to production – is now condensed into a single artifact that's guaranteed to contain the same stuff no matter where you run it.

One command we haven't used before is docker exec, which lets you execute a command inside a running container. This is useful if, for some reason, you absolutely have to inspect or modify a running container:

```
docker exec -it my-dockerpy /bin/sh
```

This launches and attaches to /bin/sh in the container (most production containers will only have a minimal shell at /bin/sh, and won't ship with something as full-featured as Bash).

Let's stop the server with the last command we'll cover here, which is docker kill:

```
docker kill my-dockerpy
```

This sends a SIGKILL (Signal 9) as opposed to a SIGTERM (Signal 15) to the process and stops it immediately without giving it the chance to shut down gracefully.

Containers vs. virtual machines

You've now gotten a taste of the workflow that you'll use to create and work with Docker images. However, it pays to know a bit about the underlying differences between containers and virtual machines. This knowledge can make a difference when you're troubleshooting operational issues, and it's also a common interview question to gauge how well you understand the principles underlying containerization.

Virtual Machines (VMs) allow you to run complete operating systems like Linux, Windows, or DragonFly BSD on top of another host operating system. VMs run independently of the host system. In fact, running Docker on macOS will transparently use a VM to provide the Linux OS that's needed for Docker.

As a result, a virtual machine runs a full operating system like Linux, which in turn uses an init system like systemd. Because of this, you manage services and processes exactly as if your VM were a physical machine. In terms of day-to-day use, everything that applies to a physical machine also applies to virtual machines. However, this is not how containers are typically used.

Docker containers usually contain single applications; in fact, they frequently contain only a single process. If there happen to be multiple processes inside a container, this is typically because of a multi-process application that has spawned child processes (web servers or command runners usually do this). Since the widely agreed-upon best practice is for a container to run only a single process, and to exit as soon as that process exits, any kind of internal process supervision and management would be wasted here.

Instead, you'll find that the jobs typically done by an operating system's init system have moved outside the container runtime environment, to the external systems *managing* the containers, such as Kubernetes, Nomad, and others.

In this new model, containers are what operating system processes used to be, and container orchestrators play assorted OS and scheduler roles.

In a Docker container, PID1, which is the init system on a full Linux operating system, is whatever your CMD or ENTRYPOINT is. Usually, that's the main process of the software you're running. Typically, a container is expected to run a single process. While there are scenarios where people intentionally run their containers in a different way, running a single process and having the container halt when the process halts is the expected behavior. Especially when simply containerizing a service to be run in production, one should make sure to follow this approach. There are exceptions to this rule, especially when running software that predates the popularization of Docker containers, but in these cases, you'll likely be aware and often base off containers made for this purpose.

A quick note on Docker image repositories

We've been working quite a bit with the nginx image in this chapter. But where exactly is this image coming from? By default, Docker attempts to download images from Docker Hub (https:// hub.docker.com/), which is a central repository of public Docker images. Docker Hub works like a Linux package repository, which contains uploaded Docker images ready for you to use. Most popular server software can be found there and can be downloaded and used as easily as you just saw with nginx.

Not all applications are public, however, and it's normal to use private repositories to store Docker images. There is an ever-changing list of Docker image repository providers, so we won't list them here, but it's enough to understand that they all work the same way as Docker Hub.

Painfully learned container lessons

As you start building your own containers, you can avoid many problems by keeping in mind the best practices discussed in Docker's official documentation here: https://docs.docker.com/ get-started/09_image_best/.

That said, we've compiled a small list of the most egregious containerization mistakes we've noticed, and how to avoid them. This section is the result of many sleepless nights, outages, and learning things the hard way.

Image size

Start with minimal images, like Scratch or Alpine. To deploy most applications, it's a good idea to try to stay away from big images and distributions like Ubuntu. When build dependencies are required, removing these, or using intermediate build containers when building larger/multi-container projects, is recommended.

Small, minimal images don't just mean faster download speeds and less resource usage, but also make it a lot easier for you to manage. If an image doesn't include software and libraries you don't need, that's less for you to keep updated, less surface area for criminals to attack, and fewer noisy warnings from container security scanners.

C standard library

Be aware of which **C Standard Library** (also known as *libc*) you're using. Many Linux distributions use glibc; some, like Alpine Linux, use musl or others. The libraries and any resulting binaries might not be compatible across those. For example, on Alpine, you may need to compile less popular tools yourself. If your projects depend on certain libraries being available via packages on your base image, you might run into incompatibilities. Of course, upgrading, downgrading, or switching base images completely might cause similar issues.

However, because Alpine and musl have been steadily gaining adoption, these sorts of issues are becoming less likely (and, at the very least, more googlable!). If you don't depend on any C libraries, this usually won't be an issue. Also, statically compiling your code can make you more independent of the underlying system and therefore the base image.

Production is not your laptop: outside dependencies

Don't depend on local mounts or other local containers. The environment for a deployed container will likely be very different from your laptop. Just because you've got a database container next to your web app container on your laptop, doesn't mean these containers will be scheduled on the same machines in production.

The same thing goes for data volumes – these outside-your-container touchpoints are where you'll have to do some planning with your Ops/DevOps co-workers. You'll likely be hooking into service discovery, health checking, and shared volumes via a scheduler or other DevOps tooling construct.

Container theory: namespacing

If you're wondering how some of this container magic works underneath, or just worried that you'll have to troubleshoot a container environment under pressure one day, it's useful to familiarize yourself with the concept of namespacing. You can skip this section if you're not interested in how the container abstraction is built on Linux.

Namespacing is an overloaded term, used to mean different things in different technological niches. In the context of Linux containers, the idea of namespacing is best explained via chroot (change root). chroot is an old utility for Unix and Unix-like operating systems that allows a user to change the root (the / path) of the filesystem.

The usage of this tool is really quite simple: chroot /some/path will set whatever is in /some/path to be the new /. In addition to allowing OS installers to change into the system that is currently being installed to run commands, it also allows for basic namespacing. In fact, various software and the configuration of various Linux distributions have been making use of this to enhance security, because using chroot essentially excludes parts of the filesystem from the currently readable scope – it makes anything outside the new root inaccessible. So, if an attacker uses an exploit that allows for remote code execution on a web server running inside a chroot environment, the system and any files outside this directory will remain unaffected.

The technical primitives used to implement containers on Linux and other operating systems have changed significantly over the last decade, and will likely continue to change. Thankfully, the low-level implementation is not critically important for you as a software engineer who is mainly a consumer of containerization, as opposed to an operator or implementer of this technology.

The "container" abstraction relies on underlying technologies like:

- Filesystem namespacing (for example, with chroot).
- User and process namespacing, making processes outside the container invisible from within the container. In other words, root and PID 5 in the container would respectively map to an unprivileged user and another process ID outside of the container namespace.
- Resource grouping and accounting technologies such as cgroups.
- Network virtualization/namespacing, so a container can't access a network interface directly, but also so that port number overlaps can be handled. For example, you can run two different containers that expose port 8080; there won't be an error about the port being already in use, because the containers' networking stacks are independent of each other.

How do we do Ops with containers?

Although this is not a book for system administrators or site reliability engineers, you should know the basic context in which containers are generally run. The main idea is that containers are largely stateless "functions" that process inputs (web requests or HTTP messages from other services) and produce outputs (web responses, side effects, and logs streamed to STDOUT). In a well-run operations environment, containers can be thought of as an analog to Linux processes, or to functions in programming.

Containers are usually "scheduled" onto hosts by a third-party tooling layer such as Kubernetes, Nomad, and others. If containers are like processes, then these fill the role of the operating system scheduler (the whole thing is a distributed system instead of a single host).

Container output is usually captured by the same tooling and redirected to logging solutions such as Logstash, Graylog, and Datadog. Metrics from all running containers may be extracted and fed into tools like Prometheus for analysis and troubleshooting.

Conclusion

In this chapter, you got a whirlwind tour of the most important things you need to know about working with Docker, and containers in general. Although individual technologies may change – which container scheduler is in vogue, or how log streaming is best handled – we've tried to stay focused on the core theory and skills that every modern software developer should have.

We hope that you take away a few main ideas from this chapter. First, we hope you have an intuitive grasp of the problems that containerization solves for people, mainly by controlling complexity and packaging dependencies into a single artifact.

It's also important to remember the difference between images and containers, and to get some practice building your own Dockerfiles from scratch, using the official documentation.

We hope that visiting a few more advanced topics, like how virtual machines and containers are different and how namespacing works, comes in handy during troubleshooting or a job interview. The best practices we discussed will come in handy there, too.

Finally, to cement your learning, we recommend that you practice these skills by containerizing one of your own applications. You'll learn a lot and it'll be much easier to start while all of the information from this chapter is still fresh in your mind.

Learn more on Discord

To join the Discord community for this book – where you can share feedback, ask questions to the author, and learn about new releases – follow the QR code below:

`https://packt.link/SecNet`

16

Monitoring Application Logs

Welcome to the world of Linux logging! As software developers, understanding logging in Linux, especially with tools like systemd and journald, is crucial. Here's a breakdown of what you need to know.

Logs are records of events happening in a software application or operating system. It's a flexible format and unique to each application, but how logs are processed, stored, and retrieved is more uniform on modern systems. It's essential for you to understand logs as a developer because the logs you can access in Linux provide insights into the behavior of the operating system and all applications running on it. You'll use this knowledge to understand errors, track application performance, and debug. Logs are your first line of defense in troubleshooting, so prepare to get comfortable with them.

In this chapter, we'll give you an overview of Unix and Linux logging, and show you the most common ways that software developers interact with logs. You'll see:

- How logs are emitted by the system and applications running on it
- Where logs are collected on most modern Linux systems
- Some historical knowledge about how logging worked in the past, which still comes in handy on many production systems you'll run into
- How to find and view logs when you're troubleshooting an application
- How logs are being centralized at companies and when services are deployed in cloud environments

We'll also give a few tips on getting the most out of structured logging while avoiding some common pitfalls that developers often fall into.

Introduction to logging

As we saw in the introduction, **logs** are simply informational messages – records of events happening in a software application or operating system. Like many Unix concepts, there are few hard and fast rules: if you write a two-line script that writes a timestamp into a text file, that might count as a log. Some logs are simple plaintext strings sent to well-known file locations on the system, and others are highly structured binary data managed exclusively by a daemon such as systemd.

As a developer, you're probably familiar with **log levels**, which are labels that indicate the urgency of events on your software. Think "error," "info," and "debug" messages, which you've surely seen scrolling past in the terminal while developing software. We'll cover these common log levels later, but for now, you should be aware of three main *sources* of logs in a modern, full-featured Linux environment: **system**, **service**, and non-service **application** logs. The source of the log can give you important contextual information about what's happening in a specific log message.

System logs are logs sent by the operating system ("the kernel") itself. These include errors, messages about hardware events, resource consumption and limits, configuration and security, and noteworthy changes in the system state.

Service logs are emitted by the services running on a system. Specifically on Linux, they are emitted by the services managed by the systemd init system, which do their logging through a service called journald. They can provide insights into the health and status of various services.

On the systems you're likely to encounter, system and service logs are both commingled in journald. We'll learn all about systemd and journald (and journalctl) as we progress through this chapter.

Non-systemd-managed applications are the outliers that don't generally log through journald. You'll have to find their log files via documentation for each application, although well-behaved applications usually write their own log files in a directory like /var/log/$APPLICATION_NAME/, where $APPLICATION_NAME is the name of the application.

As we go through this chapter, the importance of understanding journald and journalctl commands will become apparent. However, before we go into that, we should note a few details about Linux logging.

Logging on Linux can get... weird

You've seen by now that Unix-like systems are tremendously flexible. If you don't like the default way that things are done, you can break with convention and configure things to work the way you want.

This is also a tremendous downside when you're learning the basics of Unix and Linux. Many things – from software configuration to default user settings – can be configured in many different ways, and there's no way to know what the convention is in a new environment except to ask (and sometimes, troubleshoot).

Nowhere is that truer than when it comes to logging, which has been especially affected by the recent shifts in how companies do their computing. Logging was done a certain way for decades, when most companies directly purchased, configured, and managed long-lived physical servers with a single OS installed on them. As workloads have shifted to the cloud, and things have shifted to many operating systems per physical machine (VMs) and even many environments per OS (containers), traditional ideas of how logging should work have shifted as well.

That's all to say that when it comes to figuring out logging in a new job or team, the question is not, "How is logging done on Linux?" but rather, "How is logging currently done here?" It really depends on decisions made by the developers of the software you're using. When learning about logging in this chapter, we advise that you keep this in mind.

Sending log messages

While, in most situations, services will log either through a library or by simply writing to stdout, Unix-like systems provide a command that logs to a syslog server. We'll look at what that means below. Since both syslogd and systemd provide a syslog server no matter what kind of system you are using, there is a unified command to send a log message:

```
logger Hello World!
```

This will log Hello World. The logger command has many options, and it can be a valuable tool when debugging any issues, when wanting to log in a shell script, or when explaining how logging works.

The systemd journal

When a system uses systemd, journald takes over the logging side. When you're troubleshooting a Linux machine running systemd, this is the first place you should be looking for logs. By default, journald captures all output from supervised processes. Anything emitted on stderr is treated as an error. So, unless the software is configured or hardcoded to log to a location that's not stderr/stdout, you will find the logs in the systemd journal.

Logs logged to journald can be queried via the journalctl command. It provides a means to query based on individual services, time, and system restarts and allows one to use options similar to the tail command. Let's jump in and get some practice using journalctl.

Example journalctl commands

The basics of working with journalctl are simple. Think about it; when you're troubleshooting an application, what do you need to be able to do with its logs?

First, you'll want to be able to find and view the current set of logs. journalctl will give you that, but you'll quickly realize you didn't actually want *all* the logs, just the most recent ones. So, let's filter with the -n flag.

To get a look at the last 100 log messages in journald, try this command:

```
journalctl -n 100
```

This will print out the last 100 lines logged to the system. You will notice that this is similar to the tail command explained earlier in this book. If you followed along, these lines will likely contain the "Hello World!" message from above.

Following active logs for a unit

You might also want to see logs in real time. For example, following your application logs during startup can help you see exactly when things go wrong:

```
journalctl -fu unitname
```

The -f flag stands for "follow," and the -u flag stands for "unit" – the system unit (or "service") that you want to filter logs for.

Filtering by time

Even when you filter down to a specific unit that you're interested in, you may still be overwhelmed by the number of logs that match. Filtering by time can be useful here, especially when you are trying to correlate a known external problem (outage, error, and so on) to the application logs from that moment in time forward. Use --since and --until for this:

```
journalctl --since "2021-01-01 00:00:00"
```

You can also use some shorthand for this, like today:

```
journalctl --until today
```

You can also use –until to set an end time for your filter and mix these up to get pretty specific. For example:

```
journalctl --since "2021-01-01 00:00:00" --until "1 hour ago"
```

Note

One caveat to viewing and filtering logs by time is that you'll almost always want to use the `--utc` option for `journalctl`, which displays timestamps in UTC. When you're helping an ops team troubleshoot an outage, this is almost exclusively done using UTC times to prevent timezone-related confusion.

There are additional filters for things like user/group ID.

Filtering for a specific log level

If you know you're looking for an error, you can tell `journalctl` to show you only errors (or any of the other log levels listed at https://wiki.archlinux.org/title/Systemd/Journal#Priority_level in descending order of criticality: `emerg`, `alert`, `crit`, `err`, `warning`, `notice`, `info`, `debug`):

```
journalctl -p err
```

Inspecting logs from a previous boot

Sometimes things get really wild, and a fault actually causes a reboot. In those cases, you'll want to see logs from a previous boot of the system. You can view all available boots with `--list-boots`, like so:

```
journalctl --list-boots
```

Then select a specific boot from the list with the `-b` argument. In this case, we want the one labeled 2:

```
journalctl -b –2
```

By itself, the –b flag means "the current system boot."

Kernel messages

In the introduction, we mentioned that system-level log messages are sent by the operating system ("the kernel," in Linux jargon). To see just those messages, use the `--k` (or `--dmesg`, for historical reasons) flag.

Logging in Docker containers

In a Docker container, the most common way to treat logs is to simply assume that the container's main process is the one we want output from and that it's logging to the standard output (stdout). Container orchestrators (that is, tools like Kubernetes and Nomad), as well as various cloud services that are responsible for executing containers, will assume stdout to be where relevant logs will go and, depending on the configuration, will forward it accordingly. We will go a bit more into this in the *Centralized logging* section below.

Syslog basics

Compared to the systemd/journald logging we've shown you, syslog may seem a bit archaic. We prefer to think of it as having a *storied history* – although it's been around since the 1980s, it's still a useful, flexible, and widely-used logging tool. More importantly, you're almost guaranteed to come across it on real production systems, so it's worth knowing the basics to avoid being caught off guard during an outage where time is critical.

On a Unix-like system, logging to syslog is often equivalent to logging to a file in /var/log, with the majority of messages typically going to /var/log/messages. Keep in mind, however, that not everything you find in /var/log necessarily went through syslog. Various pieces of software also implement their own way of writing log files, skipping the syslog daemon entirely.

This works by syslog ingesting all the logs sent to it and depending on various parameters, like the facilities mentioned below, outputting them into a file. On virtually all systems, the default for this is /var/log/messages. If you followed along and your system uses syslog, then this is also where you'll find the Hello World! message from above.

Syslog is a standardized protocol for logging. While, at the time of this writing, syslogd mostly deals with log lines, the current standard [RFC 5424] also allows for structured logging. However, since this isn't widely supported, we will just briefly go over its basic concepts as a protocol for line/message-based logging. If you don't interact with syslog at all, feel free to skip this section.

As mentioned earlier, syslog is a protocol. While it's most frequently used for software, such as databases that want to log locally, production setups usually have a centralized logging server that logs are shipped to. Being only a protocol, various software (such as PostgreSQL, nginx, and so on) can emit logs using this protocol, and various logging-related software, like Logstash, Loki, syslogd, syslog-ng, and others can ingest its logs. It usually uses either port 514 (UDP) or port 6514 (TCP).

Facilities

Since syslog is a very old protocol from the 1980s, some of its concepts might look archaic. It uses pre-defined *facilities* to specify the type of log message. Each facility has its own code:

- 0: kern – Kernel messages.

- 1: user – User-level messages. These are often used by processes.

- 2: mail – Mail system. Mostly useful for mail servers, SMTP, IMAP, and POP3. Spam-related daemons and software usually log here.

- 3: daemon – System daemons. Daemons, especially ones related to the OS (such as for NTP), log here.

- 4: auth – Security/authentication messages. You will typically find login attempts, for example, locally, via SSH, but also for various other services here.

- 5: syslog – Messages generated internally by syslogd. These will be messages related to syslog itself.

- 6: lpr – Line printer subsystem. Printer-related logs.

- 7: news – Network news subsystem. This is historical, and not typically used anymore.

- 8: uucp – UUCP subsystem. This is historical, and not typically used anymore.

- 9: cron – Cron subsystem. Logs related to cron jobs. These can be very useful for debugging cron jobs.

- 10: authpriv – Security/authentication messages. This is similar to auth but is usually considered to be logged to a more restricted set of destinations. Most Linux software logs here instead of auth.

- 11: ftp – FTP daemon. Mostly historical. Logs for FTP servers.

- 12: ntp – NTP subsystem. Logs for the **Network Time Protocol (NTP)**, so clock synchronization.

- 13: security – Log audit. Security-related events.

- 14: console – Log alert. Messages related to the "local console."

- 15: solaris-cron – Clock daemon.

- 16 to 23: local0 to local7 – Locally used facilities, meaning local software. PostgreSQL, for example, logs to local0 per default when logging to syslog.

On many systems, you'll find files in /var/log/ that are named similarly to these facilities. So, for example, if you need to debug a cron job on a system not using journald, you'll likely find the output in /var/log/cron, /var/cron/log, /var/log/messages, or similar.

Keep in mind that what exactly is logged in each facility is not standardized. You will likely come across situations where different operating systems or similar software might not agree on which facility to log to.

Severity levels

This is a concept you are probably more familiar with. Messages come with a severity of one of seven different levels:

- 0: `emerg` – Emergency
- 0: `alert` – Alert
- 0: `crit` – Critical
- 0: `err` – Error
- 0: `warning` – Warning
- 0: `notice` – Notice
- 0: `info` – Informational
- 0: `debug` – Debug

As with facilities, what exactly constitutes each severity level depends on the software used.

Configuration and implementations

Syslog has many implementations. These typically allow you to configure filtering, and save and forward messages based on facilities and severity levels. Some systems come with a service called `syslogd`, `rsyslog`, or `syslog-ng`, which can be configured in `/etc/syslog.conf`, `/etc/syslog-ng/`. Loki, Logstash, and other distributed log management tools have their own respective ways of configuring logging, usually in a three-fold structure, with one place to define input, another to filter and transform, and a third to store or forward the output.

Tips for logging

Everyone does logging a bit differently and what is considered best practice can vary across projects and time. However, there are some things you should be aware of.

Keywords when using structured logging

When using any kind of structured logging, try to make sure to share common keywords, such as request and user IDs, while also trying to avoid conflicting keywords used for similar, but not exactly the same, things. Depending on the backing database, you might also run into issues with types here, for example, in a situation where user might be the key for an integer, a string, or its own nested structure, like a JSON object.

Sometimes it's possible to avoid any overlaps by creating per-service namespaces and keeping a list of "globally used" keys, along with definitions for them.

Severity

When developing software, it makes sense to have some internal document explaining which severity has which meaning. This avoids situations where failed login attempts to a publicly reachable service, or 404 error codes from crawlers requesting obsolete websites, raise an alarm and wake a colleague in the middle of the night. But even if that's not the case, it can make debugging and being aware of problems a lot easier.

For this reason, it's a good idea to clearly distinguish between the following:

- Situations that *might* indicate a problem
- Situations that should not happen, but *can* happen
- Situations that clearly indicate a bug or more severe problem

Logs have the tendency to become more complex as software grows and services get added, so it's a good investment to be clear about what to log and when from the very beginning.

Centralized logging

In a corporate setting, it is typical to centralize logs. This makes it easier to connect the dots when debugging issues. It also means that in a distributed application, not every log on each physical or virtual machine or container has to be looked at individually. These centralized logging services typically make it easy and fast to query large amounts of logs, especially when the company uses structured logging and services adhere to a uniform log structure.

These logging services are either their own products, such as rsyslog, Loki, the ELK stack (Elastic Search, Logstash, and Kibana), and Graylog, or they are managed services. These can, for example, be the hosted variants of the services we just mentioned or cloud-specific logging solutions, such as Google's operations suite (formerly known as Stackdriver), AWS CloudWatch, or Azure Monitor. There are many similarities between these systems in that they provide mechanisms to "ship" logs from files or via some kind of API, filter and restructure them, and eventually, save them into final storage, ready to be queried.

In microservice architectures, it's common to pass along context, such as a request ID, so a request from a client can easily be traced through the various services, which is essential for debugging architectures that involve many services.

As mentioned, most of these systems have mechanisms to ship logs to the central log server or cluster. They go by names like Logstash (the L in ELK stack) and Promtail (used with Loki) and typically provide multiple ways of ingesting logs. For example, they might be configured to create an HTTP server, act as a syslog server, tap into journald, read from any other log shipping services, use cloud APIs, or simply tail files. They are run either as additional daemons on systems, as a Pod in Kubernetes, or as part of a Nomad setup. Since they are meant to allow centralizing logs no matter what software is in use, they tend to allow for a variety of log inputs and are typically very flexible on the setup side – for example, allowing one to create a hierarchy by forwarding between individual log-shipping services. On container orchestrators like Kubernetes and Nomad, this is often implemented with a "sidecar container" that runs next to your application containers and captures logs from all containers in that Pod/allocation/node before shipping them to their destination.

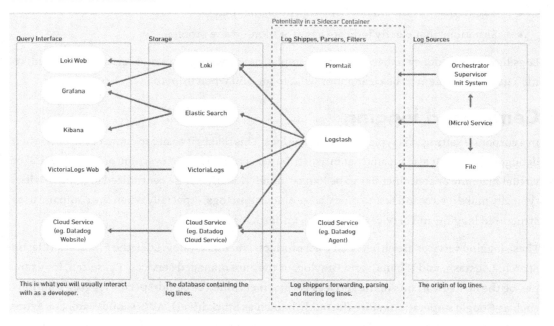

Figure 16.1: Container orchestration with a sidecar container

As you can see, while there are many technologies and products surrounding logging, they all fall into at least one of the categories described above, so when you centralize logging in your environment, this should give you an idea of how the parts relate to each other.

Conclusion

Logging can be a moving target in modern production environments. Learning and experimenting with the basics covered in this chapter should give you a good foundation. It is our hope that getting comfortable with syslog and journalctl will also equip you with a low-level understanding and historical perspective that will make it easier for you to work out how tomorrow's logging-as-a-service solution actually works under the covers.

We think you'll find that the skills you learned in this chapter give you a practical, measurable advantage when it comes to designing, debugging, and optimizing the applications you create and deploy. Mastering the basics of journald, as you just saw, lets you swiftly diagnose and pinpoint issues, whether they are related to your application specifically or to the larger Linux system around it. Having some understanding of alternative and historical Linux logging approaches will help when you're troubleshooting systems (or people) that haven't been updated in a long time.

It's not just about solving issues; it's also about making your life easier and your work better. Plus, it's a skill that makes you stand out. In short, knowing your way around Linux logs makes you a smarter, more effective developer.

Learn more on Discord

To join the Discord community for this book – where you can share feedback, ask questions to the author, and learn about new releases – follow the QR code below:

```
https://packt.link/SecNet
```

17

Load Balancing and HTTP

We're going to take a slightly different approach with this chapter, so buckle up. On the one hand, we're going to review some background on the **Hypertext Transfer Protocol (HTTP)** and focus on some misconceptions that trip up many web developers in the real world.

On the other hand, we're going to keep this practical and cover one of the most powerful standard HTTP tools that's available on the command line, curl. Specifically, we're going to teach you the basics of curl in the context of how you can use it to troubleshoot common web application issues.

We assume that if you're a web developer, you already know your way around HTTP. So, while the goal of this chapter is not to teach you the absolute basics of this protocol, we are going to review some of those basics to get you up to speed if it's been a while. If you *are* totally new to HTTP, there is lots of excellent documentation on the web that you can use. For what it's worth, we highly recommend MDN by Mozilla as your source for this information.

Instead, we want to focus on the common misunderstandings and pitfalls around HTTP and how it's used in the real world, which often catch people by surprise. These misunderstandings often come from the fact that as a developer, you write web applications in a very simple local environment but run them in complicated production setups that look quite different from the laptop you built and tested them on.

This difference between what an application interacts with when in development on a local machine, and the infrastructure around it after it has been deployed to a staging or production environment, is the source of much confusion and many subtle bugs.

In this chapter, we'll cover the most important of these differences: you'll learn about gateways, upstreams, and other concepts that intersect with the infrastructure layer around a modern website or web application. Then we'll cover some of the most common mistakes people make with HTTP that cause hard-to-debug issues with headers, status codes, and more. We'll look at some of the modern security features that have been added, such as **Cross-Origin Resource Sharing (CORS)**, along with the history of HTTP and the versions you're likely to come across. Finally, you'll learn a bit about how load balancing is done: knowing the basics will prevent you from having an incorrect model of the client request path in your mind, which is a common source of design problems at the application/infrastructure boundary.

You'll learn:

- Some basic terminology that you'll need to understand the more complex web infrastructure we discuss later in the chapter.
- Common misunderstandings about HTTP statuses, which when fully understood, can help you write cleaner and more correct status-handling code.
- HTTP headers, and some related problems you might see in your own web applications.
- The different HTTP versions you might encounter in the wild.
- How load balancing works, and why you need to understand it as a developer, even if you never plan on touching application infrastructure.
- How to troubleshoot web issues relating to all of these topics from the command line with a tool called `curl`.

The only prerequisite knowledge for this chapter is a basic understanding of how HTTP requests work, and a basic idea of the developer tooling that exists for web applications (for example, you should know how to use your browser's console and other dev tools to debug basic HTTP issues).

Let's start with some basic terminology that will come in handy when we get to troubleshooting.

Basic terminology

Later sections will use a few terms you may not be familiar with, so let's quickly cover them here.

Gateway

In today's world, the gateway is usually an HTTP reverse proxy, a load balancer, and frequently a combination of both. This can be an HTTP server, such as nginx or Apache, a physical load balancer in the classical sense, or a cloud variant of this same idea. It can also be a **content-delivery network (CDN)**. So, when you receive an HTTP status code mentioning an error related to the gateway, it's one of these gateway devices or applications talking to you.

Upstream

The upstream is the service that an application proxies to. In most situations, this will be the actual application or service, for example, an HTTP service you wrote. It is good to keep in mind that one can cascade or layer proxies, so there might be another intermediate proxy between the first proxy and the actual web application. For example, in many cloud infrastructures there is an ingress load balancer that handles and filters incoming traffic, behind which is an application load balancer that actually inspects the HTTP traffic and routes it to the right application server pool.

Now that we've covered a few bits of terminology that go beyond HTTP, you're prepared for the later sections of this chapter. Let's now take a closer look at a few commonly misunderstood parts of HTTP and start using the curl tool to practice common CLI troubleshooting commands.

Common misunderstandings about HTTP

When developing web applications and HTTP APIs, it can pay to be aware of a few details that many developers miss. Let's look at a few of the key areas where knowing a bit extra can really pay off in terms of the reliability of the applications you create. The curl skills we cover in this chapter will also give you the ability to start troubleshooting something as vague as "the website is down" from the command line.

HTTP statuses

In the following sections, we will cover some of the common HTTP statuses you'll encounter. We'll also consider some important information and myths about these statuses that you should keep in mind.

Don't just check for 200 OK

A common way to check for errors is only checking for a 200 or the whole 2xx range of status codes to know whether a request was a success. There are some caveats to be aware of when doing this, though.

The 200 range (2xx, as in, every status code between 200 and 299) tends to indicate success and many APIs return 204 No Content to indicate that an operation was successful, especially when the API usually returns the resource that was created or modified, but in certain scenarios, like DELETEs or when it would be a waste of resources, it does not.

Checking to see whether a response status is inside the 2xx range might be enough for some applications, but it is important to understand that application logic like "if it's not a 200, log an error" is wrong. Neither the 1xx range nor the 3xx range indicate an error, even though they aren't 200s.

It's somewhat rare to see the 1xx range without expecting it, since the most common situations involving 100s are things like switching to WebSockets, but that doesn't make them errors. The 3xx status code is returned quite often to inform the client about redirections, and while it might indicate that some action is needed – perhaps updating a path for some content that has moved – it's definitely not a failure on its own.

One status code in the 3xx range that tends to be seen a lot more often in production than in development is 304 Not Modified. This can be easily overlooked at development time and might also appear due to infrastructure changes or library updates that improve or introduce new caching behaviors. This status code is used when the client, such as a browser or an HTTP library, sends the request with an If-Not-Modified header, especially to take advantage of caching.

For these reasons, it usually makes sense to only consider status codes starting with 400 to be any kind of potential error, instead of considering only 2xx status codes to be a success. This still lends itself to neat logic inside your application: checking if a status code is greater than or equal to 400 is just as concise as checking to see if it's in the 2xx range.

404 Not Found

Something important to keep in mind is that the Not Found status code can mean different things depending on the application. 404 can be returned by (file) servers and gateways, but also by the application. It can imply that a route does not exist, but also that a specific resource (for example, a post or comment) does not exist for some reason (for example, if, it was deleted).

This is why 404 is often part of the normal response set returned by a healthy application that's working as designed. In some situations, a client might even depend on this behavior, for example to verify that something doesn't exist – before creating a certain resource or when indicating to a user whether a certain resource or resource name is already taken.

In other words, the 404 status code alone (without more context about the application and the request) isn't enough to indicate a problem. As you just saw, it may even indicate a success on multiple levels and layers. This is sometimes avoided by not using it in the application layer and signaling any "Not Found" situations differently, for example by still returning a status code of 200. What the right way is depends on both the application and what a team or standard agrees on, and which architectural style is used in your application.

502 Bad Gateway

This status code means that the gateway didn't understand what the upstream returned; in other words, the response to the request that the gateway forwarded wasn't a complete and valid HTTP response. This typically indicates a problem with the upstream service.

503 Service Unavailable

A 503 usually means that the upstream service isn't reachable on the port that the gateway is configured to try. Practically, this means that the web application might have crashed, or that it's not listening for HTTP requests, or that it's listening on the wrong port, or that it's blocked by a firewall rule or a broken routing rule, or a myriad of other reasons.

504 Gateway Timeout

When a gateway creates a connection to an upstream, this connection times out at some point. This is important because hanging processes consume resources on both ends; on the gateway *and* the service. Usually, such timeouts only occur if this is unexpected and there are no bytes being written or read.

If the upstream service has a long-running request caused by waiting for computation or something similar, one option is to increase the time a request can take until this timeout occurs. However, it is usually advisable to take a different approach. For example, making that endpoint asynchronous or starting to write bytes earlier (such as by streaming data) can help.

The reason for this is that until there is a timeout, resources are used up and the requesting side doesn't know whether the application will ever return a response. So, if the web service malfunctions, neither the gateway nor the client will know about it. This might also cause the gateway to think that the malfunctioning service is still up and running, instead of quickly detecting the problem and failing over to another instance of the service.

Introduction to curl: checking HTTP response status

If you learn only one command-line tool to help you troubleshoot HTTP, you would do well to learn curl. As we continue to talk about areas of HTTP that are useful to understand in more depth, we'll add sections like this to show you practical curl commands you can use while troubleshooting common issues related to the aspects of HTTP we just covered.

The simplest curl invocation is something like this:

```
curl https://tutorialinux.com/
```

This is just like pasting the URL into the browser – except it cuts out the browser and directly returns the web server's response on the command line. Not the most exciting way to browse the web, to be sure. Let's do something that's a bit more useful for your next troubleshooting script: checking the status of an HTTP response!

Curl can easily be used to check whether a web server is up and responding to requests:

```
curl -IsS https://tutorialinux.com/ | head -n 1
HTTP/2 200
```

Based on this output, we know that the web server is up and the / route is responding with a 200 OK status. You also see the HTTP version here (HTTP/2), which we'll discuss later. Specifically, this command issues a HEAD request (-I or --head), muting curl's progress and error messages (-s or --silent).

You'll still see error messages when something is wrong, though, thanks to the -S (or --show-error) option:

```
curl -IsS https://tutoriajsdkfksjdhfkjshdflinux.com/ | head -n 1
curl: (6) Could not resolve host: tutoriajsdkfksjdhfkjshdflinux.com
```

Finally, we're chopping off most of the headers and only looking for the status code, which is the first line (| head -n 1).

However, you'll often want to see the headers when troubleshooting. Let's look at a few header-related HTTP gotchas and then try using curl to inspect headers.

HTTP headers

Case-insensitive headers

The headers in HTTP are case-insensitive. Some software relies on this fact, and as a result certain gateways might modify and "normalize" these headers. Fortunately, it is rare for developers to directly interact with raw header values when writing a web application. Instead, they use web libraries, which abstract most of this complexity away and take care of these kinds of details. However, you should still make sure this is the case and normalize them, for example by lower-casing headers that your web application sets. This can also prevent situations where response headers are accidentally added multiple times with different letter casings.

Custom headers

When you create custom HTTP headers for an application, be aware of the prefix you decide to use. It used to be common to prefix custom headers with X-, for example X-My-Header. This practice is now considered bad (see RFC 6648, which deprecates it). Instead, it makes sense to create a custom prefix, such as the name of the project, product, or company, or an abbreviation of it. This prevents situations where that header will be reused by other developers who mistake it for an official part of the HTTP standard.

Viewing HTTP headers with curl

The -I option we introduced in the previous curl example is useful for viewing the response headers, which can help reveal caching problems, content-type mismatches, and other issues. Let's see what the tutorialinux server has to say in its headers:

```
curl -I https://tutorialinux.com/

HTTP/2 200
server: nginx/1.24.0
date: Sat, 21 Oct 2023 16:37:12 GMT
content-type: text/html; charset=UTF-8
vary: Accept-Encoding
x-powered-by: PHP/8.2.11
link: <https://tutorialinux.com/wp-json/>; rel="https://api.w.org/"
strict-transport-security: max-age=31536000; includeSubdomains; preload
```

There's nothing wrong with the server at the moment, but these headers already give me a few ideas of how to improve my nginx configuration: leaking software names and version numbers is usually a bad idea from a security perspective, and no one receiving HTML or JSON from this server needs to know that the backend is using PHP.

HTTP versions

To explain some of the newer HTTP features you'll see used, we'll give you a brief history of the protocol. HTTP has been around for a while and has changed a lot, especially in recent years as web applications have come into vogue. The main concepts and primitives have largely remained the same since HTTP's inception, however, some tricks, optimizations, and behaviors have changed. Being aware of the protocol version can help with debugging or preventing issues and reduce unnecessary or counter-productive optimizations and workarounds.

HTTP/0.9

You're unlikely to come across this version of HTTP anymore. It is the most minimal HTTP one can imagine. HTTP/0.9 allows for sending a GET request to a server and receiving what we now call the *body* of an HTTP request. No headers were sent or returned, not even a version header or a status code.

HTTP/1.0 and HTTP/1.1

HTTP/1.0 and especially HTTP/1.1 came a lot closer to what people think of when they think of HTTP today. While HTTP/1.0 added a version number and headers, HTTP/1.1 paved the way for methods and a substantial number of extensions, usually in the form of headers.

HTTP/1.1 also added (and defaults to) pipelining. This means that multiple requests could be sent using the same TCP connection. Another widely used addition is the Host header, which allows for the same server or IP to use multiple hostnames.

For example, a web server could now be configured to respond with requests for `http://example.org/`, `http://www.example.org/`, `http://forum.example.org/`, and `http://blog.example.org/` without requiring a separate IP address for each of them.

HTTP/1.1 also enabled many extensions: caching, compression, various authentication schemes, content negotiation, and even things like WebSockets. All of these are widely used in today's web.

HTTP/2

There are many articles extolling the virtues of HTTP/2. It is a huge and controversial step in a new direction for HTTP. While HTTP/1.1 was a text-based protocol that allowed anyone to create complete and valid requests in a terminal or text editor, HTTP/2 is a binary protocol that also handles streams, which are a mechanism to create a lightweight variant of a TCP connection.

The binary format and header compression mean that dedicated tools are now required to talk to an HTTP server (or client). The overall concepts, however, have remained the same as in earlier versions of HTTP, so as a web developer you'll only notice the differences in specific situations.

While HTTP/2 also adds a lot of entirely new features, many of them are rarely used in user-facing web applications and might not even be implemented by browsers.

While this isn't technically part of the official standard, HTTP/2 in the browser is typically limited to HTTPS.

In most situations, web applications will benefit from enhancements such as using a single TCP connection with multiple streams, especially when many requests, such as those for static files and AJAX, are made in parallel. This can render some optimizations, like sprite sheets or combining many files into a single one, unnecessary. When some of these optimizations lead to redundant data being transferred, they might even be counterproductive.

Some applications designed for HTTP/1.1 might require changes when switching to HTTP/2, because things like keeping connections alive might have unpredictable side-effects. For this and other reasons, it's a good idea to test web applications before converting them to HTTP/2. There are even instances where people have found that switching their applications to HTTP/2 increases page load times or increases resource use.

This means that real life tests and monitoring to compare the differences between HTTP protocols are a good idea. Since many of the benefits of HTTP/2 target real-life usage by web browsers, a simple command-line load test might not give the same results as real users accessing the web application. A typical mistake, for example, is not taking HTTP/1.1's pipelining feature into consideration.

However, for most real-life websites, HTTP/2 will bring benefits. For internal HTTP APIs on microservices, many companies are choosing to keep using HTTP/1.1 or gRPC.

HTTP/3 and QUIC

HTTP/3 builds on the developments of HTTP/2 and moves its concepts to a UDP-based transport protocol called QUIC (instead of TCP, which all other HTTP versions use).

Like the previous version of HTTP, HTTP/3 uses streams as a lightweight alternative to establishing a new TCP connection. Unlike HTTP/2 this isn't done by initiating streams inside an existing TCP connection, but rather by using QUIC, which is a protocol designed to allow for such streams.

QUIC has some advantages over TCP for common HTTP use cases. For example, because it's UDP-based – UDP is the User Datagram Protocol, a more bare-bones but faster alternative to TCP – QUIC prevents situations where the whole connection can stall because a single packet hasn't arrived (yet), even if that packet is destined for a different stream. QUIC is also optimized for quickly establishing that initial connection, including initiating TLS to secure the connection between the client and server. QUIC itself was created with extensibility and support for future versions in mind, and shortly after its standardization many such extensions were already on their way to being standardized.

Since HTTP/3 is based on UDP and designed to avoid *protocol ossification*, many traditional forms of intermediate nodes and gateways become obsolete.

Note

Protocol ossification is what happens when intermediate nodes (or anything that interacts with a protocol) require a protocol to keep a certain form, thereby making it hard to continue developing and changing that protocol (for example by adding extensions).

Let's look at how these basic HTTP concepts fit into the larger infrastructure that most of your web applications will be running in. In an architecture like this, it's rarely just a single web server and a client (like your web browser or curl): there are usually several layers of HTTP communication happening, and simple problems can compound and become hard to troubleshoot.

As usual, we'll give you the most important concepts you need to understand, followed by a few practical tips on troubleshooting more complex web infrastructures using curl on the command line.

Load balancing

Load balancing is a way to spread the load destined for a service across many instances of that service. While this is certainly not limited to HTTP and web services, HTTP is one of the most common contexts in which load balancing is used today.

It's important for you to understand how web application load balancing works, because it affects how bugs and problems show up in production. For example, in your local development environment, you are usually dealing with a single client (your browser or another API consumer) and a single server (the web application or service you're working on). In the real world, there are often multiple layers of servers between your client and the application, each speaking and relaying your HTTP traffic and possibly introducing its own problems or bugs into the flow.

The material in this section will give you a high-level understanding of the moving parts that become part of the application as a whole, even though they're not part of the application code you write.

HTTP load balancing is usually achieved by putting a layer of infrastructure in front of the application to proxy HTTP requests; usually one of the following:

1. Gateway service, such as an HTTP server supporting it (such as nginx or Apache)
2. Dedicated service (such as HAProxy or relayd)
3. Cloud service (GCP's Load Balancer, AWS's ELB or ALB, and so on)
4. Hardware load balancer

Sometimes, engineers choose to use a custom service or a DNS-based solution, especially in the context of regional load balancing which is often used as an additional layer in front of one of the other methods mentioned above. Container orchestrators and dedicated service discovery mechanisms also usually provide yet another mechanism for load balancing.

Introducing load balancers into the mix pulls in a few other concepts to understand – specifically around how these load balancers actually map requests coming from a client to a server running an instance of the web application that you lovingly crafted.

Session and cookie management becomes complex, because long-running sessions are no longer guaranteed to hit the same server every time. One server in your application pool going down becomes an issue – will your users' experience be interrupted, or will they lose data? Will you, as an engineer troubleshooting your own web application, be unable to replicate an issue because it's only happening on a single server out of tens or hundreds?

Understanding how modern load balancing works is essential to avoid application design flaws or troubleshooting woes like this, and the next few sections will equip you with a basic mental model that you can use to avoid them.

Sticky sessions, cookies, and deterministic hashing

When setting up load balancing for HTTP services, one of the first questions to ask is whether a service requires sticky sessions. Sticky sessions are a mechanism for tying a client to a specific application server for the duration of the session; they're often required for applications that keep session state on the application server itself.

This is one of the reasons why it's best practice to design "stateless" applications, which write state to a shared data layer – in these applications, it doesn't matter if a client's first request is handled by a different server than that client's second request. Thankfully in today's world, especially when relying on a cloud-based infrastructure, sticky sessions are usually not required. However, this is something to keep in mind, especially when troubleshooting issues that mysteriously only crop up in load-balanced production environments.

While there are many ways to create sticky sessions in HTTP, the most common way is through cookies. This can either be via application cookies (such as session cookies) that the load balancer is aware of, or via dedicated cookies that the load balancer manages on its own.

Implementing sticky sessions by storing additional state on the load balancer is fraught with its own problems, though. If a load balancer must keep an internal mapping of IP addresses to application servers, what happens if that load balancer goes down and is replaced, losing that state? You can see that we've simply moved the state problem from the application server to the load balancer, and are hoping that nothing bad happens there. However, as the adage says, hope is not a viable strategy.

One clever way to achieve sticky sessions without dealing with the problem of needing to store state on the load balancer is to load balance using an IP hash. To achieve this, a hash of the client's IP is created and used to map request IPs to instances of a service. As long as the IP of the client stays the same, the session will be "sticky" to that particular application instance.

Now, one or many load balancers will deterministically match IPs to application servers, without needing to communicate or share state. Servers can come and go as they please, and each new server will make the same matching decisions as all other servers, since they're all using the same hashing algorithm and will always match a given IP to the same application server.

Round-robin load balancing

If sticky sessions aren't required, the most common mechanism for balancing load is round-robin. This means that every new connection or request is routed to the next instance. In mathematical terms this means that the instance is chosen by `request_count % instance_count` (% being modulo).

Other mechanisms

You now have a high-level overview of how HTTP load balancing works in the real world. Of course, there are many other mechanisms that can be chosen, such as spreading the load based on resource usage, but you should be careful to really understand the effects of added complexity – many "clever" load-balancing algorithms are not without major pitfalls.

For example, resource-utilization-based load balancers can encounter problems handling short spikes in load, which can cause underutilization of one instance and over-utilization of another, because the real-life workload the service deals is spiky and the load measurements come at the wrong time and don't even out these spikes.

Adding another layer of complexity to even out such spikes might cause other issues such as having many of these spikes stack on top of each other. If you find yourself leaving the well-trodden path of more established load-balancing mechanisms, make sure your team is putting enough technical consideration into the architecture and the context of the actual application and its usage.

High availability

While a primary goal of load balancing might be to ensure quick responses, a load balancer will typically keep track of which services are reachable. It might use health checking to verify that the servers it sends requests to are fully functional. This means that load balancing is also a way to achieve high availability and often also an integral part of a zero-downtime architecture where a service can be replaced (for example, when a new version is deployed) without clients noticing.

This can be achieved by allowing some form of graceful shutdown of instances, where connections to clients aren't simply dropped, but connections will remain active until they are fully processed, while new connections are only routed to updated instances. When the last session ends the outdated instance can be fully shut down.

Health checks allow a load balancer to determine whether a service is fully operational. The most basic check, of course, is whether a connection can be established. However in microservice architectures, an external dependency (like another service) not being reachable can prevent a service from properly responding to requests. This can also be indicated via a dedicated status endpoint.

Many application and infrastructure teams agree on a route like /healthcheck, whose status code indicates whether requests should be routed to the service. In some more complex environments, such a route might even indicate which *kinds* of requests can be routed to the instance.

When skilled application developers and platform/SRE teams get together, healthcheck routes can even be built to signal situations that require action from the infrastructure, such as the instance being critically unhealthy and needing to be replaced. If such routes are well designed, they typically also respond with additional context and information on the problem to ease debugging production issues.

As the infrastructure that supports a web application grows larger and more complex, the number of things that can go wrong increases exponentially, and is highly dependent on the specific architecture and application. One class of problem that becomes more likely the more layers of proxying and routing a web infrastructure has is redirect loops and general redirection errors.

Thankfully, this is something that a command-line tool like curl is perfectly positioned to troubleshoot.

Troubleshooting redirects with curl

As we just mentioned, redirects can be a common symptom of bugs, problems, and more generally unexpected behavior in a web application and its surrounding infrastructure. Use curl's -L (or --location) option to follow them:

```
curl -IL http://www.tutorialinux.com/
HTTP/1.1 301 Moved Permanently
Server: nginx/1.24.0
Date: Sun, 22 Oct 2023 22:58:02 GMT
Content-Type: text/html
Content-Length: 169
Connection: keep-alive
```

```
Location: https://tutorialinux.com/

HTTP/2 200
server: nginx/1.24.0
date: Sun, 22 Oct 2023 22:58:02 GMT
content-type: text/html; charset=UTF-8
vary: Accept-Encoding
x-powered-by: PHP/8.2.11
link: <https://tutorialinux.com/wp-json/>; rel="https://api.w.org/"
strict-transport-security: max-age=31536000; includeSubdomains; preload
```

You'll see that the server replies with a 301 (Moved Permanently) and the correct location, https://tutorialinux.com/. curl follows the redirect and makes a request to that new location, where it gets a 200 (OK) status.

This redirect is working as expected, but you can use this curl command to do things like identify redirect loops in an application or troubleshoot caching and routing issues in multi-layer load balancer setups.

Sometimes, though, you'll need to go deeper and send data to a web application to troubleshoot it. curl can help there, too!

Using curl as an API testing tool

Having a quick curl command loaded up in your brain for API testing comes in handy more than you'd think. Especially when dealing with JSON APIs that accept POST data, it's common to want to send some test data to an endpoint to make sure the backend is returning what you expect:

```
curl --header "Content-Type: application/json" \
    --request POST \
    --data '{"some":"JSON","goes":"here"}' \
    http://localhost:4000/api/v1/endpoint
```

This command uses a few flags that you'll want to remember. First, the --header (-H) argument lets you specify a header string to set (you can supply multiple headers by simply repeating this argument). Next, the --request (or -X) flag lets you specify the HTTP request type (by default, curl performs GET requests, but using this flag lets you change that). And when you're POSTing or PATCHing some data, as in this case, you'll want the --data (or -d) argument, which lets you send data.

In the case of --data, remember that bash escape characters play a role here, so for complex data you'll probably find it easier to use the --data option, like this:

```
curl -X POST --data "@my/data/file" https://localhost/api/v1/endpoint
```

Remember to prepend the @ character to your filepath. If you're sending complex data, read up on --data-raw, --data-binary, and --data-urlencode as well. You may need to send extra headers as well, depending on what your web application expects.

You've now seen how to get more interactive with the web applications you're troubleshooting, using curl to send them custom data. But there's one last curl trick we want to show you: TLS (short for Transport Layer Security, the way we encrypt modern web traffic in HTTPS) is not necessarily a "misunderstood" aspect of web applications, but it's a common failure point that curl can help with.

Accepting and displaying bad TLS certificates with curl

curl gives us the --insecure option, which allows it to accept invalid TLS certificates from a server, and continue the request. This can come in handy when troubleshooting misconfigured servers:

```
curl --insecure -v https://www.tutorialinux.org/
```

The --insecure (-k) option will make curl behave as if the TLS certificate is valid, even if it isn't. Obviously, this is a security risk and should only be used for troubleshooting, but it can make curl continue in cases where TLS certificate validation would fail and curl would normally abort the request.

Let's take a quick look at one last piece of HTTP that's worth learning a bit about if you have anything to do with building or troubleshooting web applications: CORS.

CORS

CORS stands for Cross-Origin Resource Sharing. That is a fancy word for saying resources, such as images, videos, HTML, JavaScript, or even **Asynchronous Javascript and XML (AJAX)** responses will be coming from a different hostname. To prevent situations where resources are loaded from a third party, the browser first asks that third party whether it is allowed to do so. This is called a pre-flight request.

A pre-flight request is an OPTIONS request that expects a response containing HTTP headers informing whether the request is allowed or not. Such a response typically has a 204 (No Content) status code and only contains the headers. If no such headers are found or the headers do not indicate that such a request is allowed, no subsequent request of the resource will be triggered.

Here is an example of what such an exchange might look like.

A browser opening `https://www.example.org/` asks whether it is okay to POST to `/api/test` on `api.example.org`:

```
OPTIONS /api/test
Origin: https://www.example.org
Access-Control-Request-Method: POST
Access-Control-Request-Headers: X-Custom-Header, Content-Type
```

An accepting response would look like this:

```
HTTP/1.1 204 No Content
Access-Control-Allow-Origin: https://www.example.org
Access-Control-Allow-Methods: POST, GET, OPTIONS
Access-Control-Allow-Headers: X-Custom-Header, Content-Type
Access-Control-Allow-Max-Age: 3600
```

Since this indicates that the request is allowed, the browser can subsequently send the original request, which is now authorized:

```
POST /api/test
Origin: https://www.example.org
Content-Type: application/json
X-Custom-Header: foobarbaz
```

In the case of a request that's not allowed, there is no response with an error status that signals a rejection per se – just a lack of the expected `Access-Control-Allow-Origin` header. In this case, the client sees that the request is not authorized and logs an error.

You can see errors like this as they happen in your browser's developer console. They'll look something like this:

```
Cross-Origin Request Blocked: The Same Origin Policy disallows reading the
remote resource at https://not-allowed. (Reason: something).
```

This is just a quick introduction to CORS, because it's a topic that's important for web developers to understand. While it's not specific to the command line, it's not out of the ordinary for a developer to have to understand these concepts and check their web client for these kinds of error logs. For a deeper treatment of this material, we recommend MDN's article on the subject, which you can find at `https://developer.mozilla.org/en-US/docs/Web/HTTP/CORS`.

Conclusion

In this chapter, you learned what you need to know to avoid some of the common misunderstandings, bugs, and frustrating design flaws that we see when web applications leave a developer's laptop and start to interact with the real world through complex infrastructure. You learned about some of the infrastructure that mediates access to your applications, like gateways and upstreams.

You also saw some of the most common mistakes that we see developers make with HTTP, and you'll be able to use that knowledge to avoid hard-to-debug issues with headers, incorrect or vague status codes, and more. You learned about **Cross-Origin Resource Sharing (CORS)** and how HTTP has evolved into its current form.

Maybe most importantly, you saw how you can level up your game as a developer by learning a command-line tool like `curl` and combining it with your theoretical knowledge of HTTP.

What you learned in this chapter makes it possible for you to quickly and accurately troubleshoot web application issues, whether it's identifying a redirect loop on a broken WordPress site, pinpointing a subtle caching issue by inspecting the headers returned by a Ruby-on-Rails application, or replicating a production bug (and verifying a fix) at four in the morning by POSTing specific JSON data to a development server.

Learn more on Discord

To join the Discord community for this book – where you can share feedback, ask questions to the author, and learn about new releases – follow the QR code below:

`https://packt.link/SecNet`

packt.com

Subscribe to our online digital library for full access to over 7,000 books and videos, as well as industry leading tools to help you plan your personal development and advance your career. For more information, please visit our website.

Why subscribe?

- Spend less time learning and more time coding with practical eBooks and Videos from over 4,000 industry professionals
- Improve your learning with Skill Plans built especially for you
- Get a free eBook or video every month
- Fully searchable for easy access to vital information
- Copy and paste, print, and bookmark content

At www.packt.com, you can also read a collection of free technical articles, sign up for a range of free newsletters, and receive exclusive discounts and offers on Packt books and eBooks.

Other Books You May Enjoy

If you enjoyed this book, you may be interested in these other books by Packt:

Mastering Linux Security and Hardening - Third Edition

Donald A. Tevault

ISBN: 978-1-83763-051-6

- Prevent malicious actors from compromising a production Linux system
- Leverage additional features and capabilities of Linux in this new version
- Use locked-down home directories and strong passwords to create user accounts
- Prevent unauthorized people from breaking into a Linux system
- Configure file and directory permissions to protect sensitive data
- Harden the Secure Shell service in order to prevent break-ins and data loss
- Apply security templates and set up auditing

Mastering Ubuntu Server – Fourth Edition

Jay LaCroix

ISBN: 978-1-80323-424-3

- Install Ubuntu Server on physical servers and on the Raspberry Pi
- Deploy Ubuntu Server in the cloud and host websites on your own server
- Deploy your applications to their own containers and scale your infrastructure
- Set up popular applications such as Nextcloud
- Automate deployments and configuration with Ansible to save time
- Containerize applications via LXD to maximize efficiency
- Discover best practices and troubleshooting techniques

Packt is searching for authors like you

If you're interested in becoming an author for Packt, please visit authors.packtpub.com and apply today. We have worked with thousands of developers and tech professionals, just like you, to help them share their insight with the global tech community. You can make a general application, apply for a specific hot topic that we are recruiting an author for, or submit your own idea.

Share your thoughts

Now you've finished *The Software Developer's Guide to Linux*, we'd love to hear your thoughts! Scan the QR code below to go straight to the Amazon review page for this book and share your feedback or leave a review on the site that you purchased it from.

https://packt.link/r/1804616923

Your review is important to us and the tech community and will help us make sure we're delivering excellent quality content.

Index

Download a free PDF copy of this book

Thanks for purchasing this book!

Do you like to read on the go but are unable to carry your print books everywhere?

Is your eBook purchase not compatible with the device of your choice?

Don't worry, now with every Packt book you get a DRM-free PDF version of that book at no cost.

Read anywhere, any place, on any device. Search, copy, and paste code from your favorite technical books directly into your application.

The perks don't stop there, you can get exclusive access to discounts, newsletters, and great free content in your inbox daily

Follow these simple steps to get the benefits:

1. Scan the QR code or visit the link below

https://packt.link/free-ebook/9781804616925

2. Submit your proof of purchase
3. That's it! We'll send your free PDF and other benefits to your email directly